POWER
AND
ACCOUNTABILITY

Robert A.G. Monks
Nell Minow

HarperBusiness
A Division of HarperCollins*Publishers*

International Standard Book Number: 0-88730-512-1

Printed in the United States of America

Library of Congress Cataloging-in-Publication Data

Monks, Robert A.G., 1933–
    Power and accountability / Robert A.G. Monks, Nell Minow.
        p.   cm.
    Includes bibliographical references and index.
    ISBN 0-88730-512-1
    1. Social responsibility of business—United States.   2. Corporate governance—United States.   3. Stockholders—United States.
    I. Minow, Nell, 1952–   . II. Title.
HD60.5.U5M646   1991
658.4'08–dc20
                                                        91-8959
                                                        CIP

91 92 93 94 PS/HC 9 8 7 6 5 4 3 2 1

To Milly—RAGM
To David—NM

Contents

v

Acknowledgments

Someone once said that there is no limit to what you can accomplish, as long as you are willing to let someone else get the credit. While we do not claim credit for that insight, we are very much aware of all of the work done by others that served as the foundation for many of the ideas of this book. We were especially instructed by Jonathan Charkham, Sir Adrian Cadbury, Sir David Walker, Robert Clark, Alfred Conard, Peter Drucker, Melvin Eisenberg, Betty Krikorian, Adolf Berle and Gardiner Means, and James Willard Hurst. They are our inspiration.

We have also learned a great deal from our colleagues, clients, and friends, the widely disparate group of institutional investors joined together by their commitment to the beneficial owners they serve as fiduciaries and the corporate managers they direct as shareholders. They are also our heros. They include Dale Hanson, Rich Koppes, Kayla Gillan, Ned Regan, Tom Pandick, Harrison J. Goldin, Elizabeth Holtzman, Patricia Lipton, Ned Johnson, Dean LeBaron, Dick Schleffer, Sarah Teslick, Janice Hester-Amey, Maria Cercy, Roland Machold, Jamie Heard, Bill McEwen, Nancy Williams, Paul Quirk, Luther Jones, David Ball, Alan Kahn, Ralph Whitworth, William Weitzel, French Hill, and Michael Jacobs.

We are also grateful to those who spoke with us during our research, including Samuel Heyman, Abbott LeBan, Michael Klein, Graef Chrystal, Steve Wallman, Henry Schacht, Jerry terHorst, Peter Hamilton, and Josh Berman, as well as those who spoke off the record. David Apatoff and Martha Minow gave us generous access to resource materials. Stanley Frankel, Newton Minow, Dick Schleffer, Wayne Marr, Abbott LeBan, Joe Singer, Jane Barnard, Alfred Conard, Leslie Levy, and Jonathan Charkham trudged through an early draft and gave us thoughtful comments. We have tried to do them justice. We sent copies of this manuscript to many of the people we wrote about, including many we criticized. Every one of them responded with extraordinary graciousness and civility, and many made thoughtful contributions.

This book simply would not have been possible without the insight, support, and commitment of the staff of Institutional Shareholder Services. In particular, we want to thank Howard Sherman for his extraordinary wisdom, energy, and friendship; Casey Norman for his research on the automobile industry; Michael Deal, who conducted many of the interviews, drafted the section on compensation, worked many, many nights and weekends, and checked all of the citations; Lil Veraart for tireless fact-checking; and Bud Knecht, an editor's editor. Thanks also to those who uncomplainingly filled in for us and kept the company going while we were writing, including Nicholas Higgins, Francis Corcoran, Amy Nadel, and Connie Darrah. Barbara Sleasman and Pat Bradley were of inestimable assistance in assembling the manuscript and keeping track of the supporting materials.

We would also like to thank Martha Jewett and Mark Greenberg of HarperCollins. First-time authors could not hope for better guides.

Bob would also like to thank: my wife Milly for her many gifts, including patience with my occupation and preoccupation with this book; my Department of Labor successors, David Walker and David Ball, and my former colleagues, Alan Lebowitz and Mort Klevan, for their integrity in pursuit of the public good; and Nell Minow for making collaboration a joy.

Nell would also like to thank: my father, who cheerfully quoted King Lear when his fellow corporate directors asked him about his "thankless child"; my mother, who taught me to write like a writer, not a lawyer; my sisters, Martha and Mary; and their husbands Joe and James; my friends Kathy and Andrew Stephen, John Adams, Shannon Hackett, Jesse Norman, Judy Viorst, David Drew, Nadine Prosperi, Gary Waxman, Bill Pederson, Steve Freiss, and Stuart Brotman; my children, Benjamin and Rachel Apatoff; and my husband, David, the best person I know. I also want to thank Bob Monks, the perfect partner, for letting me come along for the ride.

A note about style: For simplicity, the "I" in the book is Bob Monks and the "we" is both of us. All generic male references are intended to refer to females as well, and vice versa.

Some of this material has appeared in different form in *Legal Times* and other publications.

"This is the part of capitalism I hate."

Source: Drawing by J. Mirachi; © 1965 The New Yorker Magazine, Inc.

PART I

How We Got Where We Are

1

Shareholders and Stakeholders

I was driving through Maine one late summer day when I stopped to admire a river running through a pretty wooded area. I noticed big, slick bubbles of industrial discharge corroding the vegetation along the riverbank, and I wondered: Who wants this to happen? Not the owners of the company, the shareholders. Not the managers or employees, who want to live in a healthy environment. Not the board of directors, not the community, not the government. I could not think of anyone connected with the company emitting the effluent who wanted the result I saw. This was an unintended consequence of the corporate structure. The very aspects of the company's design that made it so robust, so able to survive changes in leadership, in the economy, in technology, were the aspects that led to this result—pollution that no one wanted, and everyone would pay for.

I realized I was part of the problem some time later, while in my office at the Boston Safe Deposit and Trust Company, where I was Chairman of the Board. I was looking over the proxies that it was our responsibility, as trustee for $7 billion in assets, to vote, and I was preparing to do what we had always done—vote with management on all of them. I picked up the proxy for the company that produced the industrial sludge I had seen, and I realized that if I voted for management, I was endorsing this activity. Those of us who managed money on behalf of others had the opportunity, and the responsibility, to tell management that this activity was unacceptable. But none of us was doing it.

3

No Innocent Stockholders

There is no such thing to my mind . . . as an innocent stockholder. He may be innocent in fact, but socially he cannot be held innocent. He accepts the benefits of the system. It is his business and his obligation to see that those who represent him carry out a policy which is consistent with the public welfare.

Louis Brandeis

Many companies violate the law. Beech-Nut sold sugar water as apple juice for infants. Alleco was convicted for price-fixing. E.F. Hutton pled guilty to 2,000 felony counts in 1985. An Exxon ship spilled 240,000 barrels of oil in Prince William Sound.[1] Over $2 billion was spent on cleanup by Exxon as of January 1991.[2] Other companies operate within the law, but they abuse their investors with outrageous compensation packages for management or entrenchment devices that prevent a beneficial sale of the company. These activities are not just bad for the shareholders; they are bad for the market, bad for the community, and bad for the economy.

This book is about how these kinds of things happened, and why, and how to make it harder for them to happen again. It is also about how changes in the composition of the shareholder community over the past decade have made it possible to restore the corporate organization to its original design. And this will revive the management accountability that is the best guarantee not just of corporate performance in the public interest, but of competitiveness and productivity as well. If all of our recommendations are followed, does that mean there will no longer be pollution in a remote river in Maine? No, it doesn't. But it does mean that it will be much more difficult for corporations to ensure their survival by making everyone else pay the costs.

"The Business of America Is Business"

We begin with some background about the development of corporations in this country. Corporations have an immeasurable impact on every aspect of American life—not just what we buy, where we work, and which diseases we cure, but much, much more.

Retailing corporations were responsible for changing the date on which we celebrate the oldest of American holidays. In 1941, Congress moved Thanksgiving up a week to create more time for Christmas shopping.[3]

It has been said that "I Love Lucy" is playing somewhere in the world every moment, 24 hours a day—sort of the twentieth-century equivalent of "the sun never sets on the British Empire." The people across the world who watch that program will think that the word *lucky* does not exist in the American vocabulary. The sponsor banned it because it was the name of a rival cigarette. Corporations fund, and therefore help to direct, our universities, our charitable institutions, our political campaigns. More than that, they are, in a way, our art form.

The United States has not yet produced a Michelangelo, a Beethoven, a Plato, or a Mohammed. The great genius of our republic has been in creating and preserving a free and open environment in which citizens can prosper. The most conspicuous demonstration of this goal is the surge of America over the last century to a leadership position in worldwide manufacturing and commerce. The very land and air of America has not only ensured domestic prosperity but also has enticed and inspired hard-working immigrants from many lands. Their names and accomplishments are key components of the national soul.

The idea of the private corporation was not unique to America back in the eighteenth century, but it was perhaps uniquely suited to America, the first country established as a constitutional democracy. Ours was the first society where a person could achieve the highest levels of fortune and status through commerce, and it is no coincidence that the United States and its corporations have been very good for each other and to each other. Capitalism was as much a part of America as the frontier; both were infinite resources waiting for someone to tame them. The famous statement of former General Motors president Charlie Wilson at his confirmation hearing for secretary of defense still rings with his absolute conviction: "For years I thought what was good for the country was good for General Motors, and vice versa."[4] He was not the only one who found it unthinkable that there could be any conflict of interests between the corporate good and the national good.

An impoverished Scottish family named Carnegie arrived in Pittsburgh in the middle of the nineteenth century. The spirit that had been ground down by centuries of marginal existence in Dunfermline, Scotland, acquired in the New World such vigor and purpose that it brought forth in Tom and Andrew Carnegie a new breed. The importance of commerce was already established. Just emerging was the realization that new technologies could cure disease, alleviate burdens, improve communications, and change the physical aspect of the world. Openness was the key—openness to new people, new ideas, and new ways of doing things. It was as if the commercial potential of the human spirit had been given its first real opportunity.

America welcomed all the "wretched refuse" and provided the framework for commercial accomplishment that made those that succeeded not merely rich but themselves world leaders, entitled to the respect of every man, emperor, pope, and field marshal. Carnegie lived long enough to direct the application of this tremendous wealth into public libraries, a World Peace Palace, and great foundations endowed to ensure the permanent enrichment of public dialogue. The immigrant boy grew into a man who called the kaiser of Germany "Bill."

Can We Still Compete When the Business of the World Becomes Business?

What Americans like to think of as the generic aspects of the national character—energy, self-confidence, a certain naivete, tinkerer's skills, and courage—incarnate the elements necessary for business success. Those elements still exist in this country, but apparently they are not enough. In the last few decades, we have had to accept that American business is no longer competitive, a realization that is profoundly conflicting with our deepest notions of ourselves.

Evidence of our decline is inescapable. World consumers—even Americans—prefer automobiles, television sets, cameras, clothes, and virtually all kinds of products made in other countries. Across the entire spectrum of industry we are confronted daily by the reality that others are doing better what we did best in former times. We may have expected that we could not maintain our position of dominance after World War II, but after only a few decades our advantages in a limited number of areas, such as computers and aircraft manufacturing, suggest a return to the earliest days of the republic, when the colonies were the "hewers of wood and drawers of water." This is more than just a commercial failure, a loss of money; it is as if the very essence of Americanism, so long the envy of the entire world, has been tested and found wanting.

There have been many places to assign blame. Some people suggest that our government policies are at fault, while others point to the lack of skill of labor and management, the cost of capital, or even the seeming invincibility of our foreign competitors. The inefficiencies of our educational system and our tax and accounting policies, as well as the vagaries of currency valuation and short-term profit orientation by managers and shareholders, are also frequently named factors in our predicament.

Much can be—and should be—done about each of these problems, but even improvement in all these areas seems inadequate to the scope of the problem. And some of the complaints are so narrow in focus that they obscure the point. Can cost of capital really be the ultimate problem in a time when the largest American corporations are buying back their own common stock? When some "experts" blame it on a weak dollar, and others blame a strong one, the problem has to be something else. Is the diversion of management attention to the risk of a hostile takeover more harmful to competitiveness than an atmosphere of entrenchment?

Our failure is so pervasive, so broad across all sectors of industry, that the problem must be dysfunction of the corporate system. The source of its failure is found in its success. The corporate structure was as important in transforming commerce as the assembly line. Both were based on the same principle, specialization. You didn't need to know how to make a chair to work in a chair factory; all you needed to know was how to put the chair leg into the chair seat. And you didn't need to know how to make a chair to invest in a chair company; all you needed to do was buy some stock. But either system works only if it is based on accountability. The foreman needs to make sure that the workers are putting chairs together correctly, or the customers will stop buying them. And the company has to produce returns, or the investor will sell out.

The Key to Corporate Vitality

The genius of the corporation, the factor that accounts for its almost universal use in the modern industrialized world as the preferred form for large commercial enterprises, is its internal dynamic of accountability. The corporation's vitality is based on trust, bridging law, tradition, and management theory—trust that managers will work loyally and effectively to realize the full potential of value for the owners, and that the owners can be counted on to ensure that the venture operates in their interest, their interest standing for everybody's interest. If the corporate structure is inadequate to maintain that trust, then all of the changes in laws, monetary policy, and trade agreements cannot solve the problem. In this book, we demonstrate that it has been inadequate.

Trust has been more myth than reality. The aspects of the system designed to help the corporation preserve itself have worked, but the aspects of the system designed to make sure that this self-preservation was consistent with the public interest have not. As we document in Part II, state government, local government, boards of directors, and even the marketplace itself have all been unable to keep the interests of the corporation aligned with those of the community, or, to put it another way, to keep the corporation from making everyone else pay the costs of its profits.

But we have found that there is still magic in America, not only in the justly fabled products of individual genius—the Polaroid of Edwin Land, Steve Jobs' Apple, and Ross Perot's many ventures—but also in those companies that have remained faithful to the discipline of trust and the spirit of openness. We want this book to be read in the context of our unshakable optimism and our conviction that what is wrong with American business can and will be fixed.

The exciting story of America's post–World War II economy is how many new companies have been started, how many have prospered and grown. The new, the open, and the energetic are as welcome as in the most expansive days of the republic.

What Works: The Tyco Example

As a director since 1985, I have had a front-row seat to watch one good example of corporate success, Tyco Laboratories. In the creative atmosphere of greater Boston in the 1950s, it was said that two men, a wheelbarrow, and an abandoned textile mill were all that was needed for a successful new venture. Throw in a few Ph.D.s, at a million dollars a pop, and you could have a successful public offering of the nascent company's stock. Arthur Tyler's idea was to provide organization and financing for inventors, and thus Tyco was born. With worldwide sales of $3.5 billion, it is one of the *Fortune* 200. The company has been far afield, from joint ventures with Mobil to a variety of attempted hostile takeovers before the concept was popular. The company has grown rapidly in recent years, under the leadership of John Franklin Fort, into an integrated worldwide leader in automatic sprinkler equipment. Fort, a Princeton engineering graduate with an industrial management degree from the Massachusetts Institute of Technology, has risen through the operating ranks of the company. There is no corporate jet, there are no corporate clubs, and there are only 35 employees at the corporate headquarters in Exeter, New Hampshire. A simple incentive system is key to the decentralized management style. Compensation is based on profits of individual business units.

Tyco's acquisition record is impressive. All four of its acquisitions in the last five years fit its current business mix and offer genuine merger benefits without causing dilution of earnings. Acquisitions are not made to increase size; they are made to further industrial integration and to improve profits.

The company demonstrates many of the elements that have given American business its deservedly high reputation in the years following World War II. These include strong leadership from a chief executive officer who focuses on technology, operations, and profits. Compensation is direct and to the point; there are no footnotes on the corporate balance sheet for yachts, farms, consultancies, and the like, just direct grants of stock on top of a modest cash base. The company has an industrial purpose. Corporate resources are not diverted to unrelated technologies.

There will certainly be times when the Tyco story is not as favorable as it is today. However, a company with a worldwide product niche, no frills, and a 23 percent compound growth rate over the past five years makes a compelling example.

There is nothing "magic" in Tyco's technology. There is no reason any well-run manufacturing company could not approach Tyco's performance record. Shareholders should reasonably expect their directors to choose managers who can either emulate the "lean" management style or explain the correlation between higher expenses and profit realization.

Discipline in business should emanate from adding value, from quality, and from productivity, but discipline is diluted by management style that is circumscribed by numbers. The problem is that, at some point in growth or in the conglomeration of unrelated businesses, the discipline of having an industrial purpose is lost, and management becomes a matter of numbers. Even the most reputable accounting systems can be manipulated. The very mass of numbers tends to cloud the capacity to require specific accountability.

Tyco shows us one answer to those who denigrate America's companies and management. It can be done; it is being done. Like Smith Barney's celebrated advertisement about making money "the old-fashioned way," the Tyco secret is focus—focus on producing quality goods to meet customers' needs at a competitive cost.

Tyco has its biggest challenges ahead. It is not a mature company. It has not had to struggle to maintain the keenness of youth. Like other companies, it will need to continue to evaluate whether yesterday's choices will work for tomorrow. For now, though, it is thriving in an environment that other companies find prohibitively restrictive.

Legitimacy and Accountability:
The Tie That May Not Bind Enough

Many of these restrictions faced by companies like Tyco can be traced back to concerns about power being exercised by private entities. The early days of corporate development reflect a deep suspicion of private power. This power was made legitimate in the same way as the exercise of public, or government, power—through a system of accountability to those affected.

At least, that was the theory. However, it became clear that corporations did not have the human capacity of responsibility. Limiting the liability of investors in corporate enterprises to the amount of their investment had a potentially pernicious effect in decreasing the personal responsibility on which the integrity of democratic institutions depends. But, as we show in Part II, this did not fit well with the corporation's tendency to act in its own interest without reference to individual concerns.[5]

There were thus two continuing challenges to maintaining some connection between management and ownership (as representing the public interest). The first was limited liability, and the second was the fragmentation of ownership into shares so small that the whole concept of ownership was diluted to the point of disappearance. Shareholders were

---

Citizenship in Corporate America

He discovers, in fine, that citizenship in his country has been largely metamorphosed into membership in corporations and patriotism into fidelity to them.

John P. Davis

Source: Corporations, Capricorn Books, New York, Vol. 2, 1981, p. 280 (originally published in 1905).

no longer owners so much as investors or even speculators. No institution for collective action by owners developed. The absence of a human element in corporations made necessary the design of other mechanisms to limit corporate power. But, as we describe in Part II, none of them has been successful.

The combination of state and federal governmental power is not sufficient to ensure that corporations act in the public interest. In Chapter 4, we discuss the trend characterized as the "race to the bottom," which has eliminated substantive requirements in the state laws authorizing corporate formation and operation. It has now found its international counterpart in the domiciles of convenience for modern corporations seeking tax and regulatory leniency. The sociological trend will lead to a time when where one works is a more important affiliation than the country where one holds citizenship.

Rights of the Corporate Citizen

A State grants to a business corporation the blessings of potentially perpetual life and limited liability to enhance its efficiency as an economic entity. It might reasonably be concluded that those properties, so beneficial in the economic sphere, pose special dangers in the political sphere. Furthermore, it might be argued that liberties of political expression are not at all necessary to effectuate the purposes for which States permit commercial corporations to exist. So long as the judicial branches of the State and Federal Governments remain open to protect the corporation's interest in its property, it has no need, though it may have the desire, to petition the political branches for similar protection. Indeed, the States might reasonably fear that the corporation would use its economic power to obtain further benefits beyond those already bestowed.

William Rehnquist

Source: Dissenting opinion, *First National Bank of Boston v. Bellotti,* 435 U.S. 765, 825, 826 (Sup. Ct. 1978).

The Corporate Citizen

As corporations have become increasingly large, the confusion in American society about an appropriate role for them is still evident, at least in some contexts. The Supreme Court of the United States has made a number of rulings reflecting concerns about the role of corporations in politics. In March 1990, a bitterly divided court upheld a Michigan statute that prohibited the use of general corporate funds (contrasted with PAC funds) for independent expenditures in connection with state elections.[6] The issue was whether corporate managers can use shareholder assets to promote a political agenda. The language of the majority opinion was surprisingly shrill. Justice Marshall referred to the "corrosive and distorting effects of immense aggregations of wealth that are accumulated with the help of the corporate form and that have little or no correlation to the public's support for the corporation's political ideas. . . . We emphasize that the mere fact that corporations may accumulate large amounts of wealth is not the justification for [the challenged statue]; rather, the unique state-conferred corporate structure that facilitates the amassing of large treasuries warrants the limit on independent expenditures."[7] The Court spoke

---

Pro: Corporations Bring Ideas to the Marketplace

The advocacy of [AT&T or General Motors] will be effective only to the extent that it brings to the people's attention *ideas* which—despite the invariably self-interested and probably uncongenial source—strike them as true.

Justice Antonin Scalia

Source: Dissenting opinion, *Austin v. Michigan State Chamber of Commerce* (#88-1569), March 27, 1990, p. 5.

Con: The People Who Pay for It Might Not Approve

While the State may have no constitutional *duty* to protect the objecting chamber member and corporate shareholder in the absence of state action, the State surely has a compelling interest in preventing a corporation it has chartered from exploiting those who do not wish to contribute to the chamber's political message. "A's right to receive information does not require the state to permit B to steal from C the funds that alone will enable B to make the communication."

Justice William Brennan

Source: Concurring decision, *Austin v. Michigan State Chamber of Commerce* (#88-1569), March 27, 1990, p. 7.

of "the special benefits conferred by the corporate structure," referring to "limited liability, perpetual life, and favorable treatment of the accumulation and distribution of assets,"[8] and concluded: "These state-created advantages not only allow corporations to play a dominant role in the nation's economy, but also permit them to use 'resources amassed in the economic market place' to obtain 'an unfair advantage in the political marketplace.'"[9] As Justice Brennan pointed out, the problem is that corporate managers can use corporate assets to promote views not necessarily shared by the corporation's owners. Indeed, the American tradition of denying express power to government encouraged the belief that power granted to corporations would further the interests of the individual against the state.

Free speech as contemplated in the Bill of Rights bears little relationship to the use of a corporation's resources to amplify its "speech" without any guarantee that it accurately reflects the views of the corporation's shareholders or even its employees.

The Tower of Babel

Through the centuries, corporate power has been the focus of a great deal of scholarship and debate, but each of the professions has described the phenomenon in its own language. Lawyers, economists, financial analysts, political scientists, ethicists, and managerialists are like the builders of the Tower of Babel, all working toward the same goal but unable to communicate because they speak different languages.

The problem that all of them try to address is that managers will never be as scrupulous in creating value for investors as they will in creating value for themselves, yet that is precisely what the corporate structure requires—investment of the capital from one group, the labor of another, and the management skills of a third, all geared to maximizing profit, with the primary obligation to the investors. All of the disciplines recognize that there must be some accountability from those who exercise power to those who are affected by it. All try to provide for and characterize the optimal accountability. But, as we will show in Part II, the corporate structure was so successfully designed for self-preservation that it has been able to counter every attempt at imposing accountability. And the Babel of languages has only obscured the picture.

The language of economics calls this accountability problem one of "agency costs." Economics has stressed that managements, acting as agents, will be imperfectly linked to their owner principals. It has suggested a set of institutional cures for this problem that ranges from better structuring of managerial contracts to adjusting the workings of the market for corporate control.

The law calls the same problem "conflicts of interest," because each party wants its own interests to come first. And the law has developed its highest standard, the fiduciary standard, to govern the relationship of managers to owners. But the language of law is the language of contracts, and the law has also traditionally viewed corporate governance within the framework of the duty of management to a number of constituencies with contractual claims on the corporate entity. Legal precedents have established the right of shareholders to hold management accountable through a system of voting and, when all else fails, through litigation. Litigation has its own language, very process-oriented, with a lot of emphasis on "standing" to sue, and the timing of the suit [it can be thrown out if it is too early (not "ripe") or too late ("moot")].

Management studies show that companies, confronted with conflicting pressures and opposing interests, actually make decisions in the interest of the companies' continuing existence, without reference to the concerns of the traditional constituencies. Political science and economics have provided evidence on how the system of public power—the political system—tries, with limited success, to hold management accountable to changing social and political mandates over time.

Ethicists have described how corporate structure and corporate culture further, or fail to further, "moral" conduct and decision making among managements.

Those standing in different spots in the corporate structure also have fragmented understanding, something like the blind men and the elephant, each one interpreting the part he is holding on to as the whole. Those who represent corporate management conclude that "shareholders will do better if management tends to all these responsibilities."[10] In other words, "trust me." Shareholders claim they are management's allies, at least good management's allies. In other words, "trust me." The financial community wants to decide which management deserves support. In other words, "trust me."

In the current environment, these contributions, important as they are, are too specialized and too divisive to serve as a broad conceptual framework for analyzing corporate governance problems. We lack the capacity to understand the problem because we lack the language. The problem is beyond our capacity to describe and understand because it transcends the specialized disciplines that have been developed to analyze, govern, and monitor corporations.

What is needed, instead, is a reexamination and synthesis of the language, concepts, and evidence of corporate governance research as contained in economics, finance, political science, law, and other disciplines. This kind of reexamination can create a new framework for understanding the concept of the corporation and the power it exercises, and for developing new theories about how to ensure that it is exercised responsibly. The violence of the market for corporate control over the past decade, and its resulting turbulence, lend urgency to this effort. The 1980s may not have been the decade when traditional governance notions were first eclipsed by developments in finance, policy, and law, but it was the decade that made it indisputably clear that what was left was just not working.

To begin to understand the problem and develop a solution, we must step back and look at specific aspects of corporate governance within a historical and economic framework. At the core, there is a common theme: the need to understand the exercise of private power by modern corporations in the United States—how it is created, how it is used, and how it is manifested. The relationship between power in the private and public sectors continues to be the central question of our political system. Some on the right are inherently suspicious of government and want as much as possible to be established privately. Libertarian extremists even urge that the government get out of the "business" of schools, highways, and everything else but defense. Some on the left are inherently suspicious of private power in general and corporations in particular. They want policy to be made by the government. Those decisions that are left to the private sector must be heavily influenced by government, through regulation.

Strange Bedfellows

However, debates over the appropriate limits on private power do not always reflect party lines. Despite his Republican credentials, Richard Nixon reflected the political spirit of the time by presiding over the creation of some of the most intrusive regulatory agencies ever to sit across the table from American business, including the Occupational Safety and Health Administration, the Consumer Product Safety Commission, and the Environmental Protection Agency. He also instituted wage and price controls. Jimmy Carter, running as a Washington outsider, decried government regulation and promised to reform it. But it was Ronald Reagan who really began to dismantle government regulation on a large scale, creating the Presidential Task Force on Regulatory Relief and issuing reports that tracked the declining number of pages in the federal register. Reagan's first secretary of the interior, James Watt, presided over a massive plan to privatize many of the department's programs. Eight years later, the controversial rollbacks in regulation of the environment and the financial industry have led the chairman of that task force, George Bush, to begin to reregulate.

Despite its prominence in political debate, corporate power and its systems of checks and balances are not well understood. Corporate power at its current level was not foreseen by early lawmakers and constitutional scholars, and its foundation in law is uneasy and inconsistent. But it is clear that the question of the legitimacy of corporate power in the United States has been transformed. Originally, the government had to review and specifically approve each corporate charter as being essential for a specific purpose that was in the public interest. Now one does not ask so much as notify the state that a corporation has been created. Anyone can incorporate for any activity that is not illegal. And the corporation, granted at least some of the constitutionally protected right of free speech originally contemplated for individual citizens, has now been accorded the right to question and challenge whether government is acting in the public interest.

In fact, government is now as much a creation of business as the other way around. Businesses grew so fast that there was no opportunity for other national institutions to develop adequate power to filter the impact of commerce on civil life. So Big Business begot Big Government. Because the goals of business are not always identical to the goals of society (which is partially a failure of the corporate governance system, as we will show), some institution was needed to harmonize the undoubted benefits of active commerce with the various needs of other constituencies. In the United States, this organization was the federal government, the only other major national institution.

There have been three principal eras of federal government regulation of business: (1) turn-of-the-century antitrust legislation; (2) "New Deal" bills of the 1930s addressing particular elements in the economy that had failed (the securities and banking industries, for example); and (3) health and safety "externality legislation" of the 1960s, which established new federal standards and enforcement mechanisms for business impact ranging from the environment to workplace safety to discrimination in employment.

The number of federal employees engaged in business regulation, the number, length, and complexity of proposed rules, and the expense of lawyers, arbitrations, and court proceedings have created the impression of a constantly increasing federal "control" over business. But, as we discuss in Part II, in virtually every case business has neutralized or even co-opted these efforts. The expense of confrontation between business and government may be one of the critical reasons for American noncompetitiveness in the world economy, but the actual impact of all the laws, all the regulations, and all the bureaucrats on large corporations is surprisingly small.

Although there is a plethora of organizations representing every element of private life, there is no single credible spokesman for the capitalist system, the industrial sector, or the interests of business as a whole. The Business Roundtable represents management. The unions represent labor. Trade associations represent their members. And, in general, the stakeholders in American corporations—investors, customers, workers, and the community—have traditionally used government as the medium through which they relate to each other. In the United States, we do not have institutions to force business to resolve conflicting claims; competing interests have been reconciled through the law. By contrast, other countries have private structures to resolve such issues, as we discuss in Chapter 7.

Accountability, Trust, and the 900-Pound Gorilla

In a way, economic legitimacy (competitiveness) and political legitimacy (accountability) are two sides of the same thing. The foundation of our concept of corporations is our belief that because shareholders can be counted on to require that their own long-term interests be accommodated, corporations will be directed along the lines most beneficial to society. This accountability allows us to give corporations enormous power to make decisions that affect every aspect of our lives.

For that reason, it is worthwhile to examine the nature and extent of the accountability. For instance, if owners are entitled to the residual benefits from corporate activity, why are they not accountable for its liabilities? Limiting owners' liability to the extent of their investments, combined with the development of liquid markets, has changed the essential character of shareholders. Having only a day-to-day interest in the value of a piece of paper, they have lost any long-term interest in the value of the company and now bear little resemblance to the owner so venerated by tradition and law.

But, as we describe in detail in Part III, we are now witnessing the reagglomeration of ownership of the largest corporations, so that long-term shareholders are well on the way to majority ownership of America's companies. They are, of course, the institutional shareholders, who invest collections of individuals' assets through pension funds, trusts, insurance companies, and other entities.

We recognize that there is an irreducible difference of objectives between owners and managers. This has resulted in notorious failures in the system during the recent decade of hostile takeovers. Both owners and managers have, on occasion, acted in outrageous disregard of each other's rights. Coercive bust-up takeovers on the one hand and outrageous compensation and entrenchment tactics on the other have all demonstrated the absence of an effective and constructive relationship between owner and manager.

Individual shareholders can make their own trade-offs in deciding whether to exercise their rights as owners of a corporation. But as fiduciaries, institutional investors have no such out. Institutional shareholders are the famous 900-pound gorilla, entitled to respect on account of size and might. More important, as fiduciaries, they are legally obligated to use that muscle and act as owners. For institutions, ownership is not so much a right as a responsibility. That is a key distinction. So long as voting and other ownership characteristics were seen as rights, failing to exercise them was considered at worst inconvenient, but not as harming or diminishing the value of the property. When ownership is recognized as a responsibility, the legal liability for failing to exercise it is undeniable.

The evolution of the market has produced, in institutional investors, a small group of easily identifiable owners who have the capacity to understand and act. They also have two indisputable motives for paying close attention to ownership: avoiding liability for breach of fiduciary duty and enhancing portfolio values by promoting management accountability. There seems every reason to reestablish the accountability of management to ownership that has been the historical underpinning of capitalism.

The violence of hostile takeovers in the 1980s challenged all the myths and realities, all the historical and legal theories of corporate existence. The question "to whom are the mangers of the great corporations accountable?" has not yet been satisfactorily answered. If trust is to be reestablished, initiative and sustaining energy will have to come from the institutional investors. That is what the next five chapters will show. The last chapter will show how it is done.

2

Why Bad Stock Happens
to Good Investors

I remember going to my great-grandfather's office as a child and being told solemnly that the great man never purchased any security other than common stock, and that I shouldn't either. To do otherwise was not merely a poor investment, it was a breach of faith. When Nell was born, her Russian Jewish immigrant grandfather gave her two shares of common stock in AT&T, as close to a piece of America as he could find to present to his first grandchild. She still holds them.

Common stock turned out to be one of the most successful "products" ever marketed in this country. It continued to be an attractive investment even into the 1970s and 1980s, when exotic variations like puts and calls were developed to tantalize Wall Street. But some of the aspects of common stock that make it attractive have been eroded, even eliminated. In theory, common stock's unique advantages account for its value. In reality, the problem is that some of those advantages are more theoretical than real.

Equity is the only investment with a limit on liability and no limit on returns. Microsoft, the innovative software company in Bellevue, Washington, did not just make founder Bill Gates wealthy. The prescient investors who bought stock when it went public at $21 a share in 1986 found these shares worth $300 a few years later. One hundred shares of IBM stock in 1925 would now be 300,000 shares. The rising tide that lifts all the boats lifts the shareholder's most of all. Because everybody else gets paid first, the shareholder is uniquely at risk, to the limits of the investment. To pursue the metaphor: In a falling tide, the shareholder is the first investor to drown.

Creating the "Artificial Citizen"

The Corporation Defined

Corporation. An ingenious device for obtaining individual profit without individual responsibility.

Ambrose Bierce

Source: The Devil's Dictionary, Dover Publications, New York, 1958, p. 25.

We rarely ask ourselves today whether private corporations are a good thing for a society to have. Indeed, our only concept of life without them is the stereotype of the Soviet Union—consumers standing in line for hours for products that only come in one style, brand, and flavor, and even that is all gone by the time you get to the front of the line. But free societies prospered without corporations for many years, and the original concept of ceding influence to private entities was deeply troubling in the eighteenth century, a time when the legitimacy of the exercise of any kind of authority was being questioned.

The United States was founded by people who wanted something different from the old world. European tradition for many centuries involved a competing presence of "artificial individuals"—nobility, guilds, church, professional army, professional bureaucracy—so that the emergence of business corporations in the nineteenth and twentieth centuries represented simply an addition to a centuries-long continuum of accommodating large, powerful institutions. The prior history of municipal corporations, ecclesiastical corporations, guilds, joint stock companies, and educational and philanthropic corporations provides a backdrop in which the private exercise of power was familiar. Life in the new world reflected individual rather than establishment concerns.

The thinking of Revolutionary War–era leaders was based on a suspicion of power. This involved the development in the area of public power of an elaborate written constitution explicitly designed to balance different elements of power against each other.

But the parallel concerns about private power were addressed in a different context. The colonial-era citizens were familiar with corporations.

Indeed, the early colonies began their existence in the form of joint stock companies. The earliest history of the Massachusetts Bay and Plymouth companies demonstrates the evolution of governmental powers from a commercial charter. Thus, corporations were not in and of themselves suspect. What was essential was that the corporate form be available on a free and open basis. Within this framework, the emerging corporate form of business organization was based on democratic principles. To fit the corporation for American service, attention was focused on stripping away the elements of special privilege that clung to its European form. Colonial leaders rejected the British practice of issuing corporate charters by royal prerogative. It was a substantial popular victory when the privilege of incorporation was first declared a right during the presidency of Andrew Jackson.

As concerned as they were with rights, the founding fathers did not consider the rights of "artificial citizens," and the Constitution and its attending Bill of Rights did not easily accommodate them. As recently as 1990 the Supreme Court was still trying to decide how the protections of the Bill of Rights apply to corporations.[1] Indeed, the American tradition of denying express power to government encouraged the belief that power granted to corporations would further the interests of the individual against the state.

In the central document of American history, the Constitution, the word *corporation* never appears. The makers of public policy were still very wary of the impact that private entities could have on American life. One worry was the problem of reconciling the interests of management and owners (as representatives of the community interest). Another was that a corporation's size and indefinite duration would overwhelm the interests of individual citizens. As the idea of the corporation evolved, it was designed to have checks and balances like those built into the political system, and for the same purpose: to assure stability, accountability, and legitimacy. After all, the same year that America declared its independence, English economist Adam Smith was writing in *The Wealth of Nations* that directors of publicly held corporations could not be expected to watch the company "with the same anxious vigilance with which the partners in a private copartnery frequently watch over their own. . . . Negligence and profusion, therefore, must always prevail, more or less, in the management of such a company."[2] He went on to say that for this reason publicly held companies (which he called "joint stock companies") had seldom been able to compete with privately held companies, unless they had a monopoly.

To resolve these concerns, an essential part of the system was a kind of corporate democracy, with each "citizen" entitled to vote according to his investment. If we were going to permit the government to excercise public power through the accountability imposed by the electoral system, it seemed logical to permit corporations to exercise private power on the same basis.

Louis Brandeis, in 1933, eloquently warned that it was a mistake to "accept the evils attendant upon the free and unrestricted use of the corporate mechanism as if these evils were the inescapable price of civilized life." He continued:

[I]ncorporation for business was commonly denied long after it had been freely granted for religious, educational, and charitable purposes. It was denied because of fear. Fear of encroachments upon the liberties and opportunities of the individual. Fear of the subjection of labor to capital. Fear of monopoly. Fear that the absorption of capital by corporations, and their perpetual life, might bring evils similar to those which attended mortmain. There was a sense of some insidious menace inherent in large aggregations of capital, particularly when held by corporations.[3]

So the corporation was welcome in its "enlarged conception of legal persons."[4] Clearly, the demands of emerging capitalism required a conglomeration of people, money, and property beyond the capacity of individuals. The life of the new continent required such institutions to construct the harbors, build the canals, maintain the highways, and ultimately, create the railroad that would tame the wilderness continent.

A corporation is a fictional "person" with some of the rights of a citizen but not all of them—and some rights that citizens do not have. A corporation has some of the rights of freedom of speech guaranteed by the First Amendment, but there are limitations on "commercial" speech. A corporation cannot vote in an election, but it can provide a good deal of financial support (directly or indirectly) for a cause or a candidate. Indeed, as we will see in Chapter 4, corporations have been enormously effective at rallying state and federal protection. Almost two centuries ago, the Lord Chancellor of England, Edward, First Baron Thurlow, fumed at the corporation's amorphous existence: "Did you ever expect a corporation to have a conscience when it has no soul to be damned, and no body to be kicked?"[5] It cannot be jailed. It cannot even be fined, in any real sense; even when a fine is imposed, it is the shareholders who pay it.

The Externalizing Machine

Despite attempts to provide balance and accountability, the corporation as an entity became so powerful that it quickly outstripped the limitations of accountability and became something of an externalizing machine, in the same way that a shark is a killing machine—no malevolence, no intentional harm, just something designed with sublime efficiency for self-preservation, which it accomplishes without any capacity to factor in the consequences to others. With checks and balances of the marketplace intended to keep its focus on maximizing profits, that is just what it did. But it did so in a manner quite different from that intended or predicted. Instead of maximizing profits by making better, cheaper goods, it did so in less challenging ways, by restricting competition—sometimes with the help of the government. Instead of maximizing profits for shareholders, corporate management often maximized profits for themselves, lowering dividends but raising salaries. Instead of devoting creative energy to productivity, they devoted it to ever more unbreakable entrenchment devices.

The idea of the corporation evolved slowly. At first, the states chartered each company individually and limited the kinds of ventures corporations could undertake. This system was perhaps inspired by suspicion, but it created "a process that invited bribery and corruption since it involved negotiating specific charter provisions with legislators—among others, the purpose of the enterprise, the location of its activities, the amount of capital to be raised by stock sales, and the power of its directory."[6] The many impediments—some intentional, some not—to incorporation began to fall in the late nineteenth century, less as a result of any public policy in favor of corporations than as a way to increase tax revenues for states. Businesses, seeking the protections available through trusts and holding companies, for the first time provided a political base that supported, even encouraged, these changes.

In the nineteenth and early twentieth centuries, the very absence of traditional institutions stimulated the growth of business, in terms of both its favorable and in its unfavorable characteristics. Entrepreneurial energies literally knew no bounds. By the outbreak of World War I, the United States was the premier industrial power in the world. It also was a country shaken to its core by pressures that business wealth brought to the legitimacy of the political process. State and federal governments alike had been tainted by bribery and corruption; the Erie scandals and the administration of U. S. Grant are only a few examples of the government's struggle to survive the threat of unlimited private power.

Adam Smith predicted that businessmen would try to maximize profit by eliminating competition rather than beating it. "Without an exclusive privilege, they have commonly mismanaged the trade. With an exclusive privilege they have both mismanaged and confined it."[7] He was right. Some companies became monopolistic and threatened to destroy the competitive marketplace that was the essential ingredient in ensuring that commercial pursuit would result in the public interest. At the turn of the twentieth century, this brought about the first comprehensive federal laws respecting business: antitrust and antimonopoly legislation.

Business also tried to maximize profit by externalizing costs, placing the costs of unsafe working conditions on their employees and the costs of unsafe products on the consumers. So the antitrust laws were followed by the first health and safety laws. None of these laws was antibusiness; their objective was to save business from itself, to liberate the business system to function in a manner that would result in the public good. But they represent a suspicion of business and businesspeople, which is still a strong theme in the economic and political debate.

The stock market crash of 1929, the disgrace of prominent business leaders,[8] and unacceptable levels of unemployment led to a political decision that business could not and should not be unilaterally responsible for solving the nation's economic problems. Following the election of Franklin Roosevelt in 1932, big business accepted a federal presence as a permanent factor in the pursuit of profit. A business council consisting of the principal leaders of the major corporations was organized as a part of the U.S. Department of Commerce and functioned as an official liaison between business and government from the early days of Roosevelt until the Kennedy administration. Thereafter, an independent business organization, the Business Roundtable, became the most prominent mouthpiece for the major industries.

From Common Stock to Junk Stock

In the early twentieth century, as corporations began to produce more of America's goods and services than proprietorships and partnerships,[9] it became possible for anyone with enough money to buy a share of stock and participate in the profits of the industrial revolution. Buying common stock was buying America and betting on its future. Anyone could buy a piece of the people, the inventions, and the companies that were transforming the world. As the century progressed, anyone could invest in companies that produced cars, electric lights, telephones, birth control pills, airplanes, movies, computers, televisions, rocket ships, and the Tang® they carried. You didn't have to be smart enough to invent these things, only smart enough to buy a piece of the company that made them.

The ability to participate through inexpensive, easily transferable investments also made it possible to diversify a portfolio to minimize risk. Not only did investors not have to be smart enough to invent something, they did not have to be smart enough to pick the right companies to invest in. Just spread the investments around and sell out when they started to drop, and you would do fine. America's love affair with common stock was dampened by the crash in 1929, but the government stepped in to regulate the markets, to provide a level of safety that would encourage investors to return—and they did return, in record numbers.

The expectations of a holder of common stock are clearly defined and easy to understand. After the obligations of the corporation have been settled, what is left belongs to stockholders. A shareholder's rights are also clearly defined. The holder of common stock is entitled to a share of all dividends paid that is proportional to the amount of stock owned. The shareholder has the right to transfer his shares in the market, to vote proxies to elect directors, to approve amendments to the corporate charter and changes of the state of incorporation, and to vote on resolutions proposed by other shareholders or even initiate them himself. Finally, if the directors or managers abuse the authority entrusted to them by shareholders, the holder can sue the directors and management either as an individual, on behalf of the class, or as a representative of the corporation itself. (The last form of lawsuit is called a shareholder's derivative suit, because shareholders "derive" the right to sue from the failure of management to pursue its own claims.)

These rights have had varying impact and value. Transferability of shares is essential to make the corporation an attractive investment. It allows shareholders to diversify the risk of investment among several ventures and to change the level of risk easily. Transferability has been so important, in fact, that the market has willingly, if inadvertently, relinquished many of the other rights of ownership in order to preserve it. In early days, stock certificates were like checks or like other kinds of property: you transferred stock by giving someone the actual certificate. My first job, at age 16, was as messenger for Paine, Webber, delivering the documents necessary for every transfer of stock (at least five for each transaction), all pinned together with great ceremony by a man who worked behind a cage in the front of the office.

This system worked, briefly. In the summer of 1950, for example, when I was a runner, the market never traded over 750,000 shares in a day. The system, however, was inadequate for the volume that was to come. Last year, for example, the New York Stock Exchange alone traded 292,363,500 shares in a single day. The old system proved too cumbersome and too invasive of shareholder privacy.

The Path of the Proxy Card

"Like pilgrims, the proxy card and the right to vote follow a long and tortuous path before returning home to the issuer," wrote Betty Linn Krikorian.[10] The current process (see Figure 1) begins with the company sending a notice of its shareholder meeting date to one of three depositories, the largest being the Depository Trust Company (DTC), and to the stock exchanges. The depository informs its participants (in the case of the DTC, this includes 400 broker-dealers and 200 banks) and sends to the company a list of participants that hold that stock with the bank. The company has 20 days to send cards to the depository's participants asking them for the number of sets of proxy materials they need and, if the participants are banks, a list of their respondent banks. Within one day of receiving the list, the company must send cards to those respondents, who must identify their respondents, and so on, until all the respondent banks have been contacted.

The company sends out proxy materials and voting cards to all banks and shareholders of record. It is up to the bank to determine who is the beneficial owner of each stock (and thus who has voting rights) and how many shares each owner can vote. If the bank is deemed beneficial owner, it votes according to its own policy. If the bank does not have voting power, either it can forward the proxy material to the beneficial owner within five business days of receiving the material from the company or it can forward the material with a request for instructions on how the stake is to be voted. The DTC sends an omnibus proxy to all participants, detailing the number of shares held by each participant as of the record date. Within five days, each bank must assign voting rights to their shares held for the respondent banks and notify the respondents and the company.

The bank marks, signs, and returns the proxies to the company for stock held by the bank beneficially and stock for which they have received

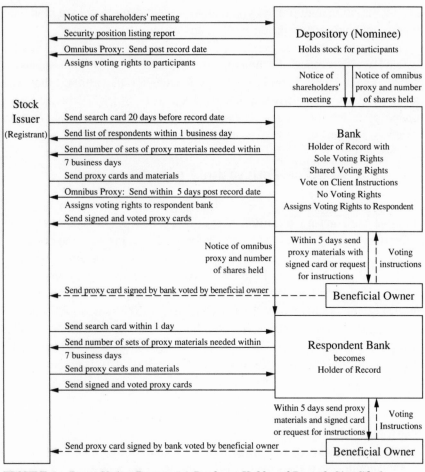

FIGURE 1 *Proxy Voting Process (a) Banks as Holder of Record, Simplified—*
No Intermediary, One Respondent Bank. *Source:* Diagram prepared by Betty Linn
Krikorian, *Fiduciary Standards in Pension and Trust Fund Management* (Butterworth
Legal Publishers), 1989, pp. 190, 191.

instructions from the beneficial owner. If the beneficial owners handle
the votes themselves, the bank signs the proxies and forwards them to
the owner.

Broker-dealers usually vote on the instructions of the beneficiary.
Thus, the broker-dealer votes a master proxy by adding the votes based
on the voting instructions received and the votes it casts internally and
returns these to the company. Due to a desire on the part of management
to communicate directly with as many shareholders as possible and to
a concern over whether shareholders are receiving complete information,

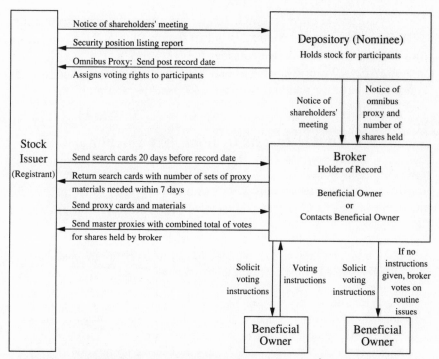

FIGURE 1 (Continued) *Proxy Voting Process (b) Broker as Holder of Record, Simplified—No Intermediary, No Layers of Brokers.*

brokers are required to ask all clients whether their identity can be disclosed to the company. Owners who refuse are called objecting beneficial owners (OBOs) and are not included on the list of beneficial owners the broker submits to the company. The names of nonobjecting beneficial owners (NOBOs) are known to the issuer company, which means that although their shares are still physically voted by the broker, they are receiving direct communications from the company on proxy matters.

The operational aspect of the process often involves a third party. A company such as the Independent Election Corporation of America (IECA) provides NOBO lists to companies and will serve as the intermediate between the owners and the corporation. IECA will also code proxies and track votes cast.

This system was great for making it easy to buy and sell stock, but it made it even harder to exercise the other rights of share ownership and, by doing so, created something of a vacuum. Wall Street, like nature, abhors a vacuum (which it refers to as a "market niche"). This one was filled by corporate managers and, sometimes, by raiders. In this chapter, we focus on the original contract between shareholders and the companies they invest in. In Part II, we consider the ways in which the other rights of ownership all but disappeared and the impact that had on companies and their stock, for which this discussion provides a context.

Junior Invests in Boothbay Harbor

The traditional relationship between entitlement to receive the benefits from a venture and responsibility for its impact on society was charmingly put early in this century, as a father advises his son in *Main Street and Wall Street:*

> Now, Junior, before you go to college I want to give you my investment in the Boothbay Harbor Electric Light Company. This concern serves our old neighbors and friends, and I want you to feel a continuing interest in, and a responsibility for, our share in this local enterprise. If properly managed it should be a benefit to this community; and it will yield you an income to be applied to your education through the next few years. But you must never forget that you are partly responsible for this undertaking. Our family had a hand in starting it. That responsibility is an inseparable part of your ownership. I read something the other day, in an opinion by Justice Brandeis of the United States Supreme Court, which bears this out: "There is no such thing to my mind . . . as an innocent stockholder. He may be innocent in fact, but socially he cannot be held innocent. He accepts the benefits of the system. It is his business and his obligation to see that those who represent him carry out a policy which is consistent with the public welfare." He is right in that. This accountability for wealth underlies and justifies the whole institution of private property upon which the government of our great country is founded.[11]

There was a certain parity in the traditional characteristics of common stock: investors could limit their risk of loss and enforce their entitlement to management's loyal attention, management could secure the capital necessary for a successful enterprise, and society could be confident that what was good for business was good for the citizenry at large. Investors, managers, and workers were all accountable to each other.

Through their power to vote for directors, shareholders have traditionally been considered the ultimate source of authority and legitimacy for corporations. Those whose money is at risk are the appropriate source of overall direction for the enterprise. The intention was that the holder of common stock would provide this guidance not by making decisions about product lines or retained earnings but by requiring that management run the venture with competence and loyalty to generate long-term value enhancement. The shareholder's entitlement was enforceable in court. So when the first Henry Ford wanted to sell his cars for below-market value out of social concern, the courts reminded him that it was wrong to sacrifice shareholder interests for social ones.[12] Nor, until the most recent times, was management legally free to make charitable contributions.[13] The theoretical capacity to require accountability is essential: "But the fact remains that the power, even if rarely exercised, and then only under extreme provocation, was there; and every once in a blue moon some resolute individual or stockholder could rise in his place and organize a protective committee or dissenting group—and, if nothing else happened, at least there was a thorough ventilation of what sometimes proved to be a musty or unsafe tenement."[14]

This remembered sense of balance is so powerful that it persists despite unmistakable proof that it no longer exists. Management accountability to shareholders is more than an economically beneficial arrangement; it is the basis on which we, as a matter of public policy, give legitimacy to the impact that private entities have on our lives. We would no more create a private entity without accountability than we would a public one; we don't want corporate dictators any more than we want political ones. But today, any remaining accountability is little more than a vestige of the original contract, the last remaining trace of the myth that no one seems to want to give up.

Practically no one has any incentive to challenge it. The myth of accountability to shareholders is like a mantra that justifies their continued passivity while allowing them to continue to invest. Management takes comfort from the same myth because it justifies their actions; after all, if there was anything wrong, the shareholders would have stopped them. Why should politicians challenge the notion of accountability to shareholders? What kind of political support can there be for such a challenge when both sides embrace the status quo?

Junior Loses Control

Academics alone have been willing to make heretical attempts to demonstrate the lack of accountability—using the helplessness of shareholders as justification for legally downgrading their "right" to primacy among corporate constituents. They sometimes express this by calling the modern shareholder "shirking" or "laggard," and they echo Berle and Means in concluding that because shareholders have abandoned their legitimating role, they "deserve" diminished rights.

A long line of distinguished scholarship points out that, to the extent the theoretical rights of shareholders do exist, they have become impossible to exercise. Berle and Means accurately put it over half a century ago: "[T]he owners of passive property, by surrendering control and responsibility over the active property, have surrendered the right that the corporation should be operated in their sole interest—they have released the community from the obligation to protect them to the full extent implied in the doctrine of strict property rights."[15]

When Berle and Means wrote their book on the helplessness of shareholders, the problem seemed insolvable. Graham and Dodd, writing at about the same time, urged shareholders to understand that the holding of stock required vigilance in the exercise of ownership rights as an investment matter. In their first edition, Graham and Dodd plainly stated that "the choice of a common stock is a single act; its ownership is a continuing process. Certainly there is just as much reason to exercise care and judgment in *being* as in *becoming* a stockholder."[16] They later admitted that being a conscientious shareholder was more difficult than it looked, noting that shareholder activity has "yet to come to grips with the real issues involved in the confrontations of stockholders and their management."[17] It seemed impossible, for the reason Berle and Means identified. With so many shareholders, it did not make economic sense to evaluate the opportunities provided by ownership rights with any enthusiasm, much less to exercise them.

It is currently fashionable in some academic circles to endorse this approach, and, as discussed in detail in Chapter 3, it appears in slightly different form in the push for "stakeholder" laws. Berle and Means pointed out half a century ago that the wide dispersal of stock, its easy transferability, and the diversification of even modest portfolios made it impossible for shareholders to play the supervisory role originally intended. So why not do away with it entirely? Why should shareholders have any more of a say than managers, customers, employees, suppliers, or the state?

Shareholders, the great short-term beneficiaries of this system, have no reason to consider the consequences of their noninvolvement, as they now freely trade the stock instead of devoting resources to monitoring and providing direction for the company, without the slightest reduction in the stocks's value on account of the costs that the companies are able to externalize. Rather than deal with the problems of pollution, public utilities and other fossil fuel–burning industries have simply lobbied government bodies, denying that the problem exists. When Ralph Nader exposed the Corvair's safety defects, General Motors did not immediately address the problem but instead hired a private investigator to follow Nader and "substantiate completely false rumors that Nader was anti-Semitic and a homosexual."[18] Those who are so willing to abandon the role of shareholder neglect the huge social cost of doing so. The long-term loser is society as a whole, like a player in an "Old Maid" card game, with each party trying to push the costs on to another.

Adam Smith's notion was that individual pursuit of self-interest would ensure the collective interest through an "invisible hand," despite his own reservations about the way this would work in a system riddled with agency costs. But the power of this "invisible hand" was such that it was used to justify freedom from government intervention needed to ensure the compatibility of corporate power and the public interest.

The High Cost of Transferability

Shareholders' ability to perform what James Willard Hurst has called "their legendary function" of monitoring has been substantially eroded, initially, as noted by Berle and Means, by sheer numbers. Management has every incentive to increase the number of holders.[19] First, to do so increases available capital and helps transferability by keeping the prices of individual shares comparatively low. Ease of transferability is not a priority for Warren Buffet, for example, whose Berkshire Hathaway trades in four figures per share. But he is a rare exception; most companies split their stock before it reaches $100 a share.

Increasing the number of shares has another significant advantage for corporate management: it reduces the incentive and ability of each shareholder to gather information and monitor effectively. Even the $250 million investment in General Motors by one of the largest equity investors in the United States, the California Public Employees' Retirement System, is not of much significance in a company with a market value of more than $30 billion. When the number of shareholders is in the hundreds of thousands—even the millions—and each holds stock in a number of companies, no single shareholder can monitor effectively. Is monitoring worth it when your investment (and liability) are limited and when, even if you do understand the issues, there is nothing you can do about them?

Universal transferability has also critically changed the nature of the shareholders' relationship to the corporate structure. As investors, stockholders had to look to corporate performance for protection and enhancement of their investments; they had to consider the efficacy of capital investments; they were directly influenced by the way the corporation conducted itself and by how society perceived it. In the absence of readily available "exit," or sale, the traditional shareholder used "voice," or ownership rights.[20] "[T]he corporation with transferable shares converted the underlying long-term risk of a very large amount of capital into a short-term risk of small amounts of capital. Because marketable corporate shares were readily salable at prices quoted daily (or more often), their owners were not tied to the enterprise for the life of its capital equipment, but could pocket their gains or cut their losses whenever they judged it advisable. *Marketable shares converted the proprietor's long-term risk to the investor's short-term risk.*"[21] The increased number of shares and ease of transferability acted as a vicious circle, because the inability to use "voice" to influence corporate activity made "exit" the only option.

The costs implicit in acting as an owner are far easier to justify in the case of a long-term holder. It is virtually impossible to argue that extensive monitoring is cost-effective for investors whose profit is principally derived from buying and selling in the short term. The prospect of buying low and selling high is so beguiling that a lucrative industry of "active money management" has flourished, notwithstanding the reality that institutional investors *are* the market and therefore cannot hope to beat its performance.

Can the Market Beat Itself?

Investment management, as traditionally practiced, is based on a single basic belief: Professional investment managers *can* beat the market. That premise appears to be false, particularly for the very large institutions that manage most of the assets of most trusts, pension funds, and endowments, because their institutions have effectively become the market.

Charles D. Ellis

Source: Investment Policy, Dow-Jones Irwin, Homewood, Ill., 1989, p. 5.

Hope always exists for a particular institution that it can be the exception and can beat the averages. This hope, rather than any statistical evidence, accounts in part for the change in the way shareholders see themselves, from owner to speculator (or investor). Another component is short-term self-interest, an objective that does nothing to encourage monitoring, which involves the commitment of resources for gains that are not immediately quantifiable (with the possible exception of shareholders who are large enough and aggressive enough to underwrite contests for control). In the longer term, this altered role has involved a high price for the business system as whole.

Transferability has had significant adverse consequences for corporations as well. It means that the interests of shareholder and manager are not necessarily the same; indeed, they are based on incompatible premises, because the investor will want to sell at the first sign that the stock may have reached its trading peak, and the manager wants stable, long-term investors. The American corporate system was initially based on the permanence of investor capital. Unintentionally, the growth of the institutional investors may have reintroduced elements of stability in stock ownership.

The market has become so complex that it is increasingly uneconomic for individuals to invest on their own behalf. Nearly half of all equity securities are therefore held by institutional investors on behalf of individuals. As a result, shareholding is now further subdivided between trustees, who are legally responsible, and beneficiaries, who are financially interested—yet another instance of agency costs in the myriad of lines between agent and principal that make up the corporation. Trustees are picked not by the beneficiaries, who pay their fees, but by the people establishing the trust—in this case corporate managers, whose interests (as we will see) are often competing with, if not directly contrary to, the interests of the people they pay the trustees to look out for.

Trip Invests in Boothbay Harbor

Let's look at a typical shareholder under this system and contrast him with Junior, who got the fatherly advice about the Boothbay Harbor Electric Light Company described in Ripley's book 65 years ago. We will begin with the largest single class of ownership, comprising perhaps 15 percent of the total outstanding equity.[22] Junior's son Trip is now an employee of Widget Co., a midsize manufacturing company with a "defined benefit" pension plan. That means that no matter what Trip puts in before he retires, once he does he is guaranteed a set retirement check every month. Let's say that Trip has been with the company for 20 years, with about another 15 to go before retirement, and let's keep in mind that his office mates—one who just started work and one who is 5 years from retirement—might have very different sets of priorities.

The concerns of Trip and his colleagues are a far cry from Junior's "sense of responsibility" for the companies he invests in; indeed, Trip could probably not say what stocks he holds, bought by several investment managers hired by the fiduciary designated by the corporate chairman. To make things even more complicated, while one of the investment managers employed by Trip's company is buying Boothbay Harbor, another is selling it; indeed, sometimes they sell to each other, leaving Trip and his colleagues with the same shares and a loss on the transaction costs. Trip "owns" a minuscule fraction of perhaps thousands of publicly traded companies. Not only has he no say about which securities are purchased on his behalf, he doesn't even find out until after the fact, and sometimes not even then. Between Junior and Boothbay there was a reliable system of communication. Between Trip and Boothbay there is an investment manager, a custodian, a trustee, a named fiduciary, and the CEO of Trip's employer, Widget Co.

Trip and the other employees whose pension money is invested really have no legally enforceable interest with respect to a particular holding of the plan; their only right is to be paid the promised benefits. Whether these come from stocks, bonds, or gold bullion is irrelevant to him. His only right is to require that the trustee act loyally and competently in his interest.

That could be complicated. The trustee, usually a bank, may have business relationships that create uncomfortable conflicts, putting Trip in a situation quite different from Junior's. For example, the trustee will be voting stock in the same companies it makes loans to or handles payrolls for. There have been a number of reports of cases where a trustee attempting to vote against corporate management was stopped by its own management. Why not? The trustee has no economic interest whatsoever in the quality of the voting decision, beyond avoiding liability. No enforcement action has ever been brought and no damages ever awarded for breach of duty in voting proxies. Trustees earn no incentive compensation, no matter how much energy and skill they devote to ownership responsibilities. And, crucially, the corporation knows how the trustee votes, whereas Trip has no idea. The trustee has nothing to lose from routine votes with management and everything to gain. Even if the trustee wanted to view ownership responsibility more energetically, it would be all but impossible as a practical matter, because of further inhibitions to shareholder activism arising out of the problems of "collective action" and "free riding," the pervasive problem of conflict of interest by institutional trustees, the legal obstacles imposed by the federal "proxy rules," and state law and state court acquiescence to management entrenchment—all described later in substantial detail.

Who Invests in Boothbay Harbor?

Meanwhile, at the top of the chain, the CEO's interest in the investment in Boothbay is also quite different from Trip's or Junior's. His interest is, first and foremost, being able to pay Trip his defined benefit when he retires, with a minimum of contribution by Widget Co. and, probably, a minimum involvement of his own time—after all, pension benefits don't have much to do with Widget Co.'s products or sales. So the CEO will push the investment managers to provide results (while he decries the "short-term perspective" of investors with other CEOs). If he is involved, he is faced with what has been called "ERISA's fundamental contradiction."[23] As a corporate manager, he would tend to favor provisions that, as a shareholder, he might find unduly protective of management, either as a matter of general principles or more specifically—he could even be a member of Boothbay's board.

In the 1920s, Trip's father, Junior, and his grandfather, who spoke of Boothbay Harbor with such proprietary interest, felt a real connection to the company they invested in. In the 1990s, the trustee, the custodian, the investment managers, and the CEO stand between Boothbay and Trip. Do any of these people "feel a continuing interest in, and a responsibility for" their share in this enterprise? Are any of them able to exercise, or even interested in exercising, the responsibility of providing overall direction for the company?

And is such monitoring by owners a "right," to be discarded if inconvenient, or is it a "responsibility"? Although academics cite shareholders' "shirking" of their responsibility as justification for their diminished status, they have neglected the consequences. The result has been that shareholders have managed to foist off all manner of liabilities onto society as a whole. Ultimately, society has paid the highest price for such "mistakes" as Rely® tampons, the Dalkon shield, and DDT. The corporate system does not provide a way for those who profit from corporate operations to share some of their bounty to pay for related social costs. We are left with three choices: legitimating the exercise of corporate power through accountability to shareholders, by enabling (or requiring) shareholders to provide their "legendary supervisory role"; finding some other kind of accountability (perhaps government) to limit the imposition of externalized costs; or leaving things the way they are, allowing those costs to fall as they do.

The Postwar Era: One Big Unhappy Family

It is a simplification, if not an outright misrepresentation, to speak of the stock Junior and Trip held in Boothbay Harbor as though Boothbay were the same company for both of them. As shareholders have changed, so have the companies they invested in. Trip's many-times-removed investment was probably not in Boothbay Harbor but in a company that had bought Boothbay and a dozen other companies—something called, say, Global Unodyne. During the era just after World War II, the fad was for conglomerates. The theory was that conglomerates would have (to use a word not popular until much later) synergy, that the various businesses would help each other, and that the diversity of interests would make the company safe from any kind of economic downturn. It was not enough, maybe not even relevant, to have expertise in the product line; a certain business expertise was thought to apply whether the product was computers, hamburgers, or hotel rooms. Put another way, the product of such a conglomerate was no longer computers, hamburgers, or hotel rooms—it was stock.

This was at the same time one of the most beguiling and one of the most damaging industrial concepts in the history of the American economy. "Tell me the story," the business school–educated analysts would ask. If the story was right, there was no limit to the stock price. Some of the cleverest people in America—Ford Motor Company's "best and brightest," Roy Ash and Tex Thornton—with their "whiz kid" credentials, brought forth to a hungry public the new phenomenon in the form of Litton Industries.

Litton was as close to glamorous as a business can get. With its former movie headquarters in Los Angeles, with Crosby Kelly, the inventor of "financial public relations," and with a record of increasing quarterly earnings for over 10 years, Litton seemed able to do anything, despite the fact that no one could single out any particular value that was added. Here's how it worked: Litton's stock would be selling at 40 times its earnings. An attractive company would be located, for example, Fitchburg Paper Company. Either the marketplace or appraisers would value Fitchburg Paper Company at around 10 times its earnings. The Litton team would descend on the shareholders (in this case, the Wallaces, the family of the founders of Fitchburg) and offer them a "premium" of 70 percent to acquire their company. How's that? Well, Litton would issue new Litton common stock to the Wallace family with a market value of 170 percent of their present holdings.

How could they do it? Assume that Fitchburg Paper had annual earnings of $5 million and a market value of $50 million. Litton would issue them stock worth $85 million and acquire $5 million of new earnings. With Litton's price/earnings ratio, this translates into $200 million of additional value for which they have only paid $85 million. So long as the market continued to accord a 40× multiple to Litton, Litton could continue to make the Wallaces of the world rich and generate "instant profits" for themselves. The Litton *principals* had charm and a sense of the dramatic. Acquisitions were seductions; work went on around the clock; the world stood still. Their goal was to acquire 50 companies a year.

Litton began by acquiring companies with related businesses in 1958. In the 1960s, however, it branched out into "typewritters, cash registers, packaged foods, conveyor belts, oceangoing ships, solder, teaching aids, and aircraft guidance systems."[24] The story ended badly. Litton's radiance ultimately became tarnished. The stock "tanked" in 1968.[25] That is, the stock fell 18 points in one week. It did not merely fall in an orderly manner; it disintegrated. The Wallaces and other shareholders were left with no company, a lot of paper losses, some fine memories, and very little of lasting value.

Other companies managed to make the conglomerate structure work by making more careful acquisitions, but the American economy is saddled with a substantial portion of its industrial capacity misorganized in the inefficient conglomerate form, from which it will take two decades to extricate itself. Here was the fertile breeding ground for the leveraged buyout, the restructuring, and the hostile takeover.

The 1980s:
Myth Meets Reality

Perhaps this system would have lumbered along indefinitely, had it not been for two unprecedented developments, on a collision course with each other and with traditional notions of corporations, management, and shareholders. The first was the emergence of institutional investors (discussed in Chapter 6), required, as fiduciaries, to take their ownership responsibilities seriously and big enough to begin to surmount the problems that had prevented effective exercise of ownership rights in the past. The second was what made such exercise so important—the takeover boom. The creation of securities to make a takeover of just about any size possible gave ownership rights a more immediate value than they ever had before. Such takeovers were in part made possible by the separation of ownership and control, which had created a value gap (the "control premium") between the market value of the shares and their absolute value. Junk bonds enabled raiders or managers to cash out the difference between the two, and inevitably, shareholders noticed that it was their money—or should have been.

In 1969, Saul Steinberg seized the commercial world's attention with a $9 billion tender offer for the Chemical Bank. The Wall Street establishment's ability to cripple this effort by shutting off Steinberg's sources of credit reinforced the conventional wisdom that hostile takeovers could not be done in America. In the intervening decades, prosperity in Europe and Asia increased liquidity substantially. Worldwide financial sophistication has developed, and the U.S. establishment no longer has the capacity to prevent foreigners from putting together bank syndicates to provide virtually limitless amounts of money to close deals. And many scholars studying the "market for corporate control" became convinced not only that hostile takeovers were tolerable, but that they were essential as the only real way in which managerial power could be held to accountability—after all, shareholders could not do the job, and raiders, or the threat of raiders, could.

Political and economic theory required that the marketplace be the ultimate judge of management. It was clear that accountability couldn't really be achieved by holders' selling shares of companies that did not perform satisfactorily. As Edward Jay Epstein points out, "just the exchange of one powerless shareholder for another in a corporation, while it may lessen the market price of shares, will not dislodge management—or even threaten it. On the contrary, if dissident shareholders leave, it may even bring about the further entrenchment of management—especially if management can pass new bylaws in the interim."[26] As discussed in detail in Chapter 3, shareholder lawsuits to enforce the fiduciary duty of managers were ineffective. The overwhelming advantages of incumbency made contests for control through the electoral process virtually impossible. So the only basis for ensuring management's commitment to profit maximization was vulnerability to hostile takeover. Takeovers were not only feasible, they were legitimate—almost.

The comfortable legal balance that had for a century provided a nurturing framework for the financing of corporations and the increasing of share values was brutally tested in the commercial environment of the 1980s. As is often the case with myths, the theories behind the corporation served a useful purpose long after they ceased having more than a tenuous relationship to reality. Although in theory shareholders could get relief from the courts if a conflict of interest with managers or directors could be proven, an appropriate context proved elusive. The intrinsic character of a business corporation involves conflicting interests: managers want to pay themselves more, owners want higher dividends; managers tend to favor size, owners profitability. Under the business judgment rule, courts would defer to the decisions of management and directors, as long as there was no obvious self-dealing or fraud.

Milken's Money Machine

Hostile takeovers in the 1980s arose primarily because virtually unlimited amounts of money were available to entrepreneurs who had energy and were willing to play. The difference between the takeovers of the 1980s and Saul Steinberg's 1969 attempt was simple: all of the funds could be provided. This "money machine" was the work of one man: Michael Milken. An utterly focused and creative financial mind combined with energy and ruthlessness made Milken the dominant financial force in America. Coming out of the Wharton School into the sleepy ranks of the Drexel bond department, Milken quickly demonstrated the elements that would in short order make him the most highly compensated individual in the world—and appear to be underpaid at that.

He negotiated a personal compensation arrangement with Drexel that depended entirely on his own production; he would be paid a percentage of the gross, no matter how high. In 1988 alone, his salary was reportedly $552 million,[27] which did not even include the value of the warrants he kept from various deals.

Finally, he negotiated the move of his operation to Los Angeles, to a building that he—not the firm—owned at the intersection of Rodeo Drive and Wilshire Boulevard. As would become apparent in subsequent criminal investigations, the move meant that Milken was effectively beyond the supervision of the "home office" in New York, which was all too content with the lavish fees of the new business to pay much attention.

He understood a new way of valuing "high-yield" (junk) bonds. What he "proved" was that the interest rate spread between so-called junk bonds and bonds of "investment grade" was so large that a buyer could, with a well-chosen portfolio, self-insure against the higher risk and still be substantially better off with junk. In other words, the rate was so high that you could afford to have a few failures in the portfolio; the successes would more than make up for it. From the perspective of 1990, this analysis seems badly flawed.

For many years, insurance companies had made loans of the same kind that Milken was now "discovering," except that they were called "private placements." What Milken did was create a public market for these loans and, in doing so, lower the costs for the borrower. In keeping with the theme of mythology, Milken's most powerful innovation was not in what he created, but what he called it. He changed the name for the financial instrument from a loan to a "security." The consequences were as astounding as if that were an incantation.

Three critical elements were there for anyone to see, but only Milken saw them. Combined, they created a capacity to raise money quickly in volumes never before dreamed of. The first was essentially eliminating the restrictions on loans. Government regulators worked to maintain a tolerable level of risk in the financial system by controlling debt-to-equity ratios.

Milken took what had traditionally been known as a loan and made it into a security, a bond.[28] As a consequence of this name change, it was considered an investment for the bank, part of its capital like any other bond, and therefore not subject to limitation on account of the traditional regulatory loan ratio standards. Thus, so long as a financial institution could get cash, it could acquire Milken's "bonds," as the Reagan administration's widely ballyhooed deregulation program permitted ever-greater latitude for investment.

The cash was close at hand. The second element of Milken's package was the Reagan administration's extension of federal insurance of bank deposits to $100,000 per account. Deposit insurance had been considered one of the enduring reforms arising out of the Great Depression, essential for creating confidence in the banks. Bank accounts were insured up to $40,000 until 1983, when the amount was raised to $100,000. Deposit insurance in its new guise set off a major "feeding frenzy." All the best

Wall Street houses tried to interest their customers in the magical new security—$100,000 bank deposit, *fully guaranteed by the federal government,* but with interest rates substantially more attractive than for other available securities backed by federal credit. The financial institutions could not believe their good luck—deposits flowing in on the one hand and Milken's bonds available on the other. It was a banker's dream—no work, no risk, and a huge spread between what they paid for money (as the deposit cost was subsidized by the U.S. government) and what they could get by investing it in huge quantities of available junk bonds. Milken invented the ideal merchandise for an ever-willing buyer.

The money machine was now in place, and Milken was quick to exploit the third element, his understanding that the market value of many American companies was substantially below their "real value." Some of this was due to a rather depressed stock market. A great deal of it was due to the fact that the stock market valued each share of stock as a minority share in a company. If one could acquire enough shares to exercise "control" over the company, values could be realized that, on a share basis, were substantially above the publicly quoted price. "Control" plainly was worth a premium, at least at a company with perceived inefficient management. It conveyed the right to determine the corporation's strategy, its capital structure, perquisites for management, and control over its cash flow. Because shares traded in the marketplace with no expectation on the part of the buyer of being able to achieve the control premium, prices did not reflect the underlying value of the business. Thus, for someone in a position to make an offer for all of the stock, a substantial premium over market could be paid and still leave enormous profit. This was the ultimate posture of the hostile takeover movement of the mid-1980s, Milken's money machine in search of the raiders—and targets. Nelson Peltz's takeover of National Can, William Farley's successful raid on Northwest Industries, and Stephen Wynn's refinancing of Golden Nugget are only a few of the many examples of Milken's enormous power in this arena.

The Investors Who Can't Say No and The Offer They Can't Refuse

Milken's money was one side of the deal. But all the money in the world cannot buy something from an owner who does not wish to sell.

Milken's buyers found the perfect sellers, and they were able to make shareholders an offer they couldn't refuse. As noted earlier and explained in detail in Chapter 6, by the 1980s a substantial portion of equity securities were in the hands of institutional investors. If Milken had tried to peddle to Junior, tried to get him to give up his Boothbay Harbor investment, he might not have gotten very far. But Milken and the people he funded made their offers to institutional investors, and their nature is an important element in understanding the appeal of the hostile takeover.

Institutions are fiduciaries and are therefore risk-averse. No one ever got the "Fiduciary of the Month" award for coming up with a new idea; fiduciaries are most secure when they are doing what everyone else does. Trustees are paid a fee that is usually a percentage of the assets under management; trustees do not earn incentives through superior performance.[29] There is no level of performance that entitles them to a meaningful participation in gains. They have an incentive to manage the property as well as others, so that they will be able to compete for new business, but the laws prohibiting fiduciaries from having interests in conflict with their beneficiaries do not permit payment at a level that would make risk attractive. A trustee thus has no upside potential but has a downside exposure if he acts differently from others similarly situated.

In that context, consider that a tender offer for shares may be at a price substantially higher than cost, market price, or, in many cases, projections for years to come. How can a fiduciary refuse? A good example is the comment by a money manager on the late 1990 AT&T offer for NCR. "As a stockholder, I have to say 'Take the money and run . . . '" It's a major premium on the market by a qualified buyer. I don't see how they can say 'no.'"[30]

Trust law tends to penalize those who lose money by acting differently than other fiduciaries similarly situated, so a cash tender has its coercive aspects in the context of large institutional investor holdings. With this behavior pattern, large institutional ownership in a company came to be taken as the equivalent of a "for sale" sign. Although the government agencies with jurisdiction over institutional investors have consistently said that pension fund trustees are under no "legal" obligation to tender stock to a high cash bidder (most recently in a joint statement by the secretaries of labor and the treasury in the first week of the Bush administration, in 1989), it has had no real impact. Why should it? Is there any possibility they will be at risk for tendering? Not really. Has such a case ever been brought? No.

But the legal question is not the real problem. Suppose that an institution had owned MD Oil for several years at an average cost of $20 per share and that a "raider" offers $40. The management may be entirely correct in pointing out that the pro rata value of shares as a percentage of the total value of the company is in excess of $40, but this is cold comfort to a trustee who must periodically account to his beneficiaries for his performance. Suppose that he fails to tender and the tender fails. The price will probably drop from near $40 back to around $29. How is he going to explain his performance? How many years will he have to wait for the full value to be achieved, and how many clients will he lose while he waits? Is he compensated for taking this risk? What does he lose by tendering? In the answers to these questions lies the success of the hostile takeover movement of the 1980s.

In Britain, the country with an institutional ownership pattern closest to ours among OECD nations, hostile takeovers never assumed the epidemic proportions seen in this country. One reason is that in Britain, a shareholder can vote against the tender and still get the tender price if the deal goes through. The system is less coercive. But a possibly more important reason is that the British institutions are in touch with each other, have some shared sense of value, and therefore have the ability to avoid being "cherry-picked" by the acquirer. The impediments to collective action present in this country are minimal over there, which gives British institutions more of a connection, more of a relationship to the companies they invest in, and which thus makes them more like Junior than like Trip. In this country, risk-averse trustees have not yet discovered how to act collectively and how to gain for their beneficiaries a substantial portion of the value gap between market price and the control premium.

Essential to the success of hostile takeovers was the emergence of a class of well-financed "risk arbitragers." These were the mirror image of the institutional investors, the other half that helped make a perfect whole. Arbs, financed by the banks, were precisely the converse of the fiduciaries. Their entire business was to take huge risks—from which they stood to profit hugely.

When a deal is first announced, the market appraises its likelihood of being consummated. The stock price rises to some amount, usually higher than the previous trading price and lower than the offer, to reflect both the probable final amount and the likelihood of its being paid. In the instance of UAL, investors drove the price up and down based on "whether or not the airline would be sold."[31] Returning to the MD Oil example, suppose the price rises to $35 on announcement of the proposed tender; what is the position of the institutional investor? Should the investor wait for the last buck, thus taking the chance that something will go wrong and the deal will not be consummated, or sell out and ensure a handsome profit (though less than might be realized by waiting)? This is what is called a market niche, and the arb arrives to fill the niche. Arbs run risks; that's how they make money. Is the fiduciary worried about what to do? Uncle Arb is here to take the risk away.

Here is how it is done: The arb borrows $35 to take the stock off the fiduciary's hands and then sees to it that a transaction does in fact take place; whether it is in the original form or another is only a matter of time and money. The arbs end up with control over the company long before the final denouement. Thus, the offer, by triggering the flight of the fiduciary to the safe profit and moving control to the arbs, is self-fulfilling.

Corporate management see it that way, too, which is why they react so strongly to hostile offers. When Donald Trump made an offer for American Airlines, the airline tried to stop him by going to the United States Congress for special legislation. I spent an afternoon calling American's largest shareholders, asking them what their reaction was. Every one of them agreed that if there was ever a time to support management, this was it. American's management was excellent, and Trump's offer was, to put it kindly, not credible. Every one of them agreed that they would make such a commitment to management, if asked. By the end of the day, I had lined up enough shares to block any hostile offer. But not one of them had been called by management at American Airlines, who were sure that the institutions would have to take any offer that was made to them. After all, when Cummins Engine, trying to protect itself from a potentially hostile acquiror (Hanson), offered its largest institutional investors a seat on the board if they would agree to hold their stock in Cummins for six years, every one of them turned Cummins down.

We use the word *shareholder* to describe institutions and arbs, individuals with a few shares, and individuals who have enormous blocks and are seeking more to describe both "passive" investors versus "active" investors. But it is clear that we are dealing with very different concepts of equity ownership. On the one hand are the active investors who intend to appropriate control. On the other hand are the institutions who have in effect concluded that they cannot or should not afford to be more active.

With all these pieces in place, all but the largest American corporations were fair game. The amounts involved were so large that the effect was seismic. A fee structure arose for bankers, lawyers, and investment professionals of every kind that quickly converted any question from whether a deal should take place to how it should take place. Bryan Burrough and John Helyar's *Barbarians at the Gate* (Harper & Row, New York, 1989) pinpoints with devastating accuracy the intrigues and machinations on all sides as everyone wanted a piece of the biggest deal in history.

Without going into detail about the tax advantages of debt financing and purchase price allocation among depreciable assets, we can agree with Michael Blumenthal that "[s]ome would argue that even if the distinction between 'good' and 'bad' deals is correct, nothing should be done. In a free-market environment, investors are best left to their own devices. No regulation or interference should or could save them from their folly. I have much sympathy for that viewpoint, but the problem is that we already have interfered with the free functioning of the market for deals. We have built artificial incentives into the system and created systemic distortions which induce people to make deals that should never be made, or to structure them in irresponsible or dangerous ways."[32]

Management Defends

Corporations are ideally suited for self-preservation, which is the definition of the externalizing machine. When they saw what Milken was doing, corporate management proceeded to do whatever was necessary to protect their capacity to direct enterprises, and they found that protecting themselves from raiders meant protecting themselves from shareholders and squeezing any remaining semblance of accountability out of the system. As described in detail in Chapter 3, the notion of management having an enforceable obligation to maximize the interests of ownership was submerged in the expansion of the "business judgment rule." The courts also permitted the creation by management of new captive artificial shareholders, leveraged employee stock ownership plans (ESOPs), literally in the middle of an attempted takeover, with a sufficient percentage of total ownership to block it. The ultimate death of the corporate myth, the theory under which management owed shareholders a greater duty than they owed themselves, came with the widespread acquiescence to the so-called management buyout (MBO).

There were dozens of other colorfully named devices that management used for protection against the hostile takeover deluge. Collectively, they were known as "shark repellents." Some of them were utterly justified, by any standard.[33] For a while there was an unconscionable practice called a "two-tier tender offer," which was an all-out robbery of shareholders. A two-tiered tender offer was used to accomplish the largest non-oil takeover in history, R. J. Reynolds' $4.5 billion acquisition of Nabisco in 1985. In such a deal, a buyer would offer, for example, $10 per share over the market price to everyone who tendered—until 51 percent was received. The last 49 percent to line up would be left, like Oliver Twist, asking for more, and with no better chance of getting it than Oliver had. What they would get would be thinner than Oliver's gruel, for example, notes for the tender amount but not payable for 15 years. Present an offer like this to a group of institutional investors and watch them push and shove their way to the front of the line, for all the reasons just described. After all, fiduciaries were being given a choice between $10 now and $10 in 15 years. The better choice, the $15 or $20 that the buyer would realize from this transaction, was not available. These offers were inherently coercive, as trustees in particular could not legally turn down the offer.[34]

These offers can be compared to the classic "prisoner's dilemma," where two coconspirators are captured and placed in separate rooms by the police. They are each told that if neither confesses, there will not be enough evidence, and both will go free. If one confesses, only that prisoner will get a reduced sentence. If both confess, both go to jail for a reduced term. Each must sit, unable to communicate with the other, and decide what to do. The dilemma is that an action that may benefit the individual making the choice (whether silence or confession) may have adverse consequences for the group (prison), whereas an action that benefits the group (silence) may have adverse consequences for the individual (prison, if the other confesses). This kind of situation is deemed "coercive" because someone is receiving an inappropriate incentive to do something contrary to his best interests.[35] By exploiting self-interest, the police could obtain confessions from both prisoners. If the prisoners could have communicated, however, they would have undoubtedly remained silent. Similarly, a shareholder facing a two-tiered tender offer knows that what is best for the group is for all shareholders to turn it down. But with no way to identify—much less communicate with—the other shareholders, the only choice is to try to get in the front of the line for the first tier of the offer.

1,000 Poison Pills

Quite properly, lawyers for corporate management came up with a way to stop two-tier offers. Corporate managers call them "rights plans." Everyone else calls them "poison pills." Nearly 1,000 companies have adopted poison pills,[36] most of them since November 1985, when the Delaware Supreme Court upheld a company's right to adopt a poison pill without shareholder approval in *Moran v. Household International*. The plans generally take the form of rights or warrants issued to shareholders and that are worthless unless triggered by a hostile acquisition attempt. If triggered, pills give shareholders the ability to purchase shares from or sell shares back to the target company (the "flip-in" pill) and/or the potential acquirer (the "flip-over" pill), depending on the circumstances, at a price far out of line with the fair market value. Unfortunately, they not only protect shareholders from coercive tender offers, they also protect managers from shareholders. Even though they are designed as protection and not intended ever to be triggered, the pills are poison, indeed.

The basic function of pills is, simply stated, to confront a hostile purchaser with immediate and unacceptable dilution of the value of his investment. The pill is a "doomsday device," with such potent wealth-destroying characteristics that no bidder has ever dared proceed to the point of causing a pill actually to become operative. Sir James Goldsmith circumvented the Crown Zellerbach plan by acquiring control through a creeping acquisition. In 1985, Goldsmith ignored the threshold set by Crown Zellerbach's pill and boldly bought enough shares in the conglomerate until he had control. Although the pill made it impossible for him to merge with Crown Zellerbach, he permitted its shareholders to swap their Crown Zellerbach stock for stock in divisions of the conglomerate, thereby dismembering the company.

The remaining chunk was sold to a third company, which operated it as an uncontrolled subsidiary. Thus, no company actually "acquired" Crown Zellerbach, so no purchase rights could be flipped over into an acquiring company.[37] A more recent example is Instron. Management and family members purchased 39 percent and then issued a statement stating that they would collectively resist any change in control. As a result, a shareholder filed suit (the case has since been dismissed) claiming that the directors have acted as a "controlling group" and inadvertently triggered their own pill. Metaphorically, pills have the impact in corporate wars that nuclear weaponry had in the Cold War: they could not be used.

Depending on the type of pill, the triggering event can either transfer a huge amount of wealth out of the target company or dilute the equity holdings of the potential acquirer's preexisting shareholders. In either case, the pills have the potential to act as doomsday machines in the event of an unwanted control contest, providing a target's board with veto power—all the board has to do is refuse to redeem the pill—over takeover bids, even if they are in the best interest of target shareholders. The power of redemption is the crucial issue for shareholders. To date, the courts have allowed target company boards great leeway in deciding when a pill must be redeemed, even in the event of bona fide offers. However, the courts indicated there are limits.[38] This is widely believed to be the reason for the 1990 Pennsylvania statute, discussed in Chapter 3, specifically permitting directors to act for nonshareholder constituencies.

Pills have changed form considerably since their inception, in response to court challenges, shareholder complaints, and the development of strategies that have been used successfully in overcoming earlier versions. Currently popular pill plans do not have the strategic shortcomings that were manifested in, for example, the Crown Zellerbach plan.

The widely used flip-over plan gives target shareholders the right to purchase shares of the potential acquirer's common stock at a steep discount to market value, usually 50 percent, should the acquirer attempt a second-stage merger not approved by the target's board. Since the built-in discount would encourage all of the target shareholders to exercise their rights and purchase shares from the acquirer, and since the potential acquirer's shareholders would be prevented from participating, the result would be that the acquirer's preexisting shareholders would find their own equity interests substantially diluted once the pill is triggered and the rights exercised. This is the "poison" in the flip-over plan.

The flip-in plan is often combined with a flip-over plan. Upon the triggering event, rights in a flip-in plan allow target company shareholders to purchase shares of their own company at a steep discount, again usually 50 percent. The right is discriminatory in that the potential acquirer cannot participate. As in the flip-over pill, the potential acquirer is excluded from participating should the flip-in be triggered by a transaction not approved by the target's board. Despite their similarity to discriminatory self-tender offers, flip-in plans have been found to be exempt from Williams Act strictures because they are in the form of a rights plan. The poison in the flip-in is a substantial dilution of the acquirer's position in the target company, which makes the acquisition much more, if not prohibitively, expensive.[39]

All poison pills raise questions of shareholder democracy and the robustness of the corporate governance process. They amount to major de facto shifts of voting rights away from shareholders to management, on matters pertaining to the sale of the corporation. They give target boards of directors absolute veto power over any proposed business combination, no matter how beneficial it might be for the shareholders; all the board has to do is refuse to redeem the pill, and no bidder would dare trigger its poison. Yet because they are implemented as warrants or rights offerings, the plans can be put in place without shareholder voting approval, under state law, which controls corporate governance.

Managements claim that although the potential for abuse is there, poison pills will not be used against shareholder interests. They say that pill plans are merely designed to ensure shareholders equitable treatment in the event of a takeover bid, specifically, to ensure that two-tier and other coercive acquisitions will not occur. However, effective protection from coercive offers can be obtained through the adoption of a fair price amendment, which provides a far more straightforward protection than does a pill plan, by stipulating equal but not unreasonable treatment for target shareholders. The fair price amendment had been part of the charter of many American corporations. In general terms, this required that a person who acquired a given percentage of a corporation's shares would have to pay a fair price for the balance. With a bit of focus, fair price provisions could have stopped all two-tier offers. In addition, fair price proposals must be approved by shareholders, which means that management has some incentive to design them to ensure shareholder support.

The evidence to date on the value of pills has been inconclusive. One type of study has examined the price movement of company stock following the adoption of a pill. Some have suggested that adoption of a pill increases share value; some say the opposite.[40] Another set of studies has focused on how pills are used in practice. Some of these suggest that companies with pills generally receive higher takeover premiums than companies without pills; others disagree.[41]

Without voting approval, poison pills constitute not just another, more potent takeover defense, but a fundamental threat to the process of corporate governance. They signal that management is able, unilaterally, to substantially redefine the shareholder-management contract.

Why poison pills? Great Britain, as stated earlier, is the country that most resembles the United States in the pattern of public ownership of its largest corporations (since the denationalization efforts of Margaret Thatcher) and the predominance of institutional investors. The same elements of vulnerability to hostile takeover are present there. But Britain's solution through its Take-Over Code has been very different. An acquirer who reaches the 30 percent threshold level is required to make a cash offer for all the remaining shares, and management is barred from interfering with the ultimate offer being communicated to shareholders, who make the ultimate determination. That this entirely sensible solution was not adopted in America is attributable to two factors: the skill of our corporate lawyers (who, after all, are hired and paid by management, not shareholders) and the vagaries of our federal system.

Lawyer's Poker

Why this solution was not adopted here is another fascinating chapter in the continuing corporate wars. As managements found themselves threatened, they turned to their lawyers and investment bankers for help. Lawyers behaved like businesses and created new and improved products—endorsed as "fair" by investment bankers—to replace last year's model. Takeovers quickly lost the characteristics of business transactions and became the province of lawyers and investment bankers.

Thus, the solutions and the fees charged for their creation soon lost any relationship to traditional patterns. Management came to believe that their very survival depended on hiring the "best" lawyers and the most aggressive bankers and following their advice beyond any limits thought reasonable in the past. T. Boone Pickens, the consummate raider of the 1980s, found himself relying on the omnipotent Manhattan lawyers to complete his run at Cities Service: "The day was the low point in the [Cities Service] deal; I felt helpless. Then I thought of someone who might be able to help and called Joe Flom. . . . We got to his office early Wednesday morning. Joe seemed glad to see us and a bit amused; he seemed to be saying 'What took you so long?' "[42]

What is legal has never been limited to what is right. But at no time in commercial history have the top leaders of American industry been so utterly in the thrall of lawyers that concern for enduring or long-term values simply dropped off the agenda. Survival was the imperative; the lawyers were the indispensable means. The future would take care of itself.

Who the "best" lawyers are is no secret; they are very well known. Within the top ranks of corporate America their names are household words. It is genuinely noteworthy for a handful of rather scholarly professionals to acquire the level of influence over a wide spectrum of the country's business as was achieved by Manhattan takeover specialists in the 1980s.

We should pause to meet three of them who were on everybody's list: Joseph Flom of Skadden, Arps, Slate, Meager & Flom; Martin Lipton of Wachtell, Lipton, Rosen & Katz; and Arthur Fleischer of Fried, Frank, Harris, Shriver & Jacobson. On first examination this is an unlikely trio to control corporate America. At the start of the 1980s, they were all respected and their firms were solid, but they were not the "cream of the corporate bar," this distinction being reserved to the old-line firms of Sullivan & Cromwell; Cravath, Swaine & Moore; and Davis, Polk, & Wardwell. Although the three individuals had some promotional skills, they were scholarly rather than flamboyant. Fleischer had worked at the SEC and was the author of a widely respected treatise, and Lipton authored a case book and published law review articles; but there was something special about Flom.

The ascetic-appearing Harvard Law School graduate accomplished nothing less than total revolution in the legal community. So great was his reputation and expertise that American corporations by the hundreds had his firm on retainer simply to ensure that he would not be involved on the other side. When Flom started to practice law, a large firm had 100 lawyers and a single office. At the peak of his career he had managed to build a multinational firm with nearly 1,000 lawyers. Lipton kept his firm substantially smaller, but year after year it achieved the highest earnings per partner of all firms, averaging over $1 million for each of the 46 partners.

These were bold, imaginative, and ingenious people; their capital was in developing new weapons and defenses in the frenzied pace of the corporate wars. They worked hard, prompting Lipton to conclude that if they were smarter than investment bankers and worked harder, they should be paid as well. His $20 million fee in the Philip Morris–Kraft merger for two weeks' work established a new sense of the "value" of lawyers to corporate America.[43] As time passes, one can question whether this kind of expense is metaphor for the increasing noncompetitiveness of American industry or for the decline in the reputation of lawyers. It was a rare major transaction that did not involve these three—Flom for the attack in later years, Lipton for the defense. Fleischer probably most of all gave the impression of "fairness," of a wider view, of a traditional role as counsellor.

Flom v. Lipton

The formal law reports say that the "poison pill" was first upheld by the Delaware Chancery and Supreme courts in the case of *Moran v. Household*.[44] The case would more appropriately have been called *Flom v. Lipton*. This time Marty Lipton won, and it was a very significant victory: it resulted in the adoption of poison pills by almost all major American corporations within a very few years, and, more important, it was another significant blow to the few remaining rights of shareholders.

John A. Moran was a partner in the firm of Dyson, Kissner & Moran, which very quietly and very effectively had been doing leveraged buyouts, takeovers, and reorganizations for 30 years. It is hard to imagine people less likely to involve themselves in such a public brouhaha as a major lawsuit. Dyson had been a partner in one of the Big Seven accounting firms, and Kissner, first in his class at Harvard, had a world-famous collection of rare books. Over the years, they had bought and reorganized literally hundreds of American corporations, becoming in the process among the richest of Americans, even if virtually unknown. Their only moment in the spotlight was when Charlie Dyson managed to make Nixon's "enemies list" by providing office space to former Democratic National Chairman Larry O'Brien on the strength of their sons' having served together in Vietnam.

DKM had merged one of its significant industrial groups into Household, thereby becoming its largest shareholder. John Moran, as director, was also the owner of many millions of dollars of the corporation's equity. Having successfully made deals all his life, it was second nature for John Moran to approach the management about a leveraged buyout of Household. Management preferred independence to well-paid service in the DKM empire. The Household board retained Marty Lipton's firm and, Moran dissenting, adopted a poison pill.

The board declined to consider a fair price amendment out of concern that they may not get shareholder approval. Part of the appeal of the pill was that it could be adopted without the requirement at any time of shareholder approval. Joe Flom argued eloquently:

> The underpinning for the Plan and the board's adoption of it was the belief, articulated by director Whitehead, that directors are better able than stockholders to decide whether an offer is fair and should be accepted. On that basis he, and the other directors, justified removing the decision from the owners of the shares and granting it to themselves. If such a fundamental right of personal property can be arrogated simply because the professional managers believe in good faith that they can better exercise it, is any stockholder right immune from seizure? More than 50 percent of Household's shares are held by institutions who are themselves fiduciary holders. On what basis do the Household directors claim to be more capable of deciding at what price to sell shares than these investment professionals? If it is in the interests of Household's stockholders to have their directors decide whether a tender offer is acceptable, why have the directors been unwilling to ask the stockholders for this power?[45]

The Delaware court knew what was at stake and chose to ignore it.[46] This decision thus holds that management, having a choice between equally effective mechanisms to deal with the problems of "coercive offers," may choose the one carrying no legal requirement to seek approval by shareholders, and that the board of directors is the ultimate decider as to whether a corporation is to be sold.

This was the first of many steps that would result by the end of the 1980s in shareholders having virtually no capacity for involvement in the important questions regarding the long-term direction of their corporation. This case illuminates the way that management, with control over the corporate pocketbook and professional relationships, has the ability to advance its own interests, even when they conflict with those of the owners. Management's agenda over the rest of the decade has been the successive denial to shareholders of even their minimal traditional rights—to elect the full board at the annual meeting, to call special meetings of shareholders, to act by referendum between meetings, to vote without revealing their identity, and even to freely transfer their shares to a willing buyer at a mutually agreeable price.

It has become clear that courts will not protect shareholder rights or values. One of the reasons may well be frustration with the automaton character of the risk-averse institutional investor and its resulting tendency of putting all corporations up for sale. During the oral argument of the Time-Warner case (broadcast live on CNN), the judges asked what percentage of stock was held by institutional shareholders. Possibly, the development of a class of genuinely long-term holders who do not "shirk" their responsibility might give judges a different perspective. But, as discussed in Chapter 3, through ignoring or even denying the self-interested nature of many management decisions, courts have broadened the deference given to boards and officers under the "business judgment rule," producing increasingly grotesque results.

Certainly, courts should not second-guess the business judgment of managers and directors, any more than shareholders should—unless those making the decision in question have conflicts of interest that provide a real or apparent impediment to their acting as fiduciaries for shareholders.

The Delaware Factor and the Polaroid ESOP

The "Delaware factor"—the commitment of Delaware to being a hospitable forum for major corporation managements—explains the otherwise incomprehensible chancery court approval of the Polaroid employee stock option plan (ESOP). The Roy Disney organization, pleasant but tenacious, headed by Stanley Gold, had been accumulating a position of slightly less than 4.9 percent of Polaroid's stock during the first half of 1988. On June 22, Roy Disney wrote asking for a meeting "to establish the ground work for a good relationship with the Company." Polaroid imposed several conditions, with which Disney complied at considerable expense, and agreed to a meeting to be held on July 13 in New York. The board hastily convened a special meeting on July 12. Polaroid CEO I. MacAllister Booth explained to the board that everyone wanted to put together an ESOP quickly because of the Shamrock meeting. "The meeting was called on less than one week's notice and, as a result, three outside directors were unable to attend and a fourth had to leave the meeting before any votes were taken. Contrary to the general practice, the directors received no written materials prior to the special meeting."[47] The directors had never considered an ESOP as large as $300 million (indeed, this was three times the size earlier discussed) or the likely impact that a 14 percent ESOP would have under the new Delaware corporation law. As a practical matter, an acquisition cannot be made unless 85 percent of the shares are obtained. The court blithely concluded: "The ESOP may mean that a potential acquirer will have to gain the employees' confidence and support in order to be successful in its takeover effort. However, there has been no showing that such support is or would be impossible to obtain."[48] Perhaps this is the place to point out that it is not the employees' confidence and support that are necessary to get the votes of the ESOP shares. The trustee—appointed by management—votes the "unallocated" shares in an ESOP, virtually all of them when the ESOP has just been created, and it is highly unlikely that they would vote those shares against themselves.[49]

In the world of common sense, when a hastily convened board meeting inadequately considers a major change in the corporation's capital structure by creating a 14 percent ESOP in the face of a potential acquirer who needs 85 percent, a "defensive" action has been taken. The practical impossibility of ever obtaining the requisite majority is manifest. But in the world of the "Delaware factor," 0.5 percent is all that is needed to manifest management commitment to shareholders.

American Keiretsu—Corporate Partners

When Shamrock Holdings indicated an interest in acquiring Polaroid in July 1988, the management of Polaroid mobilized their defenses quickly. Besides the now-classic maneuver of selling a 14 percent stake in the company to their own Employee Stock Ownership Plan and buying $1.1 billion of their stock back on the open market, Polaroid began shopping a major piece of the company to a single, friendly investor. By January 1989, Corporate Partners, a so-called "white squire" fund allocated by Shearson Lehman, agreed to purchase a $300 million block of preferred, which at the time could be converted into over 6 million shares, or 7.7 percent of Polaroid's total votes. Because of the structuring of the deal, which included pay-in-kind dividends of stock, Corporate Partners' holdings have grown over time. As of 15 January 1991, the Corporate Partners' shares could be converted into 6.97 million shares, representing 12.2 percent of Polaroid's votes. The Corporate Partners deal, however, was more than a simple management-saving device, due in part to the conscience of Lester Pollack, who heads the concern.

Corporate Partners was conceived in 1986 as an investment concern that would purchase stock in only a few companies, but would take a large and active role in each company. In all five companies Corporate Partners currently invests in, Pollack or a representative of Corporate Partners sits on the board. Investors in the $1.645 billion fund, which consists of banks, insurance companies, and public and private pension funds, in effect pay Pollack to be an active director. Because Corporate Partners' investments typically include special privileges, in effect the shareholders pay him, too. But they get what they pay for. Warren Buffett has played the same role at other companies.

David Gollub, vice president of Corporate Partners, explains Corporate Partners' approach this way: "We have a small number of investments, a deep relationship with management in those companies we invest in, a staff that can support Lester in his role as director so he can stay fully apprised of events, and a significant financial stake in each company."

In the case of Polaroid, Corporate Partners received between 11 and 11.5 percent guaranteed annual return, immediate voting rights equivalent to 6 million common shares, and two board seats. Pollack holds one seat. The other is held by Delbert Staley, the former CEO of NYNEX. And unlike the placement deals at Cummins Engine, Pollack's Corporate Partners is under no obligation to vote with management. Explains Pollack: "I entered the board unfettered, but constructive, clearly with the benefits of shareholders first. With $300 million invested in the company, if shareholders benefit, we benefit." As a board member, Pollack believed that this views "have some weight from having done the investment analysis in due dilligence and owning a major economic stake, which means I have a more active knowledge of the company and more of a stake in its stock performance than an ordinary director."

Before investing, Corporate Partners completed a review of Polaroid's books and investigated Polaroid's proposed restructuring. In effect, Corporate Partners did not come to the aid of Polaroid as much as they came to the aid of the restructuring and subsequent business plan. Corporate Partners, in Pollack's words, was an entity that "bought into the corporation's plan. We could see the benefits of a restructuring, recapitalization, and a business plan that would lead to long-term growth, all of which would increase shareholder wealth. We could buy a stake, and they could keep their leverage low." Implicit in the agreement was the fact that Corporate Partners would not necessarily be a "friendly" presence if management reneged on the restructuring.

"I see it this way," says Jonathan Kagan, Corporate Partners' managing director. "Eighty percent of institutional investors are legitimate long-term investors. Now, let's say eighty percent of corporations want to benefit shareholders. So they have the same interests, but they often miss each other in the night, and a level of distrust often exists between most corporations and their shareholders. These groups can find each other by finding someone who can bridge that gap. That's where we come in." Corporate Partners represents a new breed, perhaps a hybrid of institutional investor. While many investors purchase blocks in hundreds of companies, hoping that the economy as a whole will bring them profit, Corporate Partners selects only a few companies, and becomes a knowledgeable, active force in those companies, promoting the long-term business strategies that create shareholder value.

One of the most notorious abuses of a company's ESOP was the Carter-Hawley Hale defense against a tender offer from The Limited. When The Limited announced its offer in April 1984 of $30 per share, a 50 percent premium over the present market price, the Carter-Hawley Hale ESOP covered 56,000 employees and held nearly 40 percent of the outstanding stock. The plan was administered by the trust department of the Bank of America, a bank where Carter-Hawley Hale chairman and CEO Philip M. Hawley served on the board as chairman of the compensation committee. Bank of America had been the company's primary lender, to the tune of $75 million in outstanding loans and credit lines in

1988. Bank of America also agreed to loan $900 million to help Carter-Hawley Hale resist The Limited's offer and revised their loan agreements to provide that, if CHH suffered a change in control, all loans would be in default. Carter-Hawley Hale paid the Bank of America an up-front fee of $500,000.

The conflicts of interest were mind-boggling. As Ben Stein notes, "Bank of America was supposed to administer the plan in the interests only of the stockholder-employees. But it was simultaneously in the active, highly paid service of CHH management, a party with a life or death interest in how the shares were voted. . . . The interests of the shareholder-employees and the interests of CHH management were, at least apparently, sharply different, and the trustee for the employees was getting paid by CHH management."[50]

Bank of America had a "pass-through" policy in its contract to provide for such situations: If CHH was subject to a tender offer, the bank would detail the terms of the offer to employee-shareholders, who would then vote confidentially whether they wanted to tender. If 50 percent of the ESOP stock supported the tender offer, all the shares would be voted for the offer; otherwise, all shares would be voted against it. But when The Limited announced its offer, the Bank of America revised its policy to one that could not guarantee confidential voting. The bank also informed employees that all unvoted shares would be voted for management, as would the 800,000 unallocated shares.

The ESOP proved a vital factor in The Limited's decision to give up the chase. Management at Carter-Hawley Hale demonstrated that they would stop at nothing to retain their positions, buying nearly 18 million of their own shares in one week and selling a $300 million chunk of preferred stock, representing 37 percent of the vote, to General Cinema, a friendly third party.

The Limited picked up the pursuit again in 1986, however, and ran into problems with the ESOP again. The Bank of America had new rules for voting Carter-Hawley Hale's ESOP: In the event of a tender, employees could do nothing and have their share voted for management, or they could ask for their share certificates. Since the share certificates were kept at Carter-Hawley Hale, management could easily figure which employees did not want management to vote their shares. Furthermore, the trustee insisted that six to eight weeks were necessary to send the certificates, and The Limited's offer only lasted five weeks from the date it was announced. In all respects, members of the Carter-Hawley Hale

ESOP had no choice but passive support for management the second time around. The directors, however, still didn't let it go to a vote, turning down The Limited's $60 per share offer in favor of a restructuring.

The final word on ESOPs has yet to be written. The Department of Labor consistently takes the view that the voting of unallocated shares by "formula" violates fiduciary requirements, and yet this remains the operative provision in many plans. It is not at all clear what elements must be demonstrated to satisfy that the trustee bank is "independent" of the plan sponsor. In the absence of definitive guidelines, the field is expanding chaotically in many directions, right up to NL Industries' allegation, in connection with its 1990 proxy contest, that Lockheed's management intends its ESOP to acquire an actual majority of the outstanding capital stock and, thereby, control of the company itself.[51] When and how these allegations will be disposed of by the judicial system is unknown, but the language of the complaint itself provides the clearest indication of the theoretical possibilities of the ESOP as the "ultimate entrenchment device."

An ESOP's Fable: NL Industries' Complaint

16. The Lockheed Board of Directors approved the ESOP on April 3, 1989. That same day, the ESOP Trust was established and U.S. Trust Company of California, N.A. appointed as trustee. On April 4, the ESOP was funded through a circular series of transactions, the effect of which was that Lockheed borrowed $500 million to buy its own shares to place them in hands friendly to the incumbent directors and management.

17. The ESOP borrowed $500 million from private sources and used those funds to "purchase" 10.7 million common shares from Lockheed. Lockheed, however, guaranteed the loan and is contractually obligated to the ESOP to provide sufficient funds to pay all debt service, regardless of the company's earnings and profits. The entire unpaid balance of the loan is treated on Lockheed's books as Lockheed's debt and, correspondingly, a reduction in shareholders' equity.

18. The ESOP shares were put into a "suspense account," where they serve to collateralize the loan. Shares held in the suspense account are "unallocated." Over time, these unallocated shares are credited to the accounts of individual workers through the mechanisms of the Lockheed Salaried Employee Savings Plan Plus.

19. Under this plan, compensation contributed by participants to any of four funds is matched by Lockheed up to specified levels. Lockheed's match takes the form of contributions to the ESOP trustee to pay off the ESOP debt, which contributions then "release" shares from the suspense account. The released shares are allocated to the accounts of plan participants as "match stock."

20. No worker has any assurance that he or she will eventually own unallocated shares. If the worker quits, is fired, or retires, he or she cannot buy any more shares. Moreover, Lockheed has expressly reserved the right to terminate the ESOP at any time. In the event of plan termination, the unallocated shares—*i.e.*, the shares in the suspense account—are to be "sold back" to Lockheed or to some other person and the proceeds are to be used to pay off the loan. If there is a shortfall, Lockheed must make up the difference.

21. Even after the shares are allocated, workers do not own them. They do not have even a partially vested interest in their match stock until one year after it is credited to their accounts. Moreover, they do not have a *fully* vested interest in the match stock until four years after the date it is allocated to them. The ESOP was implemented less than a year before workers voted in this proxy contest. Thus, the match stock allocated to workers' accounts was *not even partially vested* when they voted those shares.

22. Until workers perform services to ensure the allocation and vesting of match stock, they have not paid for, and do not own, either the unallocated shares held in the suspense account or the match stock credited to their accounts.

23. So far, according to information distributed by the ESOP trustee during the proxy contest, approximately 1 million shares have been allocated from the suspense account to individual employees' accounts as ESOP match stock. Approximately 800,000 more shares have been purchased by employees directly through their salary contributions to the ESOP. Approximately 10 million ESOP shares remain unallocated in the suspense account.

24. Notwithstanding that the unallocated shares and match stock have not been paid for, and might never be paid for, Lockheed and the incumbent directors have provided that these shares shall be voted. Under the voting provisions of the ESOP, a worker who has ESOP match stock credited to his account can instruct the trustee not only on how to vote those shares, but also on how to vote a proportionate number of unallocated shares.

25. As a result, the ESOP permits salaried employees, including management, who own about 1 percent of Lockheed's outstanding shares to vote a block of over 17 percent which they do not own.

NL and every other non-company shareholder of Lockheed receives only one vote for every share of common stock purchased. The ESOP plan participants as a group, however, currently have 15 votes for every share of common stock they own through the ESOP. This is true even though there is no assurance whatsoever that an employee who votes unallocated shares or unvested match stock will ever own those shares.

26. Defendants structured the ESOP voting provisions so that *all* unallocated shares *must* be voted, even if a substantial percentage of ESOP participants choose not to vote. If any employee chooses not to vote his or her portion of the unallocated shares, the ESOP plan requires the trustee to vote those shares in the same proportions as instructions received from other plan participants. In this way, the ESOP plan places disproportionate influence over the voting of unallocated shares in the hands of senior employees and management, who may believe their futures are linked to re-election of the incumbent board, and who, therefore, have the greatest incentive to vote for management.

27. The defendants' decision to transfer supervoting power to a select employee group has been costly for Lockheed's shareholders. In 1988, Lockheed paid $71 million in matching contributions under the employees' savings plan. In 1989, when the ESOP was established, Lockheed increased the level of its matching contributions to $82 million. In addition, Lockheed paid $14 million in dividends on the unallocated shares in the suspense account and another $9 million to cover the shortfall between the ESOP's debt expense and Lockheed's matching contributions plus the dividends. No employee concessions were made in exchange for this increased funding from Lockheed.

28. There is no telling how much more the ESOP will cost shareholders in the future. The price per share "paid" by the ESOP was about $47. When an ESOP loan repayment is made, shares are released from the suspense account based on the $47 price. However, when the released shares are allocated to individual employees' accounts as Lockheed's matching contribution, they are valued at the current market price (currently about $37 per share). If the current market price is lower than $47, Lockheed must make up the difference by contributing additonal cash or shares to the ESOP trustee who, in turn, allocates more match stock to employees. Thus, the lower the price of Lockheed's stock, the greater the expense of the ESOP to Lockheed's shareholders.

29. In addition to the increased cost to Lockheed shareholders described in paragraph 28, another consequence of the ESOP is that

more shares of Lockheed stock are placed in friendly employee hands as matching contributions when Lockheed stock performs poorly than when it trades at $47 per share or higher. The poorer the stock performs, the greater the percentage of outstanding shares controlled by Lockheed workers through the ESOP.

30. The ESOP has diluted the holdings of other shareholders. When the incumbent directors set up the ESOP, they said that dilution would not occur because the company would repurchase on the open market approximately the same number of shares transferred to the ESOP (10.7 million). The buy-back program was suspended, however, after less than 7 million shares were repurchased.

Source: Complaint, *NL Industries v. Lockheed*, Case 90-1950 RMT (BX) in the United States District Court for the Central District of California.

A recent amendment to the complaint alleges that, in reality, the ESOP is contemplated to purchase not only 17 percent of the total outstanding shares but actual control of Lockheed.

Where You Stand Depends on Where You Sit

Even in the post-Milken 1990s, the market for corporate control continues—and continues to make headlines. As we write, Matsushita is acquiring MCA for $6.6 billion, the latest in a series of international business combinations. Perhaps more emblematic of the future of the corporate control market is the prospective hostile takeover of NCR, not by Carl Icahn or Donald Trump, but by blue-chip behemoth AT&T. Perhaps there was some AT&T director who sensed the irony in approving the hostile takeover; the directors include Cummins CEO Henry Schacht, Philip Hawley, who defended Carter-Hawley Hale with an excessive amount of leverage that ultimately bankrupted the company, and Drew Lewis, president of the Business Roundtable, an organization that has consistently defended management's interests. It will be interesting to see how these directors respond to NCR's claims that its corporate culture and corporate constituencies require its continued independence.

America in the Global Market

Any discussion of the role of owners in American corporations must include a global context. Both our products and our stock compete in global markets. Foreign companies are increasingly aggressive in taking over American businesses. And institutional investors, America's "sleeping giants," are increasingly investing in equity securities denominated in foreign currencies. For these reasons, it is important to examine the governance structures abroad. It is immediately clear that ours is the only system without meaningful accountability to owners.

The world can be divided into three parts. In the United States and the United Kingdom, the major corporations are preponderantly publicly owned, and accountability, to the extent it exists, arises out of the pattern of large institutional ownership. The big difference is that in the United Kingdom, the institutional investors work together and with management on questions of overall direction. There has not been a proxy fight in Britain, in recent memory. The issues are settled earlier in the process, through discussion. And the institutions have joined together to fund ProNED, a clearinghouse/headhunter organization, to recommend independent director candidates for corporate boards.

In the United States and the United Kingdom, companies rely on the marketplace as a source of capital. The majority of outstanding shares can be purchased "in the market." Elsewhere corporate control is not for sale. Takeover battles like those we saw here in the 1980s do not occur in the United Kingdom because the institutional investors are able to make "midcourse corrections" at an earlier stage. They are simply not possible elsewhere because the shares necessary for obtaining control are not in the market.

In Germany and Japan, control over major enterprises is held by "permanent" shareholders, who have very close surveillance over operations. In the continental European Community (exclusive of Germany), private and governmental ownership is the pattern. In both cases, corporate management is accountable to "permanent" owners. In Germany, the universal banks own up to 20 percent of the total of outstanding capital, and, because the custom there is to use "bearer" shares (rather than "registered" shares, as is the case here), the banks also vote enough proxies to be able to exercise voting control at shareholder meetings. The German banks are capable of exercising the most direct control over portfolio companies, as in the recent example of the Deutsche Bank changing the management of Daimler Benz.

Shareholding in Japan is an element of the industrial paradigm. Each company is "owned" by its customers and suppliers. It is interesting to note, as we shall later discuss, that this is a pattern emulated by Cummins Engine in the summer of 1990, when it sold a 27 percent stake of the company to Ford, Kubota, and Tenneco. It is an essential part of the commercial relationship. The pattern by which manufacturers relate to suppliers and customers is one of mutual dependency and accountability. The Japanese industrial groupings involve an intensive interrelationship that is not primarily concerned with profit in our sense.

In other countries there seems to be virtually no agreement as to what constitutes profit and what relationship "profit" may have to the value of the shares. Thus, in Japan, some of the largest companies are only marginally profitable in the American sense, but they have been successful in achieving huge increases worldwide in market share. Turning to the example of the American auto industry in the 1980s, one can speculate which measure of "profit" is the more meaningful. Is it the record levels of profit reported in the United States that were coupled with stock repurchase and loss of market share, or the marginal earnings reported by such companies as Mitsubishi Corporation and their expansion of manufacturing base and market share within the United States?

In the industrial companies of other countries, debt and bank capital are more prevalent as the financing modality. Figure 2, which was prepared as part of a study for Great Britain's Department of Trade and Industry,[52] illustrates the great discrepancy between the United Kingdom structure, with extensive reliance on stock market equity capital,

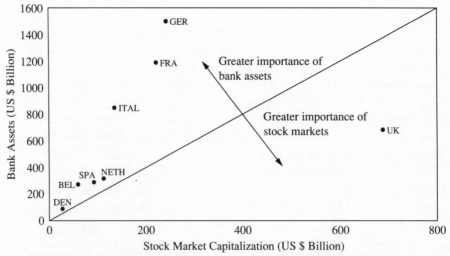

FIGURE 2 *Relative Size and Importance of Bank Assets and Stock Markets in EC Countries.*

and that of the balance of the EC countries, with far greater emphasis on banks as the source of industrial financing. This study suggests the relative unimportance of "institutional investors," as we know them, in continental Europe. They are not significant holders of equity securities and do not participate in corporate governance. "Institutional" holdings (as of 1986) are concentrated in four member states, with totals as follows (in millions of pounds): France 148, Netherlands 147, and Germany 142, which, taken together, total less than the holdings of UK institutions (580). On the continent, only the Dutch pension funds could be considered a major institutional investor, with £100 million.[53]

Privatization:
The LBO as the Model of the Future Corporation

The typical shareholder of a modern large business enterprise is different from the owner of tangible property: the ownership of the former is

---

The Evaporation of Property

The capitalist process, by substituting a mere parcel of shares for the wall of and the machines in a factory, takes the life out of the idea of property. It loosens the grip that once was so strong—the grip in the sense of the legal right and the actual ability to do as one pleases with one's own; the grip also in the sense that the holder of the title loses the will to fight, economically, physically, politically, for "his" factory and his control over it, to die if necessary on its steps. And this evaporation of what we may term the material substance of property—its visible and touchable reality—affects not only the attitude of holders but also that of the workmen and the public in general. Dematerialized, defunctionalized and absentee ownership does not impress and call forth moral allegiance as the vital form of property did. Eventually, there will be *nobody* left who really cares to stand for it—nobody within and nobody without the precincts of the big concerns.

Joseph A. Schumpeter

Source: Capitalism, Socialism and Democracy, Harper & Row, New York, 1942, p. 142.

both indirect and temporary. Treating the shareholder of a large modern corporation as a traditional owner entitled to the legal protection of his or her *unique* right of property fails to consider the gradual change in ownership over the last 50 years from the direct and permanent to the indirect and temporary.[54]

When ownership of property involves responsibility, risk and reward are properly matched and accountable to each other. An owner of tangible property is required to avoid causing nuisance to others. Yet even this limited responsibility has been obscured in the context of shareholders.

Harvard Business School professor Michael Jensen suggests that the optimal corporate mode is a company in which the managers are the equity owners and the basic capitalization is debt.[55] In his view, the debt serves as a discipline, and the alignment of managers' interests to be congruent with those of owners eliminates what the lawyers call conflict of interest and the economists call agency costs. It is this "cost" that has contributed to the lack of competitiveness of American industry. Jensen writes:

> The current trends do not imply that the public corporation has no future. The conventional twentieth century model of corporate governance—disperse public ownership, professional managers without substantial equity holdings, a board of directors dominated by management-appointed outsiders—remains a viable option in some areas of the economy, particularly for growth companies whose profitable investment opportunities exceed the cash they generate internally.... The public corporation is not suitable in industries where long-term growth is slow, where internally generated funds outstrip the opportunities to invest them profitably, or where downsizing is the most productive long-term strategy.[56]

In effect, Jensen concludes that the legal and commercial restrictions on effective monitoring by shareholders—particularly institutional investors—inevitably will lead to inefficiencies that require privatization or going out of business. Michael Jensen has looked at the same question that bothered Adam Smith and Karl Marx—the problem of making a manager care as much about the value of the company as the investor—and like them, he has decided it is insoluble. Unlike Smith and Marx, Jensen had the chance to examine years of historical and empirical data, but his conclusions are consistent with their theories. In other words, after less than a century, there is serious question as to whether the modern corporate form has become obsolete.

The Psychological Difference Between Debt and Equity

Equity is soft; debt is hard. Equity is forgiving; debt is insistent. Equity is a pillow; debt is a dagger. Equity and debt are the yin and yang of corporate finance. Equity lulls a company's management to sleep, forgiving its sins more readily than a deathbed priest. A surplus of stock muffles the alarms that should be heard when earnings decline. Forgive and forget is equity's creed.

But put a load of debt on that same company's books and watch what happens when its operating profits begin to fall off even a little bit. . . . But the actual problem is the same. . . . it just *feels* a lot more pressing if debt is at the door. . . . what a perfect device for the land of Disney and Coca-Cola, where illusion is more important than reality.

G. Bennett Stewart III

Source: *The Quest for Value,* HarperCollins, New York, 1991, pp. 580–581.

PART II

Corporate Myths, Corporate Reality

3

The Director's New Clothes

A scene in *Barbarians at the Gate* frames the question of accountability of corporate management perfectly. Ross Johnson, the man who somewhat impetuously initiated the leveraged buyout of RJR-Nabisco, met with Henry Kravis and George Roberts of Kohlberg, Kravis, Roberts, & Co. to discuss it. There was a brief discussion of the business before Johnson's central question came up. "Now Henry, if you guys get this, you're not going to get into chickenshit stuff about planes and golf courses are you?" (Johnson's perquisites included corporate jets and membership fees at 24 country clubs.[1]) Kravis was eager to gloss over this question, but Roberts was more candid. "Well, we don't want you to live a spartan life. But we like to have things justified. We don't mind people using private airplanes to get places, if there's no ordinary way. It is important that a CEO set the tone in any deal we do." Johnson stated his concern more directly. "I guess the deal we're looking for is a bit unusual." Johnson, as it turned out, wanted to keep significant control of the company. Roberts responded even more directly: "We're not going to do any deal where management controls it. We'll work with you. But we have no interest in losing control." Johnson asked why.

"We've got the money," Roberts said, "We've got the investors, that's why we have to control the deal." From the look in Johnson's eyes, Roberts could tell it wasn't the message he wanted to hear. "Well, that's interesting," Johnson said. "But frankly, I've got more freedom doing what I do right now."[2]

There's something wrong with this picture, because it took debt to make management accountable. It should have been accountable to shareholders, to the people who have "got the money."

What's wrong with this picture is the discrepancy between the expectations of the law and reality. The law generally assumes that "All corporation power shall be exercised by or under the authority of, and the business and affairs of the corporation managed under the direction of, its board of directors, subject to any limitation set forth in the articles of incorporation."[3] According to Melvin Eisenberg, "All serious students of corporate affairs recognize that notwithstanding the statutory injunction, in the typical large publicly held corporation the board does not 'manage' the corporation's business in the ordinary meaning of that term. Rather, that function is vested in the executives."[4] This reality is reflected in the erosion of the standard of performance for directors. *Barbarians at the Gate* documents in devastating fashion the way that Ross Johnson handled his boards, with a combination of lavish perquisites and meager information. While he was dazzling his hand-picked directors, who could expect them to complain about his jets and country clubs?

The corporate structure was designed to maximize profits through competition in the marketplace, but it has proven to be more successful at making profits, whether maximum or not, by imposing costs on others. Every single mechanism that has been set up as some kind of check to prevent this externalizing of costs has been neutralized, short-circuited, or co-opted. Shareholders, directors, state and federal legislatures—even the marketplace itself—all are part of the myth of corporate accountability, and all are part of the reality of corpocracy. In this chapter, we look at the convenient myth behind the mechanisms established to make sure that corporate activity was consistent with the public interest, and the more convenient reality of the failure of these mechanisms to do so.

The Essence of Business, Simplified

Business is other people's money.

Delphine de Girardin

The Myth of the Director's Duty

In a corporation, management acts as agent for the owner, but they do not always have the same interests and incentives. What can we do to require—or at least encourage—people to treat other people's property with as much care as if it were their own?

The law has tried to answer this question of agency costs by developing its highest standard of behavior, the fiduciary standard, and applying it to those who hold and manage property on behalf of others. This standard applies to several different players in the process for establishing corporate behavior, including the board of directors. At least in theory, they are fiduciaries for the shareholders. And the law books are filled with attempts, some almost poetic, to define that duty. Their actions must be "held to something stricter than the morals of the marketplace," with a "punctilio of an honor the most sensitive."[5]

That there is a fiduciary standard is perhaps the most powerful myth underlying the corporate system. Why is it so important to make clear that directors must take extraordinary measures to make sure that they are protecting the rights of shareholders? The reason is our belief that those who exercise power should be accountable to those who are affected by it. We delegate authority to the directors of private companies because they are accountable to the shareholders, just as we delegate authority to government officials because they are accountable to the electorate. Accountability is what makes delegated authority legitimate; without accountability, there is nothing to prevent abuse.

This was the conundrum that almost stopped corporations before they began. Karl Marx and Adam Smith did not agree on much, but they both thought that the corporate form of organization was unworkable, and for remarkably similar reasons. They questioned whether it is possible to create a structure that will operate efficiently and fairly, despite the fact that there is a separation between ownership and control. Put another way, is there any system to make a manager care as much about the company's performance as a shareholder does? Harvard Law School's Dean Robert Clark describes this issue when he says that the major problem addressed by corporate law is how to keep managers accountable to their fiduciary duties of care and loyalty while allowing them great discretionary power over the conduct of the business.[6]

This is a key question, for both economic and public policy reasons. The separation of ownership and control leads to externalities, imposition of costs on others—including shareholders, taxpayers, and the community. For example, a company that discharges untreated effluent into a river is making the community pay some of the costs of production, through government services for clean-up or increased health care costs. A company that uses political pull at the state level to thwart a worthwhile takeover attempt is making the shareholders foot the bill, not just for the lobbying efforts, but for the lost premium, and possibly for a less competitive company. And, of course, it was the shareholders who were paying for Ross Johnson's 24 country club memberships and (at least by one account) for his dog's trip on a jet from the corporate fleet, to say nothing of the devastatingly expensive mistake of the "smokeless cigarette."

The answer to this problem was supposed to be the board of directors, elected by shareholders and acting as fiduciaries on their behalf. The board is responsible for setting overall goals and making sure they are met, for hiring the CEO and monitoring his performance, and for watching corporate management on behalf of the shareholders, to make sure that the corporation is run in their interest. That's the theory—and the myth. The reality is that directors are "merely the parsley on the fish"[7] or the "ornaments on a corporate Christmas tree."[8] As Peter Drucker put it many years ago, "Whenever an institution malfunctions as consistently as boards of directors have in nearly every major fiasco of the last forty or fifty years it is futile to blame men. It is the institution that malfunctions."[9]

The Convenient Myth—and the More Convenient Reality

How can we justify a system in which investors purchase shares in a company that is far too big and complex to permit any meaningful shareholder involvement in governance? In theory, the accountability in our system is the enforceable allegiance that corporate directors and managers owe to shareholders. And that allegiance is enforceable in two ways. Dissatisfied shareholders can sue for violation of fiduciary duty, or, through the electoral process (proxy voting), they can throw the bums out and vote in directors who will do better.

Although difficult to believe in today's world, it is from the premise that shareholders can respond effectively to inadequate boards that much of corporate decision making gets its legitimacy. It is directors, after all, who appoint the officers and determine their level of compensation, and who set the long-term goals and make sure that management takes appropriate steps to carry them out. The fiduciary standard is supposed to ensure that they take all of these actions on behalf of the shareholders. But this is little more than a vestigial notion in modern times. As the creation of instruments to finance takeovers of any company, of virtually any size, has presented directors with the most demanding challenges in corporate history, they have found, as have the shareholders, that the traditional notion of a director's duty—and authority—was more myth than reality.

Dance with the One Who Brought You—or Else

Barbarians at the Gate detailed Ross Johnson's techniques for the care and feeding of his directors—everything from arranging for them to rub shoulders with celebrities to endowing chairs at their alma maters. Perquisites such as the use of corporate planes and apartments made it hard for directors to push him on tough questions. The same is true at most corporations. Directors are picked because the CEO knows them and knows that they are likely to be on his side. Many of them—even those termed "outside" directors, by the New York Stock Exchange's definition—have some business or personal relationship with the CEO.[10] We were once informed by an investor of a prominent electronics company that the head of the board of directors' compensation committee was the chancellor of a college. The president of the company, in turn, was the chairman of the college's board of trustees, and the company has been a big contributor to the school—a nice, cozy arrangement.

Directors are not picked for their ability to challenge management. On the contrary, they are more often chosen for their business or personal ties, or for their ability to add symbolic luster. Compensation expert Graef Crystal describes boards as "ten friends of management, a woman and a black."

A vice president of one of the nation's largest conglomerates told us that during one period his company's board included a much-loved TV personality. "He always made a hit at annual meetings, where shareholders greeted him with loud applause," said the vice president. "After the meeting, the directors would have cocktails and lunch, and the star would regale them with anecdotes and jokes. Then, when the Chairman banged the gavel, the star would put his head down on the table and sleep until the meeting was over. Someone sitting next to him would cast his vote, when required, claiming he or she had checked the star's position." On another board, a Nobel Prize–winning scientist was selected by management. An observer told us that "he always made a point to ask questions during board meetings, the kind of questions that an intelligent but uninformed layman might ask, but his material contributions were nil."

Since they are selected by management, paid by management, and— perhaps most important—informed by management, it is easy for directors to become captive to management's perspective. Information is the key, and it is often frustrating to directors to have such limited access. Former Supreme Court justice Arthur Goldberg, a member of the board of TWA, suggested that the board form a committee to make periodic reports on the company's operations and that it have its own staff of experts, including a scientist, an economist, a public relations expert, an auditor, and, perhaps, a financial expert. The proposal was turned down, and Goldberg resigned from the board.[11]

Other directors who have tried to question management have fared even worse. Those directors who cannot be shmoozed, ignored, or avoided can be silenced. Ross Perot was brought to the General Motors board just to bring the skills and experience that had made his company, EDS, so successful. When he tried to give the board the benefit of that skill and experience, CEO Roger Smith paid Perot $742.8 million—$33 a share for stock that closed at $26 7/8 on the day of the trade, plus another $346.8 million for contingent notes and tax compensation—in order to get him off the board.[12] GM even established a $7.5 million penalty to be levied if either Perot or GM criticized each other, and they set up a three-man arbitration panel to evaluate possible violations.[13] So there was no opportunity for the shareholders to find out what Perot's concerns about the company were. There was also no opportunity for them to get that kind of a price; General Motors refused to buy back other shareholders' stock for the price they paid to Perot.

An outside director of a company that went private in an MBO told us that his every attempt to question management was thwarted. The special committee convened to oversee the deal was made up of directors selected for their history of going along with whatever management proposed. The projections for segments of the company previously expected to do well suddenly became dismal, as all of the assumptions changed to justify a low price. Even if a company is operating as a public company, it has every incentive to present its most optimistic forecasts to directors and shareholders. But a buyer and a seller have two different ways of valuing assets, and in an MBO, management switches sides. The "independent" investment banking firms hired to provide "fair" evaluations of the value of the assets owe their allegiance to management. Who owes allegiance to shareholders? In theory, it is the board of directors, who, as fiduciaries, are supposed to be better to shareholders than they would be to themselves. But the theory of fiduciary duty has given way to the reality of a duty so threadbare that it covers as little as the fabled emperor's new clothes.

The Empire Strikes Back:
The Business Roundtable

> With the birth of the Roundtable, big business in the United States may at last be said to have come of political age.[14]

Source: Kim McQuaid, *Big Business and Presidential Power: From FDR to Reagan,* William Morrow, New York, 1982, p. 308.

The Business Roundtable is an association of approximately 200 of the country's largest publicly held corporations, who have joined together to examine public issues that affect the economy and to develop positions that reflect "sound economic and social principles. The objectives of the Roundtable include fostering economic policies conducive to the well-being of the nation and its people."[15]

The Roundtable came about, indirectly, because its predecessor, the Business Council, was part of the Department of Commerce—a fact Kennedy's first commerce secretary, Luther Hodges, did not appreciate. Hodges felt the council, a group that advised him as commerce secretary yet would not allow him to select its members or determine their meeting agendas, should not have a "special channel to government thinking."[16]

Hodges and the council remained at loggerheads until the council went to Kennedy and told him that they would operate as a private group. Business was then represented by different umbrella organizations over the next decade, including a revived private Business Council, the U.S. Chamber of Commerce, the National Association of Manufacturers, and the National Federation of Independent Business. From the point of view of the business community, the inadequacy of its governmental relations was never more painful than during the Nixon and Ford administrations, when wage and price controls were installed, with almost no input from the business sector. According to one scholar, it was John Connally, long an ally of big business, who made it clear to prominent business leaders that "[b]usinessmen had to improve in political sophistication and techniques in Washington or else face political impotence."[17]

In March 1972, Frederick Borch of General Electric and John D. Harper of Alcoa convened about a dozen corporate CEOs as "the March Group" to involve themselves directly in lobbying and influencing. The result was the Business Roundtable, a disciplined, sophisticated, and effective political fighting machine. Its success is attributable to the prestige and personal effort of the initial leaders: Harper, Irving Shapiro of Dupont, Reg Jones of GE, GM's Thomas Murphy, Exxon's Clifton Garvin, and, more recently, GM's Roger Smith and Union Pacific's Drew Lewis.

The Roundtable's direction comes from its executive and policy committees. The organization has three unique characteristics. First, the CEOs are personally involved. Second, membership is limited to CEOs of large companies; there are no small or medium-sized businesses whose interests and priorities might be different—or inconvenient. Third, the organization carefully avoids involving itself with a single company or a single-interest pressure group. The Roundtable speaks for "big business," and it does so through its task forces. Typically, a subject for special attention will be selected and then a "lead company" designated. Usually its CEO directs the task force, supplying the critical personnel from his or her own corporation or using people made available by other corporations. The Roundtable itself stays relatively small and discrete.

"Unable to persuade Congress to pass legislation curbing hostile takeovers,"[18] the Roundtable has devised an ambitious strategy to protect its members, including the devotion of substantial attention and energy to questions of internal corporate governance as a way of allowing what is, in essence, a hostile takeover from the inside. Although a great deal of the Roundtable's energy has been devoted to opposition to federal authority over corporate governance and support for state antitakeover legislation, one of its initiatives is noteworthy here: the recent drastic revisions of the Roundtable's own well-researched and thoughtful 1978 Statement on Corporate Governance.

The Roundtable on Governance, 1978 and 1990

There is no clearer indication of the Roundtable's views on corporate governance than in its own reports on the subject. In its brief existence, the Roundtable has profoundly changed its views, as revealed by a comparison of its papers issued in 1978 and 1990.

In January 1978, the Business Roundtable issued a statement entitled *The Role and Composition of the Board of Directors of the Large Publicly Owned Corporation.* The paper was the culmination of a project responding to a pattern of corporate criminal behavior involving illegal campaign contributions, bribery, and illicit involvement in the elections of other countries. The CEO members of the Roundtable evaluated the way in which boards of directors of business corporations are selected, constituted, and function, in order to understand and to avoid further criminal behavior.

A distinguished scholars group was chaired by Dean David S. Ruder of Northwestern University School of Law (who later became chairman of the SEC during the last part of the Reagan administration). He reported to the Roundtable's Committee on Corporate Organization Policy, chaired by J. Paul Austin (CEO of the Coca-Cola Company).

Their report was the state-of-the-art explanation in 1978 for the legitimacy of private power. It relies heavily on accountability as the safeguard from criminal and other activity that is contrary to the interests of society. The report describes the constraints on corporate action that are traditionally used to support its legitimacy. All of the limits listed in the report were more myth than reality, and more often breached by corporate management than observed. However, the most noteworthy one concerned accountability to boards and shareholders, because as that myth began to become reality in the 1980s, the Roundtable reversed its position. The 1990 version had the pomp of the earlier version, without the circumstance—no blue-ribbon panel of academics was brought in this time.

The 1978 report specified the accountability imposed by economic constraints—inadequate response to competition, both domestic and foreign—and raised the prospect of lower share prices, higher cost of capital, vulnerability to takeover, and diminished personal job security. It also cited accountability imposed by the formidable array of legal and regulatory requirements to which corporate management is subject: "Moreover, we have witnessed in recent years an increasing rigor on the part of state courts in applying fiduciary standards to evaluate behavior of corporate management. Contrary to some misconceptions, sanctions for management misconduct are in fact imposed and constitute an impressive system of deterrence."[19]

The Roundtable in 1978 was acutely conscious of the necessity of an independent board of directors. In order to have meaningful independence, the report recognized that it might be necessary to give shareholders an explicit right to nominate directors.

The Board—CEO Relationship

[T]he relation between board and the chief executive officer should be challenging yet supportive and positive. It should be arm's length but not adversary. The Board should stimulate management to perform at the peak of its capacity not by carping, but by setting high standards and providing level headed encouragement.

Source: The Business Roundtable, *The Role and Composition of the Board of Directors of the Large Publicly Owned Corporation* (available from The Business Roundtable, 200 Park Ave., New York, NY 10166), 1978, p. 22.

This may be the best definition of the role of a board of directors: "The board of directors then is located at two critical corporate interfaces—the interface between the owners of the enterprise and its management, and the interface between the corporation and the larger society. The directors are stewards—stewards of the owners' interest in the enterprise and stewards also of the owners' legal and ethical obligations to other groups affected by corporate activity."[20] If only the Roundtable had stuck with it.

The Roundtable Retreats: Corporate Governance in 1990

The transformation of the issues of corporate governance in the 1980s is reflected in the revisionist approach taken 12 years later in the

Roundtable's March 1990 report, called *Corporate Governance and American Competitiveness*. Its basic conclusion is that American business is doing just fine and does not need interference from anyone, especially shareholders. The Roundtable responded to the threat of government involvement in 1978 by emphasizing private accountability; it responded, 12 years later, to the threat of private accountability by emphasizing CEO supremacy.

Whereas the 1978 report contemplated a board of directors directly accountable to shareholders and constructively capable of independent evaluation and monitoring of management, the 1990 statement's version is closer to a structure of vertical authority, with the CEO on top and the board of directors one among several operating departments. The report contemplates the selection of directors who are acceptable to the CEO,[21] who attend meetings presided over by the CEO, and who discuss agenda items selected by the CEO.[22]

As a practical matter, the board contemplated by the report is self-perpetuating; there is no more suggestion of shareholder involvement in nominations, even informally. And the essence of the report is that owners cannot be trusted and therefore should not be permitted to make the fundamental decisions concerning the corporation's operations. "Shareholder voting on such things as acquisitions and divestitures can put immediate shareholder financial return ahead of sound longer-term growth which may have the potential of being even more rewarding to the corporation, its shareholders and its other stakeholders."[23]

This begs the question. No one is in favor of an overly short-term outlook, but *long term* may be a euphemism for something that never happens. The real question is whose perspective is riskier. Why aren't shareholders—as those whose interest is at risk—just as knowledgeable and even more entitled than directors to set the overall direction of the company? Whose perspective is likely to be longer-term—the index fund[24] pledged to hold the stock indefinitely or the CEO, who could lose his job in a change of control?

The critical question is on what basis directors and managers will make their choices. To the extent that directors have authority to allocate corporate resources on any basis other than long-term value enhancement, they are undermining the basis for the grant of power to private entities in a free society.

The 1990 Roundtable report, in all its essentials, is a wiring diagram for CEO monarchy. First, it cautions against direct shareholder involvement: "Excessive corporate governance by referendum in the proxy statement can also chill innovation and risk-taking."[25] Second, it diminishes the authority and independence of the board by depicting it as a necessarily self-perpetuating body ("Because effective corporate boards function as a cohesive whole, the directors are in the best position to recommend the slate of nominees for board membership which is presented to the shareholders for election at the annual meeting"[26]) and by implying that the chairman and presiding officer of the board must be the CEO ("To ensure continuing effective board operations, the CEO can periodically ask the directors for their evaluation of the general agenda items for board meetings and any suggestions they may have for improvement"[27]).

In the fall of 1990, the Business Roundtable further demonstrated its view of the role of shareholders by telling all of its members to refuse to respond to a survey of directors submitted by the California Public Employees' Retirement System. The Roundtable responded as if merely asking questions of directors to determine their personal views was not appropriate: "Some of the questions do not lend themselves to broad generalizations because the answers depend on particular facts and circumstances, others require a more complex response than the questionnaire's format allows, and still others suggest that directors' responses will be used to create 'good' and 'bad' rankings for director nominees in spite of the disavowal of any such intent in the transmittal letter."[28] The letter itself provides the most telling evidence of the Roundtable's vision of the role of shareholders, directors, and management: it assumes that when shareholders seek information about the directors they are asked to elect, managers have not only the right but the obligation to interfere.[29]

This is quite a departure from the earlier commitment to acting as stewards for owners. Indeed, other than a vague acknowledgment of the obligation to maximize value, shareholders are only mentioned in the context of either being incapable of providing direction or having their rights considered along with those of other "stakeholders." This diminished role for shareholders is a startling retreat for the Roundtable. It also parallels the diminished role for the shareholders' representatives, the board.

The Evolution of the Fiduciary Ideal:
Above "the Morals of the Marketplace"

It is worthwhile to contrast the current standards for fiduciaries with those established in early case law. In 1846, in a case called *Michoud v. Girod*,[30] the court decided that it was improper and invalid for a fiduciary trustee to buy assets from the trust. Essentially, the court said that the trust was to be managed on behalf of the beneficial owner, and the trustee therefore could not participate in any transaction involving the trust assets, regardless of any special care taken to ensure that the purchase was at a fair price. The theory of those times was that the role of a fiduciary was so sensitive that it was better that the fiduciary forgo any kind of a transaction with the trust, to make scrupulously clear the superiority of the beneficiary's interests over its own.

One of the most famous cases in American history is *Meinhard v. Salmon*,[31] where the plaintiff and defendant were partners, "co-adventurers," in reconstructing and operating a building. The plaintiff provided only capital; his partner, the defendant, also managed and operated the building. Four months before termination of the partners' lease, the owner of the building approached the defendant, offering to lease it. The defendant did not notify his partner and instead arranged for the new lease to be made to a corporation he controlled.

In this classic interpretation of fiduciary obligation, Judge Benjamin N. Cardozo said, "The very fact that Salmon was in control with exclusive powers of direction charged him the more obviously with the duty of disclosure, since only through disclosure could opportunity be equalized. . . . He was a managing co-adventurer. For him and for those like him, the rule of undivided loyalty is relentless and supreme."[32] It wasn't enough for the partner to behave in accordance with standard business practices; as a fiduciary, he had to do better, he had to be above "the morals of the marketplace."

Cardozo even found that the partner's fiduciary obligation continued, although the defendant could reasonably have believed that the partner-

---

The Fiduciary Code of Honor

Many forms of conduct permissible in a workaday world for those acting at arm's length, are forbidden to those bound by fiduciary ties. A trustee is held to something stricter than the morals of the marketplace. Not honesty alone, but the punctilio of an honor the most sensitive, is then the standard of behavior.

Benjamin N. Cardozo

Source: *Meinhard v. Solomon*, 249 NY 458, 464 (1928).

ship concluded at the end of the original lease and very likely acted in good faith.

These cases and many others demonstrate the extraordinary conscientiousness, scrupulousness, and diligence traditionally imposed on those who owe each other a fiduciary duty. It was with this in mind that the original corporate structure was established. But, like Humpty Dumpty, who uses a word to mean whatever he wants it to mean, those who used the word *fiduciary* gave it an entirely different meaning in applying it to directors.

The Rise and Fall of the Duties of Care and Loyalty: The Morals of the Marketplace Are Good Enough

Although the courts wanted directors to be fiduciaries, they did not want them to be hamstrung by worries that every decision would be reviewed in hindsight by a court, after the fact. So the business judgment rule was established, providing that a court will not second-guess the merits of a business decision. If it is a business decision—not outside the scope of the appropriate conduct of the corporation's affairs—and undertaken with disinterestedness, due care, good faith, and without abuse of discretion,[33] the court will not interfere.

The business judgment rule begins with the reasonable assumption that directors should not be judged in hindsight, so we should not ask that all of their decisions be the right ones. All even the strictest fiduciary standard asks is that decisions be undertaken with care, good faith, disinterestedness, and without abuse of discretion. As one court has said, "The entrepreneur's function is to encounter risks and to confront uncertainty, and a reasoned decision at the time made may seem a wild hunch viewed years later against a background of perfect knowledge."[34] In essence, the business judgment rule provides that if any rational purpose exists for the directors' or officers' decisions, they are not liable for errors in judgment, even when the decisions turn out to be wrong.

The business judgment rule can be traced as far back as 1829.[35] In that case, the court seems to have held that directors have no particular duty to try to find out if the company is being managed honorably—remarkably consistent with the claims made today by lawyers defending directors of failed banks and savings and loans. Although it goes pretty far, even by today's standards, the reasoning in the decision reflects another set of agency costs, those created as the board sets overall policy and leaves it to management to carry out. The business judgment standard was refined over the next century and a half, and it has recently been more vigorously redefined, as courts have been forced to apply it to grapple with the more complex issues of corporate control.

In general, fiduciary duty has two components: the *duty of care* and the *duty of loyalty*. We will begin with the fiduciary duty of care. It contains two elements: *alertness* to potentially significant corporate problems and *deliberative decision making* on issues of fundamental corporate concern. The duty of care is generally interpreted as a "reasonable director standard." In other words, we expect more from a director than from a simply "reasonable man"; we expect the director to behave reasonably according to the experience and expertise a director should have. We might not expect a reasonable man to be familiar with generally accepted accounting principles or earnings per share, but we do expect that of a director.

The Duty of Care

A director shall discharge his duties as a director, including his duties as a member of a committee:

1. in good faith
2. with the care an ordinarily prudent person in a like position would exercise under similar circumstances, and
3. in a manner he reasonably believes to be in the best interests of the corporation.

The Model Business Corporation Act [Sec. 8.30(a)]

Reasonableness varies according to the circumstances. A director who is a lawyer or an accountant is expected to bring his expertise to bear on the issues presented to the board and thus may be held to a higher standard than a director who does not have that training. Corporate officers who are also directors are sometimes held to an even stricter standard, because they know more about the day-to-day operations of the company. Similarly, directors of large companies are sometimes held to a stricter standard than directors of small companies, because directors of large companies are expected to be more familiar with complex corporate finance and governance issues.

There is no way to establish a clear standard for the duty of care; courts must examine the facts of each case. It is the duty of care that has been most troubling to corporations, and the one that has been cut back the most by judicial opinions (the business judgment rule) and state legislatures (limiting liability and permitting indemnification). If one examines the cases that apply fiduciary standards to boards of directors, it is difficult to connect them to the high principles of the decisions quoted previously.

In theory, the rule can be seen as another way of determining "reasonableness." Reasonableness generally relates to process. What was the basis for the decision? What experts were consulted? What research was done? But in practice, many people believe that the courts (especially the most recent decisions of the Delaware courts) have used the business judgment rule to virtually eliminate any real duty of care.

The business judgment rule gives directors a rebuttable presumption of correctness, meaning that anyone challenging a business decision has the burden of proving that it violated fiduciary standards. The courts will go to the greatest possible lengths to defer to directors' business judgment, unless there is a clear showing of fraud or bad faith.

A woman who "never made the slightest effort to discharge any of her responsibilities as a director" was found to have violated the duty of care in *Francis v. United Jersey Bank*.[36] She had never attended a single board meeting or read any of the financial statements, which clearly revealed that her sons (corporate officers) were embezzling funds. In *Hoye v. Meek*,[37] a president and CEO who stopped attending board meetings after he retired and moved away was found liable for over $1.4 million. But, as Woody Allen said, 80 percent of life is just showing up, and directors who do show up get a lot of deference.

In *Shlensky v. Wrigley*,[38] a court upheld the decision not to install lights in Chicago's Wrigley Field, despite the fact that lights for night games were the industry standard and that the decision resulted in loss of revenues from attendance, concessions, and broadcast rights.

The business judgment rule has even been applied in cases of clear shareholder opposition, as in *American International Rent A Car v. Cross*.[39] It became clear at the annual meeting that the shareholders would not support a proposed bylaw amendment. The directors called a recess and adopted the amendment themselves. The court acknowledged that the board's action "had the effect of withdrawing a vote from the stockholders," but that alone did not "automatically override" the other factors (such as the need for additional capital) that the board considered in deciding to approve the amendment.

Courts do not always allow directors to thwart shareholder actions. Directors who try to change the rules on voting find that "in circumstances where corporate fiduciaries appear to have acted out of self-interest, it is particularly appropriate to give scrutiny to the question whether they discharged their duty of the exercise of care."[40]

When Blasius Industries attempted to take over and restructure Atlas Corp. in 1987, it proposed a consent solicitation to put eight Blasius candidates on the board. Atlas expanded its board from seven to nine members, appointing two new members to the board to ward off the attempt. In *Blasius Industries, Inc. v. Atlas Corp.*,[41] the plaintiffs charged that the action by the Atlas directors was "motivated solely by an attempt to retain control of the corporation and violated the directors' duty of good faith." The Delaware Chancery Court disagreed that self-interest was involved, stating that the Atlas board found the Blasius restructuring proposal faulty and that the bond's action was "a good faith effort to protect its incumbency, not selfishly, but in order to thwart implementation of the recapitalization that it feared, reasonably, could cause great injury to the company."[42] The court did, however, refuse to defer to the business judgment of directors who interfered with the voting rights of shareholders, finding that "even though defendants here acted on their view of the corporation's interest and not selfishly, their December 31 action constituted an offense to the relationship between corporate directors and shareholders."[43]

The court also added that "the deferential business judgment rule does not apply to board acts taken for the primary purpose of interfering with a stockholder's vote, even if taken advisedly and in good faith."[44] Although the plaintiffs lost their second suit, alleging that the consent election results were improperly computed, Blasius represents a milestone in defining board responsibility to the shareholders' right to vote.

The business judgment rule does not protect directors if their "sole" or "primary" purpose is self-perpetuation. But that level of protection is not consistent. The takeover battles of the 1980s subjected a lot of defensive maneuvers to "business judgment" scrutiny, and at first the courts tried to limit its application when management's interest might conflict with the shareholders' interest. Later, as these decisions led corporate managers to consider changing to another state of incorporation, the courts quickly reversed this trend.[45]

The Corporate Miranda Warning

In the landmark case *Smith v. Van Gorkom*,[46] directors were found to have violated their fiduciary duty over the sale of Trans Union. The CEO of Trans Union, Jerome William Van Gorkom, suggested to potential buyer Jay Pritzker that $55 per share (a substantial premium over the market) would be a good offer for his company, without consulting anyone on his board. When the board did meet to discuss the deal, Van Gorkom did not tell them that it was he who had suggested that figure to Pritzker, and he did not tell them how he had arrived at it. He did not ask the board whether it was the best price, just whether it was a fair price. After about two hours, the board approved the deal, subject to two conditions: First, the company could accept (but not solicit) another offer during a "market test" period, and second, to facilitate other offers, the company could share proprietary information with other potential bidders. Van Gorkom executed the merger agreement that evening, although the court found that at the time the agreement was executed neither Van Gorkom nor any other director had read it.[47] Trans Union issued a press release announcing a "definitive" merger agreement, "subject to approval by stockholders."

The shareholders did approve the deal. The lower court upheld the actions of the directors, but the Delaware Supreme Court reversed, finding the Trans Union directors "grossly negligent" in failing to inform themselves whether Van Gorkom did a complete job of evaluating the price and negotiating the terms of the merger agreement, and in failing to understand the transaction themselves. The issue was not the substance of the decision; the court never said whether $55 per share was too low or too high. But the court did find that the directors had not taken adequate steps to evaluate it. The substantial premium over the market price, the "market test" period for entertaining other offers, the fact that investment bankers had unsuccessfully tried to get other offers before Van Gorkum approached the Pritzkers, the advice of counsel that they might be violating their duty as fiduciaries if they *failed* to approve the merger, and the approval of the shareholders were not sufficient to make up for the board's failure to evaluate the deal independently.

This was a close case. Although it was not an easy case to decide—two justices dissented, finding the directors' actions reasonable—*Van Gorkom* became the litmus test for directors' duty.

The primary impact of the *Van Gorkom* case has been on the process for arriving at decisions, not on the substance of the decisions themselves. Courts have been very careful not to substitute their business judgment for that of boards. The result is a kind of corporate Miranda warning. However, the warning has little meaning, with routine checklists considered just to make a strong record for the court, rather than for any substantive purpose. And sometimes the record does not even need to be very strong, as in the Time-Warner case, where all the steps taken to establish due care and deliberation were taken in consideration of a deal that was different in every major respect (except management compensation) from the deal that went through.

In the *Unocal* case,[48] the court said that the "omnipresent specter" that a board would act to protect its own interests when faced with a takeover offer, would subject those actions to special scrutiny.

Directors have to show "good faith and reasonable investigation" before they can be protected by the business judgment rule. They also have to show that, unlike the actions of the Trans Union directors, their decisions were "informed." The decisions must also meet another test: They must be "reasonable in relation to the threat posed."[49] Directors are not supposed to use an atom bomb to fight a squirt gun; if they do, it has to be assumed that their primary interest is their own job security.

When Revlon adopted a poison pill in reaction to Pantry Pride's offer of $45 a share, that was "reasonable in relation to the threat posed."[50] When Pantry Pride increased its offer to $53, the defensive measures were no longer reasonable. At that point, according to the court, "it became apparent to all that the break-up of the company was inevitable" and "the directors' role changed from defenders of the corporate bastion to auctioneers charged with getting the best price for the stockholders at a sale of the company."[51] Granting favorable treatment to a white knight whose offer was only $1 per share more than Pantry Pride's was wrong. "[T]he directors cannot fulfill their enhanced *Unocal* duties by playing favorites with the contending factions. Market forces must be allowed to operate freely to bring the target's shareholders the best price available for their equity."[52]

Most of these cases have been decided by the Delaware courts because most big companies are incorporated there. Some other courts have addressed the business judgment rule, holding, for example, that issuing a block of stock to an ESOP and a wholly controlled subsidiary, just to avoid a takeover, violates the duty of loyalty.[53] But, in general, Delaware has a lock on the Fortune 500, and when it seemed that decisions limiting the protection of the business judgment rule might lead companies to incorporate elsewhere, the Delaware courts began to back off.

Did We Say Marketplace?
The Death of the Duty of Care

The first relaxation of a director's duties as defined by *Revlon, Unocal,* and *Moran* came in 1989 with *Barkan v. Amsted Industries.*[54] In that case, the purchase of a block of stock by an investor led management to consider defensive actions. It adopted a poison pill and then decided that its best alternative was a management-led leveraged buyout involving an ESOP. After creating the ESOP, it convened a special committee. The court found that "although the Special Committee was given the power to evaluate the fairness of any acquisition proposal made by a third party, the Committee was instructed not to engage in an active search for alternatives to an MBO."[55] The company then terminated its pension funds, except those covering employees subject to collective bargaining agreements, so that it could use the $75 million surplus. The ESOP trustees and members of senior management then submitted an MBO proposal, which was challenged in four separate lawsuits. After some negotiation, the board accepted the MBO offer, which was later revised upward in settlement negotiations. The court found that "although difficult questions were raised by the course of events leading to the settlement, the settlement was fundamentally fair."[56]

Amsted attempted to define a director's duty of care in an auction involving only one bidder. But just because someone puts a price on a company does not mean that is the best price. How and to what extent must directors pursue the best price in the absence of other bidders? Since no bidder wants a company to be free to pursue other bids, a fundamental conflict will arise between the acquirer—who wants to close the deal as quickly as possible, and the target, whose fiduciary duties require it to take the highest bid over a certain period of time. Thus, an acquirer will attempt to engage the target in a "no shop" clause, preventing the directors from actively seeking other bids.

The rulings in *Van Gorkom* and *Revlon* implied that, in the absence of information to judge the adequacy of the offer, the directors should shop before accepting the first bid. *Amsted* allowed directors to use a "market check" or "window shopping" clause, in which a board accepts an offer but retains the right to passively receive other bids and provide information to other bidders. The court ruled that "Revlon does not demand that every change in the control of a Delaware corporation be preceded by a heated bidding contest. . . . When, however, the directors possess a body of reliable evidence with which to evaluate the fairness of a transaction, they may approve that transaction without conducting an active survey of the market."[57] *Amsted* allowed directors to accept an initial bid without actively "shopping" and without triggering an auction, because the Chancellor found that "the investment community had been aware that Amsted was a likely target," and yet no bids had been made.[58] While the court raised concerns about the "no-shop" restriction on the special committee, because it "gives rise to the inference that the board seeks to forestall competing bids" and it suggests that "a judicious market survey might have been desirable, since it would have made it clear beyond question that the board was acting to protect the shareholders' interests," these concerns were outweighed by other indicators ("timing, publicity, tax advantages, and Amsted's declining performance") of good faith.[59] Practical on the surface, this ruling nonetheless permitted Amsted directors to accept an offer quickly and quietly, inviting conflicts of interest between executives and shareholders.

The Ravages of Time

The Time-Warner case represents probably the greatest incursion in U.S. business history into the rights of shareholders. The Delaware Supreme Court allowed the directors of Time to completely redesign its proposed business combination with Warner, just to keep the decision away from the shareholders.

Time and Warner originally negotiated a stock-for-stock merger in which the shareholders of Time would have the chance to vote whether to exchange their Time shares for new pieces of paper worth approximately $125 per share. Paramount entered the situation with a cash bid of $175 per Time share, later raised to $200. Time and Warner, concerned that shareholders would not support their merger, revised their deal to no longer require shareholder approval. The revision also meant that the new company—and its shareholders—would have an enormous debt burden, at least $7 billion of new debt, and possibly more than $10 billion. Reported earnings were essentially eliminated, because $9 billion of goodwill had to be amortized.

What this means is that Time's management (1) devised and began to put into place a plan that was at least $50–$75 per share below the market's valuation of the stock, (2) refused to meet with Paramount to discuss its offer, and (3) completely restructured the deal, in a matter of days, along lines considered and rejected in favor of the original merger, to prevent shareholder involvement. They demonstrated their utter disregard for the rights of shareholders even further by establishing the line of succession for managing and directing the company, a decision that is supposed to be made by future boards of directors elected by shareholders. All of this was permitted by the Delaware Supreme Court's decision.

In that decision, the court examined the history of the Time-Warner merger as initially proposed and concluded that because it had been under discussion for more than two years, it was proper to proceed with it, even as radically revised in a very short time, and even in the face of a legitimate alternative. This approach is consistent in process but not in substance with the *Van Gorkom* case and the factors that the Delaware courts consider in other cases in evaluating maneuvers that may be characterized as defensive. It is appropriate to consider the motives of directors to determine whether such actions are taken in good faith and therefore deserve the broad protection of the business judgment rule. But it is not appropriate to give weight to an action just because it has been considered for a long time. First, this does not address the obligation to respond to something like the Paramount offer, which could not be predicted. Second, it creates a very perverse incentive for boards to have their lawyers simply read aloud a list of every possible defensive action and every possible business combination at each board meeting, just to make sure that it is on the record as having been considered, but leaving entirely open the question of whether that consideration has been at all meaningful.

The *Paramount v. Time* case presents a clear question. The court put it this way: "Did Time's board, having developed a strategic plan of global expansion to be launched through a business combination with Warner, come under a fiduciary duty to jettison its plan and put the corporation's future in the hands of its shareholders?"[60] The Delaware courts answered no, a result that must be viewed against an offering price of $200 in cash versus a price on August 23, 1990, little more than a year later, of $76⅞. When I asked Michael Dingman, an outside director of Time,

Inc., whether he thought there was a problem in giving managers such broad discretion in a deal where their own compensation played such an important role, he was characteristically direct: "To put it bluntly, I believe that the directors of Time did an extraordinary job of preventing the shareholders from getting screwed."

Monks-Dingman Exchange on Time-Warner

Original Letter, 21 July 1989

Dear (Time Shareholders):

Delaware's Chancellor William Allen, in his decision to permit the merger of Time and Warner, has not just missed the forest for the trees; he has missed the forest for the bark.

As the Delaware Supreme Court prepares to hear oral argument in the challenge to the Time decision he issued last Friday, we wanted to let you know how we see the issues. We believe that Chancellor Allen missed the central issue, which is this: Can we justify a transaction that presents directors with a conflict of interest, by protecting their employment and compensation, but denies shareholders the opportunity to express their views?

As you know, Time and Warner negotiated a stock-for-stock merger in which the shareholders of Time would end up with new pieces of paper worth approximately $125 per share. Paramount entered the situation with a cash bid of $175 per Time share, later raised to $200. Time and Warner, concerned that shareholders would not support their merger, revised their deal so that it would no longer require shareholder approval. The revision also meant that the new company—and its shareholders—would have an enormous debt burden, at least $7 billion of new debt and possibly more than $10 billion. Reported earnings will be essentially eliminated, because $9 billion of goodwill will have to be amortized. The equity deal was based on both industrial and financial logic. The debt was justified by the same industrial logic, but there was no longer any financial justification for the deal.

What this means is that Time's management (1) devised and began to put into place a plan that was at least $50–75 per share under the market's evaluation of the stock, (2) refused to meet with Paramount to discuss its offer, and (3) completely restructured the deal, along lines considered and rejected in favor of the original merger, to prevent shareholder involvement. Their utter disregard for the rights of shareholders was demonstrated even further by the line of succession they locked in for directing the company. This is one of the most important rights reserved to shareholders. All of this was permitted by Chancellor Allen's decision. He also concluded that because the merger had been under discussion for more than two years, it was proper to proceed with it. But the deal he allowed to go forward was not the one they designed during that period of deliberation; it was one they rejected and then put together quickly to obstruct Paramount. Furthermore, the original deal was developed without reference to Paramount's offer. At the very least, that offer should have forced the board to determine why it was so much higher than the share value realized in their merger. Chancellor Allen said, in one of a series of double negatives, "I am not persuaded that there may not be instances in which the law might recognize as valid a perceived threat to a 'corporate culture' that is shown to be palpable (for a lack of a better word), distinctive, and advantageous." The facts suggest that it was not the "corporate culture" that Time management was planning to preserve but the extremely favorable employment and compensation schemes they had negotiated with Warner. Chancellor Allen notes that the "Time culture" issue was of concern in setting the compensation for Time executives, but that this was resolved by paying them at a higher level, though still on the same basis, rather than revising it along the formula used at Warner.

The Time board has not fulfilled its critical role in coordinating the restructuring in an objective, independent manner, for the benefit of those to whom it owes the most scrupulous fiduciary duty, the shareholders. The court has not objected. The issue is the same one as that presented by management buyouts, a question of conflict of interests. The "Revlon mode" should be triggered whenever such a conflict arises, because that is the key issue, not some formal notion of whether the company is "for sale." At that point, the board must step back and preside over an orderly evaluation of all alternatives to decide which will provide the best long-term return for the shareholders.

When directors, due to the impact various alternatives will have on their compensation and employment, have a conflict of interest that prevents their fulfilling their obligation as fiduciaries to protect the interests of the shareholders, then the decision should be made by the shareholders. That is the critical issue ignored by the court. We hope that the Supreme Court will reverse this decision. If not, shareholders have the choice of seeking legislative change, either in Delaware or at the federal level, or using their ownership rights to reincorporate the companies they hold in states with more respect for the interests of shareholders.

We will continue to keep you posted. In the meantime, if you have any comments or questions, please do not hesitate to call.

Sincerely,
R. A. G. Monks

Dingman's Reply, 15 August 1989

Dear Bob,

Your letter of July 21st has been brought to my attention.

As you know, when it comes to shareholder value, I've believed, espoused, and supported many of the same things as you. In fact, in cases like Santa Fe, I've earned a reputation as an opponent of poison pills and entrenched management. But with the Time-Warner merger, we part company. In the main, I find your opinions to be ill-informed and off-target.

Paramount's highly conditional offer of $175 or $200 per share was not only ludicrously low but transparently cynical. In making it, Mr. Davis (Chairman and CEO of Paramount Communications Inc.) had two motives. The first was tactical. He wanted to sabotage Time Inc.'s carefully considered merger with Warner and thereby destroy or weaken a competitor that would dwarf his own newly created media/entertainment company. The second was opportunistic. If his public relations campaign succeeded, Mr. Davis saw a chance to panic the board into letting him pick up Time Inc. for a song.

He wasn't that lucky. Unlike the role played by Paramount's board in ratifying the tender offer to Time Inc., we weren't about to rubber-stamp a managerial fait accompli. That's not the way the Time board works. We had been looking at the merger with Warner for over two years and had considered the long-range payoff for shareholders, as well as the strategic and financial implications.

In the media coverage surrounding Paramount's tender offer, it was the universal consensus that the Time board was composed of eight outside directors with reputations as hard-nosed individualists, men and women equally unwilling to do the bidding of either Time Inc.'s management or Mr. Davis. In this, at least, the media were on the money.

As a participant in the board's deliberations, I was a witness to the demanding independence of the other seven outside directors. They lived up to their reputations as mavericks, asking all the tough questions and looking without sentiment or illusion at the offers on the table. In the end, all of us, without a single dissent, voted to proceed with the Time-Warner deal.

I have no regrets about that decision. *None.* We've created the strongest and potentially most profitable media/entertainment company in the world. And if Mr. Davis succeeded in changing the terms of the original deal, nothing he said or did changed its rationale. It remains an extraordinary opportunity to improve dramatically the value of Time Inc. stock.

Frankly, I find it more ridiculous than insulting for you to accuse me and the other outside directors of a "conflict of interest." No one—not even Paramount's lawyers—raised this as an issue. In fact, if you really think I'm worried about my "employment" (sic) as a Time director or depend in any way on the compensation it entails, then you are probably beyond the reach of rational argument.

The ultimate outcome of the Time-Warner situation will be decided in the near future as the managements come together to build what they set out to. Despite whatever speculative losses some investors may have incurred in betting on Paramount's bid, I do hope you and others try to make an honest appraisal of the values represented by this new company.

There's no question in my mind that the eventual outcome will resemble what happened at Disney after Saul Steinberg was paid his greenmail of $19.25 per share. Michael Eisner and his management team left the employ of Martin Davis and Paramount and brought a whole new energy and direction to Disney. At some point you may wish to examine for yourself why Eisner and other creative managers left Paramount, but this much is already certain: They have revived the company's fortunes. Disney stock is now selling at $120 per share.

Dick Munro, Steve Ross, and Nick Nicholas have proven records of attracting and holding the best talent in the media/entertainment business. They have shown that they can create substantial value for shareholders, and now that the fight with Paramount is over, they will make an immense success out of their new venture.

I don't mean to oversimplify all the issues that surrounded the Time-Warner deal. It was a complex transaction that required some very tough judgments. And, in my opinion, the press did such a miserable job of covering the facts and issues involved that I can't really blame you and your colleagues—never mind the ordinary shareholder—for being confused.

To put it bluntly, I believe the directors of Time did an extraordinary job of preventing the shareholders from getting screwed. And except for a few major shareholders like Capital Research—who understood the real values at stake and stood by their beliefs—they did it alone.

I look forward to seeing you in the future and discussing this at greater length. In the meantime, I felt it necessary to express my personal opinion concerning your previous letters.

Sincerely,
Mike Dingman

Monks' Reply, 23 August 1989

Dear Mike,

I very much appreciate your thoughtful response of August 15, to my letter about the Time-Warner decision issued by Chancellor Allen, and since then upheld by the Delaware Supreme Court. Although you described my "opinions to be ill-informed and off target," I think we agree more than we disagree. I can support many of the points you made, and still think that the courts (and the board of Time) were wrong to disregard the rights of the shareholders. And I suspect that both of our positions lead to the same ultimate diagnosis, even the same solution.

I agree with you that the directors of corporations should have the power to consummate mergers; however this must be done in a way that recognizes the clear conflicts of interest that exist for top management in such situations. Even though it imposes an additional burden on the "outside" director, I see no alternative to their taking over the merger process, much in the same way and for the same reason that they have been required by this same Delaware court to take over the "auction" process, as in RJR and Macmillan. The chief advantage of outside directors is that they can bring some objectivity and discipline to the process. (I agree with your characterization of the Time Board. Indeed, I have frequently cited *your* involvement as conclusive evidence that the problem is systemic and not personal.)

Here is where I think we disagree. To my way of thinking there is a world of difference between "outside" and "inside" directors. The Time Board apparently chose to conduct the merger (acquisition) negotiations without limiting the participation of the "inside" directors. That the "outside" acquiesced in and supported direction of the transactions by "insiders"—and not that I am "beyond the reach of rational argument"—is why I refer to a conflict of interest by the Board.

Corporate reorganizations ultimately devolve into a question of who gets how much. There is no objective standard—no Mosaic decalogue—that proscribes how much to shareholders, how much to management and how much to other corporate constituencies the total consideration should be allocated. When, as I am sure you will agree was the case with Time, the consideration to be paid the principal executives is not immaterial, isn't it better practice to limit their role in leading the negotiations? Should anybody be in the position of being the ultimate arbiter of his or her own entitlement? Should those with the largest personal stake continue to select and direct the professional advisers and thus the information reaching the Board? I think of the transaction as one in which the top management took the top dollar for itself, whether or not it was in the long term best interest of the company and the shareholders as parties whose interest is far more genuinely long term than that of the people who put this transaction together.

Let's look at the transaction for a moment. It is ironic that the original proposal required shareholder approval, under the rules of the New York Stock Exchange, while the revised plan, far worse from the shareholders' perspective because of the debt burden, did not. Time was easily able to take the choice away from the shareholders, by redesigning the deal to make it much worse for them, and the shareholders did not have any way to get it back.

The court gave great deference to the fact that the merger with Warner was negotiated over a period of two years. However, the business combination that was actually executed was put together in days, in response to the Paramount offer, on terms that were explicitly considered and rejected during that two-year period of deliberation, terms that left the company with a gigantic burden of debt. The fact that the record showed compensation and succession of the top management to be the most contentious issues (apparently the only contentious issues) did not suggest to the court that perhaps self-interest might have been the primary factor in setting the terms of the merger. It does suggest it to me.

You could very well be right that the merger between Time and Warner makes more sense than a merger between Time and Paramount. The question is who makes that decision. You suggest that it should not be shareholders, because they are uninformed and only look to the short term. I suggest that it should not be top management, acting without meaningful accountability, because they have a fundamental conflict of interest. I have the same problem with MBOs. There simply cannot be a level playing field when one party has all of the resources and all of the information. In this case, Time's management also had all of the power.

I do not think that institutional shareholders are irretrievably short term in their orientation. If they take short term gains, they then have to find another place to invest them, and that is a real problem. Furthermore, most institutions have highly diversified portfolios, with major investments in thousands of companies. Many of our clients were investors not only in Time, but also in Warner and Paramount, not only in stocks, but also in bonds. They must look to the net impact of any proposed transaction, as fiduciaries and as prudent investors. This militates against a short-term orientation.

I agree that the institutional shareholders have a way to go before they can persuade those, like you, who are convinced that they look no further than the quarterly returns. In this regard, it is important to note the escalating portion of institutional investments today are *de facto* or *de jure* indexed. Over the last few years, the index funds have performed better than the managed funds, which makes them hard for any "prudent and diligent" asset manager to ignore. Earlier in the year before the Markey subcommittee, I recommended that indexed investments be deemed, per se, prudent under ERISA. It is essential to take some step to encourage (possibly, even, to ensure) that the largest class of institutional investor— one for whom liquidity serves no private or public objective—to be a genuine "long term" holder and source of "patient capital," and, therefore, begin to function as a permanent shareholder. I recognize that a gap exists today between my desired world of a solid core of long-term institutional shareholders and the arbitrageur driven world of contemporary takeovers.

If the arbs were the only institutions, I would find it difficult to argue that a governance system be organized for their benefit; on the other hand, I see no reason to disqualify ownership as the fundamental object of governance just because arbs are involved. No one has suggested that newly elected CEOs have any less authority because of the brevity of their tenure, nor are directors required to serve an apprenticeship period.

I suggest that to the extent that the institutions have a short term orientation, it is in large part attributable to the failure of the governance system. If you were an investment manager with a large holding in Time, your alternatives would be quite limited, even under the terms of the original deal with Warner. But if you had a real voice, a real relationship with management based on real accountability, to give you confidence in the long term, there would be no incentive to go for a short term gain.

Under the current system, managers and boards and shareholders face real impediments to making the best long term decisions on these issues. But the obstacles to shareholders can be removed, while the essential conflicts presented to managers and boards will always be there. As Professor Roberta Romano has noted, "we focus on enhancing shareholder value because when looking at a corporation, it is difficult to conceive of who else's interests would be appropriate for determining the efficient allocation of resources in the economy." That is why it makes more sense to entrust these decisions to shareholders than to the people whose employment and income is at stake.

I am not at all convinced that the Delaware Courts consider these issues fairly. (You and I have been in agreement on this point in times past!) I am certain that the "Delaware interest" factor played an important role in the Time decision, as it did in Polaroid and many others. Delaware risks losing its title as champion of the race to the bottom. The Pillsbury and Macmillan decisions led to Marty Lipton's call to reincorporate elsewhere, and the Supreme Court's CTS decision gave the domicile states' authority a boost. Pennsylvania and other states are moving quickly to pass laws even more accommodating than Delaware's, with the "stakeholder" laws being the latest fad.* I testified before the Delaware state legislature, arguing against adoption of the antitakeover law, along with every other

* This is a standard to which one cannot be held accountable. He who is responsible to many is responsible to none. "We hope more states, especially Delaware, where so many major corporations are incorporated, will explicitly adopt broader constituency laws." Jay W. Lorsch with Elizabeth MacIver, *Pawns or Potentates: The Reality of America's Corporate Boards,* Harvard Business School Press, Boston, 1989, p. 187.

shareholder representative. When the parade of CEOs came in, saying that they sure would hate to have to reincorporate elsewhere, it was no contest. In order to protect Delaware's economic interest in accommodating the Fortune 500, the courts have created a special language of takeovers that has no base in law or economics, and they make that language go through all kinds of acrobatics to make precedent appear to apply. This gives us the "Revlon" and "Unocal" modes. And it gives us the contortions that Chancellor Allen went through to keep Time out of those modes.

Another element of Delaware's special language is the "business judgment" rule. Certainly, managements need and deserve the widest indulgence of courts in deferring to their "business judgement." No one thinks that they should second-guess these decisions. But the courts should be there to make sure there is a process in place that promotes fair treatment— or at least one that does not impede it. Shareholders deserve a level playing field, too. The original Time-Warner proposed transaction can and should be supported. This represents a determination by management that ownership values can be maximized within the framework of a merger company, virtually debt free, that can be the aggressive competitor in a multinational world. The Time management has made three judgments for its owners: (i) the business of Time can best be carried out in tandem with Warner; (ii) the merged businesses can best be conducted with a solid equity base, permitting capital investment and acquisitions on a global basis; and (iii) that this merger is the best way to bridge the "value gap" for Time shareholders. At this point, the Paramount offer gave some public indication of the exact size of the "value gap." Paramount offered $200/share and was willing to offer more; Time management dismissed this as inadequate notwithstanding that the market valued common stock in its proposed merger at $120/share. Time then decided to buy Warner. While this preserved the face of the "business logic" of the merger, clearly a "debt encumbered" survivor is not going to be able to pursue the course of multinational aggressive dominance that was the apparent keystone of the original merger. Management thus has turned 180 degrees from an equity heavy company to one drowning in debt.

Should there not be some common sense limit to the extent of deference paid to "business judgement" when deference is paid both to a business strategy based on all equity and then it is paid again to a strategy based on all debt? Conceivably, one of these is correct. Both cannot be, and yet deference is paid to both. And, can the courts ignore arithmetic? How many years, and at what implicit rate of return, does a holder of Time common have to wait until his stock will achieve the levels that Paramount offered in 1989 in cash? Should there be any limit to this, or should deference extend indefinitely? Chancellor Allen conjures up only the most unsatisfactory "red herring" of limits based on fraud.

What is to be done? The Time-Warner decision represents a real failure of the system of governance. America cannot simply give over the assets and power of the private corporation system to managers who are not meaningfully accountable to anyone. I personally have little appetite for the federalization of corporate law, and yet I recognize that "Delaware interest" decisions like Time-Warner will tend to make federal preemption more appealing.

What I have been interested in for the past several years is fortuity of large fiduciary ownership. What seems to me to be a beginning point is to require that institutional owners act as such; that those with long term interests be required to be long term investors; that we stop regulating institutional fiduciaries in the interest of service providers and that we elevate the interests of the beneficiaries, who constitute an adequate proxy for the national interest.

Of one thing do I feel certain, had Michael Dingman been a large shareholder of Time, the transaction would not have been consummated without the meaningful involvement of owners.

I look forward very much to the opportunity to spend a few hours together to talk of this and so many other things of mutual interest.

With respect,

Your Friend,
R.A.G. Monks

Dingman's Reply, 31 August 1989

Dear Bob,

Thank you for your letter of August 23, 1989. If we keep this up, we'll be able to publish a book—*The Monks-Dingman Correspondence!*

You're right. We agree on more than we disagree. But not on everything. For example, you believe that once a corporate merger comes under consideration, management and the inside directors should at some point turn the process over to the outside directors. (In your words, "Even though it imposes an additional burden on the 'outside' director, I see no alternative to their taking over the merger process. . . . ") Then, at some later point—again unspecified—the outside directors should step aside and let the shareholders decide.

I believe this would turn corporate governance into a muddle. More to the point, it has little bearing on the case of the Time-Warner merger. The outside directors were in charge. Every step was reviewed and approved by us, and we weren't the empty vessels you seem to believe we were, filled with whatever ideas and information management cared to pour in our ears. We challenged management every step of the way. We asked the kind of questions that we would ask of our own employees, and we didn't settle for stock answers. In the end, we agreed that the merger was a magnificent opportunity that should be pursued.

You use the word "acquiesce," i.e., "to accept quietly or passively." We did a lot of things in the unfolding of the merger. Argued. Probed. Questioned. Inquired. Cross-examined. It went on and on until we were satisfied. But we never acquiesced.

One final thing. The central issue in the Time-Warner deal was neither debt nor compensation. Paramount would have loaded on more debt than Time's acquisition of Warner, and provided a far less significant cash flow with which to service it. And Michael Eisner and Frank Wells were offered an extraordinary package by Disney, and they've proved themselves worth every dime. If Steve Ross can deliver the same return to Time-Warner that he has for Warner, a company he built from scratch, his compensation will be more than justified.

The board wanted to build Time Inc. so it could provide the very best return for shareholders. I think we did.

You raise a number of interesting points in your letter and, if I had the time, I'd like to look at them all. But I don't. The reality of creating shareholder value doesn't leave much space for dwelling on theories. Sometime in the future, when we can manage it, I look forward to sitting down and discussing the whole matter of Time-Warner, as well as its wider implications. I hope that we'll both learn something.

There is one thing I am absolutely against and that is the federalization of corporations and/or the establishment of more government rules concerning how businesses, managements, shareholders, et al. interact. I hope we agree on this point as well, and please stay away from Mr. Metzenbaum.

Again, thank you for your thoughtful response to my letter.

Sincerely,

Mike

A great deal of financial data was introduced to the court with various extrapolations of projected long-term value. It boils down to this: The Warner transaction valued Time stock at $125, and the Paramount offer was $200. It almost makes one feel the need to suspend disbelief to understand how an investor could not do better with $200 cash, which she would be free to invest in any venture of her choice, than with a

$125 investment in Time-Warner, even with the most competent management ever known. How could any factfinder ignore the simple fact that starting with 60 percent more capital is virtually certain to make more money? What this suggests is that the case is not about money; the Delaware courts have devised a language to resolve disputes that does not include a vocabulary for maximizing owners' value. What are owners left with after *Time*? Michael Klein, who argued as special counsel for Bass Brothers in this case, put it: "When the marketplace has put a 25-percent or 30-percent premium on one answer as opposed to another, why should the legal system be constructed so as to deny institutional and other shareholders the opportunity to accept that premium? What's heinous about this case is the manipulation of the corporate machinery by the directors of Time to accomplish an avoidance of the shareholder franchise."[61]

In this case, as in *Household,* management deliberately structured the transaction to avoid having to seek shareholder approval. The issue here was not merely the difference between antitakeover provisions; it was the very essence of the transaction. Time conceived of the deal as providing a capital base that would give it the capacity to be an aggressive worldwide competitor. As the Supreme Court of Delaware found: "Time representatives lauded the lack of debt to the United States Senate and to the President of the United States. Public reaction to the announcement of the merger was positive. Time-Warner would be a media colossus with international scope."[62]

Following Paramount's initial $175 a share offer,

"[C]ertain Time directors expressed their concern that their stockholders would not comprehend the long-term benefits of the Warner merger. Large quantities of Time shares were held by institutional investors. The board feared that even though there appeared to be wide support of the Warner transaction, Paramount's cash premium would be a tempting prospect to these investors. In mid-June, Time sought permission from the New York Stock Exchange to alter its rules and allow the Time-Warner merger to proceed without shareholder approval. Time did so at Warner's insistence. The New York Stock Exchange rejected Time's request. . . .[63]

Thereafter, "Time's board decided to recast its consolidation with Warner into an outright cash and securities acquisition . . . to provide the funds required for its outright acquisition of Warner, Time would assume 7–10 billion dollars worth of debt, *thus eliminating one of the principal transaction-related benefits of the original merger agreement.*"[64] The decision utterly to alter the capital structure of the surviving company to heavy leverage was made in a matter of days and appeared to undercut the purported rationale of the entire transaction.

Furthermore, Time's commitment to the merger with Warner was less than its commitment to making sure Ross had a fixed retirement date. Negotiations were broken off for several months, until Ross was induced "to reevaluate his position and to agree upon a date when he would step down as co-CEO."[65] The agreement reached was that Ross would retire five years after the merger and that Nicholas would then become the sole CEO of Time-Warner. (So much for the role of shareholders and the boards they elect in selecting management.) The decision found that "[o]ther aspects of the agreement came easily."[66] Despite the evidence about the importance of compensation and succession (these parts of the deal remained as the rest of it was completely restructured), somehow Chancellor Allen found that "there is no persuasive evidence that the board of Time has a corrupt or venal motivation in electing to continue with its long-term plan even in the face of the cost that course will no doubt entail for the company's shareholders in the short term."[67] The concerns he referred to as "corporate culture" seemed to be focused only on compensation.

An enterprise and its equity securities are a function of two components—the businesses and their capitalization. There is an enormous difference between an equity-funded worldwide communications colossus and a debt-ridden venture. That the courts would base a decision on the long-standing plan respecting the businesses and ignore the quickly cobbled-together complete change with respect to capitalization means that Delaware courts will endorse any action of management, even if self-interested. "Finally, we note that although Time was required, as a result of Paramount's hostile offer, to incur a heavy debt to finance its acquisition of Warner, that fact alone does not render the board's decision unreasonable so long as the directors could reasonably perceive the debt load not to be so injurious to the corporation as to jeopardize its well being."[68] Rarely has the irrelevance of shareholder interest been so clearly articulated.

Why pretend that there is such a thing as shareholder rights? In the lower court decision, the chancellor stated, "I am not persuaded that there may not be instances in which the law might recognize as valid a perceived threat to a 'corporate culture' that is shown to be palpable (for lack of a better word), distinctive and advantageous."[69] Of course there is an instance in which the law recognizes the validity of a "corporate culture." The instance is in the value that corporate culture provides to shareholders. Time shareholders want the company to be able to reap the benefits of its culture, whether alone or in a productive synergy with another company. But it is difficult for Time to claim that its culture and editorial independence could not have been preserved with Paramount, since they did not even meet with Paramount to discuss it.

Chancellor Allen was correct in saying, "Directors may operate on the theory that the stock market valuation is 'wrong' in some sense, without breaching faith with shareholders."[70] But they may only operate on that theory if they base it on fact. Let them demonstrate to the shareholders that they can do better. Without that, we abandon any pretense of a market test, in favor of "expert opinion" paid for by management, usually with a contingent "success factor." Even Chancellor Allen was appalled at the company's estimated valuation of $208–$402 for Time-Warner stock in 1993, calling it "a range that a Texan might feel at home on."[71] Are there any limits, short of explicit fraud or corruption, to the deference that the court will give to management's determination of value? Is there any level to justify, even require, judicial intervention?

The obvious reluctance of courts to involve themselves in second-guessing management of enterprises is understandable, even justifiable. But the result denied owners both the right to vote on the merger of Time with Warner and the right to sell their shares to a willing buyer at a mutually agreeable price.

The Time board did not fulfill in an objective, independent manner its critical role of coordinating the restructuring for the benefit of those to whom it owes the most scrupulous fiduciary duty, the shareholders. The court did not object. As Michael Klein pointed out, the Time-Warner decision theoretically allows companies to "create a high threshold of risk, and then do everything deliberately to deprive shareholders of any alternative. The Time-Warner directors did not even need to confront, evaluate, or compare alternatives."[72] The "Revlon mode" (requiring directors to preside over an auction) should be triggered whenever a conflict of interests between shareholders and management arises, because that is the key issue, not some formal notion of whether the company is "for sale." At that point, the board must step back and preside over an orderly evaluation of all alternatives to decide which will provide the best long-term return for the shareholders.

The Death of the Duty of Care, Part II:
Limited Liability and Indemnification

Cases like *Van Gorkom* triggered huge increases in insurance premiums for directors if, in fact, coverage was available. Increasingly, companies confronted an inability to purchase E&O (errors and omissions) insurance for fiduciaries at any price. To protect themselves, directors passed bylaw amendments limiting the amount for which they could be held liable. First, of course, state legislatures had to authorize such caps on liability. Delaware did so immediately after the Van Gorkom decision, and other states soon followed suit, in yet another example of state legislatures accommodating managers. A number of states have adopted very broad laws limiting the liability of directors, even for negligent acts. This effectively eliminates a duty of care. Nevada, New Jersey, and Virginia permit limitations on the monetary liability of officers, in addition to directors. New Mexico even allows limited liability for gross negligence. Some states allow the corporation to cover a director's legal expenses, plus damages, even if the court finds that the director violated his duty. In states where indemnification provisions are overly broad, a significant problem arises since shareholders who challenge directors are in effect picking their own pockets. An unsuccessful defense by an indemnified director can lose the shareholders more through recovery and reimbursement than they had originally suffered in damages.

Did We Say Morals?
What's Wrong with These Pictures?

In 1989, the board of Occidental Petroleum voted to spend $86 million of the corporation's funds to build a museum for Dr. Armand Hammer's art collection. Many people believed that this was an inappropriate use of the corporation's assets, especially since only part of it was a deductible charitable contribution, and also since Dr. Hammer reneged on his commitment to donate the collection to the Los Angeles County Art Museum, considerably diminishing any goodwill from the construction of a museum at the corporate headquarters. But what was even more clearly an outrage was the lawsuit brought by "the usual suspects" of the Delaware bar. They tried to settle it quickly. The settlement would have provided no benefits for the shareholders, would have given the museum at least $96 million from the corporate treasury (more than the original allocation), and would have paid the attorneys $1.4 million for a few weeks of work.

This settlement would have gone through immediately but for the intervention of plaintiffs Alan Kahn, a money manager, and two public pension funds, the California Public Employees' Retirement System and the Pennsylvania Public School Employees' Retirement System. Kahn noted that the shareholders had now been abused twice, once by Occidental directors and once by the lawyers who were supposed to be representing the shareholders. The settlement was stalled, and discovery was allowed to go forward. Discovery produced many additional revelations, including the fact that some of the artwork in Dr. Hammer's personal collection was paid for by the corporation and the fact that at least one of the members of the committee of "independent" directors who approved the museum expenditures had no understanding of the financial consequences of the deal. Nevertheless, the same lawyers came forward with the same settlement, only now for up to $120 million. This included payment of seven years' worth of Dr. Hammer's salary directly to the museum after his death, a sort of "coffin parachute."

Despite the protests of many major shareholders, and the court's finding that the benefits to shareholders were "meager," the Delaware Chancery Court approved that settlement. Although the judge expressed strong reservations about its terms, he said that the likelihood that the museum expenditures would be approved under the business judgment rule made it impossible for him to do anything else. The judge took the unusual step of expressing his concerns about the outcome by cutting the attorney's fees nearly in half. He also said that "If the Court was a stockholder of Occidental it might vote for new directors, if it was on the Board it might vote for new management and if it was a member of the Special Committee it might vote against the Museum project."[73] But he said that, because the expenditures would likely be upheld under the business judgment rule, the case had to be settled. The business judgment rule has now been extended so broadly that it can bar a trial on the merits, despite evidence that corporate funds were used for personal acquisitions. If a clerk did that, it would be called embezzlement. If Armand Hammer does it, it is business judgment.

This demonstrates shareholders' utter helplessness under Delaware law in suits for breach of directors' duty. A small group of lawyers, representing "shareholders" with token investments, file almost daily lawsuits, with complaints that are photocopies of yesterday's suits against other companies, based on whatever is reported in the financial press. Then they settle, quickly, for small awards and high attorney's fees.

The majority of shareholder lawsuits are brought by a small group of people, who hold a small group of shares, working with a small group of law firms, and the conclusions are generally favorable only to the lawyers. For example, in the recent settlement of a shareholder lawsuit against CBS, the plaintiff, who held 12 shares, received $15,000, or $1,250 per share. His attorneys got $1.5 million. CBS got about $4.5 million from its own insurer; we do not know whether that sum covered more than its expenses.

To make things worse, corporations sometimes welcome these suits because they can be settled quickly and cheaply, extinguishing the claims of all shareholders. Insurers push for settlement. According to a letter we received from CBS, "neither CBS nor the individual defendants participated in those (settlement) negotiations." Buying off the "Delaware regulars" is a small price for directors to pay to protect themselves from a serious lawsuit. Even if they do not think so, their insurers do. One disadvantage of indemnifying directors is that decisions such as these are then made by the insurance companies.

In the Occidental case, even the protests of shareholders with millions of dollars invested in the company were not enough to stop an outrageous settlement. If the Delaware courts cannot find enough merit in a challenge to a $120 million expenditure for a personal monument that is a twentieth century equivalent to the pyramids to even allow it to go to trial, despite evidence of improper use of corporate funds, then Delaware does not deserve to be the jurisdiction for these challenges. Shareholders should insist that the companies they invest in incorporate in states that will give them a chance to challenge directors who violate the duties of care and loyalty.

The Death of the Duty of Loyalty

Although "care" is vague and hard to define, loyalty is a concept that is simple to understand and enforce. Courts examining violation of this duty have occasionally held that a transaction undertaken by directors who have a conflict of interest is void, even if the corporation and shareholders are not harmed (for example, if the CEO buys equipment the company was planning to sell, and he pays a fair market price). More often, the court will let these transactions stand if there is no harm. The burden is on the party claiming a breach of the duty of loyalty to prove that there was a conflict of interest (in the preceding example, that the shareholders had an interest in getting the highest price for the equipment, and the CEO had an interest in buying it for the lowest price). Then the burden is on the director or officer to show that the transaction was fair (that he bought the equipment for the same price as it would have realized on the open market).

For example, Marriott Corporation decided to acquire some companies who were owners or lessees of real property leased or subleased to Marriott. The owners of these companies were members of the Marriott family. The payment (313,000 shares of Marriott stock) was established by independent appraisers, evaluated by independent analysts, unanimously approved by outside directors, and then approved again by the shareholders. The transaction was upheld by the court. That was appropriate. The evidence showed that the directors had the opportunity to use their advantage to profit at the expense of shareholders, but the directors showed that they took every possible step to assure scrupulous fairness. Therefore, the duty of loyalty was not breached.

Playing Both Sides: The MBO

An MBO is a transaction where management sits on both sides of the table, on one side representing shareholders, on the other side representing itself. Management claims that they will run the company better when they are running it on their own behalf. But isn't fiduciary duty supposed to make them run it better for shareholders than they would for themselves? And buying out the company does not necessarily mean that they will be running it on their own behalf. When Edward K. Finklestein took Macy's private at $68 a share, he took a $9,755,280 profit on his stock options. Of that, he put $4,375,000 back in. He ended up with less of his own money in the company than he had before.

Management controls the timing and the information and then submits the deal to the board they have selected. The Macy's board initially asked for $70 a share but backed down later to Finklestein's proposal of $68, even though the stock had risen in the interim, and even though the company's own projections showed that investments of several hundred million dollars were about to pay off. Macy's had listed eight shopping malls as worth $100 million. Finklestein's group valued them at $250 million. Three months after the buyout, he sold them for $555 million.[74]

Can anyone claim that it was his newly revived entrepreneurial spirit that gave him this idea only after the MBO? Can anyone claim that this money did not rightfully belong to the shareholders?

The MBO is practically the definition of a conflict of interest. As long as management is free to be involved as a principal in an MBO, it has an interest in the company having a low stock price. Management can make sure there is a gap between "real" and "market" value. If management's participation in LBOs is to be justified by the increase in values attributable to its initiative, management has the strongest possible incentive to time its MBO when values are the lowest. What remains of the duty of loyalty when managers can buy companies from shareholders at just about any price above market? Management's significant advantages make any effort to "shop" the company around to get a competitive price almost meaningless.

A classic example of unintended consequences (i.e., management's use of its insider status to make money for individual managers rather than the company or the shareholders) can be traced back to Mary Wells in the early 1970s. Wells took her advertising company—Wells, Rich, Greene, Inc.—public in 1968 at $17.50 a share and sold a new offering in 1971 at $21.75. When she went private in 1974, the stock was at $5.50 in the aftermath of the 1973 recession. Shareholders got $3 cash per share and $8, 10-year debentures.[75] The SEC, concerned with managers taking such blatant advantage of depressed stock prices, responded with Rule 13e. This rule, by explicitly prohibiting certain types of actions, gave legitimacy to all others, allowing fiduciaries to feel secure that, as long as they complied with 13e, they were being fair and just and were protected from charges of breach of their duty as fiduciaries. Rule 13e, instead of a warning, became a blueprint.

The result has been a string of abuses, with some particularly disturbing examples. Loral Corporation sold two of its divisions to its own CEO, Bernard L. Schwartz, despite a higher bid from an outside company, Banner Industries. Banner's complaint in its lawsuit against Loral says that it first expressed interest when Loral acquired the two divisions in 1987; Banner was told that Loral did not want to sell them and that it would contact Banner if it ever decided to sell. When Banner read in the press that the divisions were being acquired by Loral's CEO, it offered a higher bid. Banner says that it was denied access to the information about the divisions necessary for due diligence in submitting a formal bid, however, and was never permitted to meet with the special committee of the board convened to oversee the "auction" of the two divisions. Banner's complaint also charges that it obtained additional information demonstrating that the two divisions are worth even more than it originally thought, and that would have supported even a higher bid. The CEO and the special committee were both aware of this information.

Schwartz has stayed on at Loral while he runs his two units, renamed K&F Industries. In addition to his $1.7 million salary from Loral, Schwartz and four Loral executives split $200,000 a month in "advisory" fees, for work Schwartz himself estimated takes him 10 hours a month.[76]

UAL: A Wolf in Wolf's Clothing

The UAL MBO attempt that failed in October 1989, prompting a minor stock market crash, in many ways perfected the breach of trust by taking the process to the next logical step: total protection of management and its team of lawyers and bankers. According to the *National Review of Corporate Acquisitions,* "The original unsuccessful transaction will long be remembered as a glaring case of overreaching greed and questionable judgment."[77] Management at UAL acted on its own behalf, at shareholder expense, on two fronts: management compensation and exorbitant legal and financing fees, both vital parts of the MBO plan to support management interests. Stephen Wolf, CEO of UAL, followed the example of Steve Ross at Warner and included in his MBO a healthy compensation package totaling $22.5 million in shares plus $54.176 million in unexercised stock options, fully protected in the event of a change in control.[78] The new company that Wolf would head was designed to keep UAL out of play. Wolf and John Pope, CFO of UAL, stood to gain $114.3 million in a successful MBO, although UAL executives planned to reinvest only $15 million in the new company.[79] Taking into consideration that all of these managers also have lavish golden parachutes, it becomes apparent that MBOs have become a vehicle for guaranteeing extraordinary rewards for management while protecting them from any risk.

Adding insult to injury—and adding further injury, too—it is the shareholders who must pay the bills of the lawyers and investment bankers hired to carry out the MBO, even if it is designed to benefit management at shareholder expense, and even if it fails. In the case of UAL, the bill was more than $50 million. Lazard Freres alone took over $8.25 million.

One *Wall Street Journal* journalist calculated that UAL was paying each Lazard Freres banker $41,045 per day. Citicorp and Chase received a combined $8 million; Salomon received about $8 million, plus an additional $3 million for a bridge loan commitment; the law firms involved on the deal took over $15 million; and $16 million went to repay a fund created for an ESOP.[80] All this for a group that failed to raise the $6.79 billion necessary for the MBO to occur.

The UAL deal demonstrates how far you can stretch an unfair principle when no one is watching. The shareholders are taking the risk, even paying for management's support teams, whether they win or lose.[81] Case after case demonstrates that management is taking advantage of its insider status to keep legitimate bids from shareholders. The problem is that this advantage is inherent. There simply is no way to conduct an MBO in a manner that is fair to shareholders. Although Loral and UAL are good examples of the astonishing level of abuse possible in an MBO, it is important to keep in mind that even those MBOs conducted by responsible management, making every effort to ensure scrupulous fairness, are wrong because there simply is no process that will guarantee a level playing field when one of the parties controls the information and the agenda. Management cannot bargain with itself, representing both the shareholders and its own interests. The fiduciary responsibilities of a CEO are not compatible with entrepreneurial efforts to preserve or attain individual power through corporate assets. You can't sit on both sides of the table.

This may, in fact, have contributed to the failure of the UAL deal. Some observers believe that the original financing failed *because* of management's self-centered behavior. "The bankers [who turned down the UAL proposal] said that UAL's management and advisers pushed too hard, trying to keep too much of the potential profit for themselves."[82] It may be that the bankers realized that a good CEO is one who is not an MBO artist.

Management does not even have to bear the risks of its offer, as outsiders usually do—if it fails, let the shareholders pay for it. Management has a great deal to gain and literally nothing to lose. Shareholders, on the other hand, have a lot to lose—not just an adequate price for their stock, but the loyalty of directors as well.

Clearly, an MBO is not a surefire way of enhancing revenues for the company and the shareholders when it (1) involves paying over $53 million to lawyers and financiers who actually fail to complete the MBO (as in UAL), (2) depresses a stock price so that management can realize a thousandfold profit on a public-private scheme (Wells, Rich, Greene, Inc.), or (3) keeps the company from selling at the best price in order to give it to the CEO (Loral).

There have been several MBOs where the value gap between what management paid and what they shortly realized was shocking. One such transaction was the privatization of Metromedia that made John Kluge the richest man in the United States. Writes Benjamin J. Stein, "The list of cases in which management has made millions, hundreds of millions, even billions from LBOs is sadly long. Metromedia. Burlington. Amsted. Narragansett Capital Corp. Triangle. Many, many others. (Triangle's was a particularly brilliant LBO in which management did not have to put up any money.)"[83] A "fairness opinion" that underestimates realized value by 80 percent is perhaps the newest candidate for the quintessential oxymoron.

The MBO at GAF

Sam Heyman and GAF were different. The MBO at GAF is interesting because it demonstrates that good people with all of the right values, following all of the rules, can still face significant conflicts. Heyman, after graduating from Harvard Law School, worked for Robert Kennedy and served as an assistant U.S. attorney in Connecticut, then went on to a career as a real estate developer. Heyman became involved in the management of GAF the hard way. In 1983, with just 5 percent of the stock, he waged a bitter and successful proxy contest to elect his nominees to the board. The company flourished, making over $1.5 billion over the next five years. Two bold Heyman initiatives alone—efforts to acquire Union Carbide and Borg Warner—produced over $350 million of profit.

There can be no question that Heyman's energy and brilliance were the principal contributing factors to the realization of this incremental value for GAF shareholders. No one who invested in Heyman lost money; indeed, some made a very great deal. GAF made $1.5 billion in increased values for shareholders during Heyman's tenure, and the stock price increased sevenfold. Harold Simmons, later to try to take over Lockheed, invested shortly after the proxy contest and sold before the privatization. Net profit—in excess of $100 million. The capacity to create value of this magnitude raises the question: From Sam Heyman's point of view, what sense does it make to channel his energy through a public company?

Ultimately one has to ask: How much money does he have to make for other people before he can be allowed to take the company private? It is clear from the public documents that the directors' committee and their counsel made serious efforts to get more for the outside shareholders. Indeed, it is noteworthy that these individuals, all of whom came to GAF through Heyman's proxy contest, struggled so tenaciously that conspicuously among all the MBO transactions, this one stands for the kind of arm's length negotiation contemplated by the law—no less, but no more. Heyman conferred with directors in August 1987, stating his intention to take the company private and quoting a possible price as "north of $75."[84] When he announced his bid in September, however, it was $64.00 in cash, $2.50 in debt.[85] At this point, the directors became wary. One director reflects: "I think we led him to believe that since we hadn't raised much objection when he proposed it, when we went along with who he selected as the committee, when we went along with his choice of the law firm, in essence . . . it looked like a no brainer."

But the directors at GAF came alive, and a lengthy battle for a fair price for GAF was waged over the next year. Heyman dropped his $66.50 bid before the market opened on October 19, 1987.[86] That day the stock market crashed. When Heyman submitted a new bid on December 14, 1987, it was for $40.00 cash, $8.50 in debt.[87] True, it reflected a premium over the current stock price of GAF, but the intrinsic value of the company had not changed, only people's perception of it. Until the deal closed in March 1989, the board scrapped with Heyman, inching the price up to a final bid of $46.00 in cash, $7.00 in debt.[88]

Managers face conflicts of interest when taking the company private, both those who are and are not participating in the buyout. When the directors interviewed the managers, one who was not invited to participate told the board that, in his opinion, one of the divisons alone was worth Heyman's bid, which at the time was in the low $50s. He charged that Heyman, in essence, was getting the other divisions at no cost. A similar situation occurred at RJR, when the head of the Nabisco division, John Greeniaus, was cut out of Ross Johnson's MBO plan. Greeniaus went over to the rival bidders, Kohlberg, Kravis and Roberts (KKR), and gave them accurate figures on the RJR-Nabisco operations. KKR won the bidding war, and Greeniaus still heads Nabisco.[89]

At GAF, the board dealt with the inherent conflicts by spending 18 months trying to find another buyer. According to one source, they wanted to find another buyer, if only to confirm that there was no favoritism. Unable to find one, they concluded that Heyman's offer was in the best interests of the shareholders.

After the GAF deal had closed, there was the issue of the dividend, which had come due. Heyman, who would own the company in a matter of weeks, did not want to pay it, but the outside directors felt it had to be paid. From Heyman's perspective, the directors were talking about distributing his money. The directors disagreed, believing that the money was the shareholders' until Heyman actually assumed control. The directors voted in favor of the dividend.

The GAF MBO demonstrates the conflicts that lie at the heart of an MBO. Sam Heyman is a brilliant manager with a gift for maximizing profit. The board of GAF was a group of capable, intelligent, and honest men. Yet the CEO and the board found themselves at loggerheads when the MBO process began, when suddenly the managers were no longer working solely for the interests of shareholders.

In an MBO, the CEO, on the inside, has the advantage. He decides the parameters of the MBO: when, where, and at what price. He retains control of the corporate information machine and pocketbook and hires the experts. The imbalance tilted in management's direction is too great for even the most diligent and energetic efforts of independent directors to correct.

The Death of the Duty of Loyalty, Part II:
Stakeholders

A previously unheard-of doctrine, the stakeholder concept, has recently taken strong hold in corporate America. In essence, it says that corporate directors owe a duty to a host of constituencies beyond shareholders: local communities, employees, suppliers, creditors, and others. This is in contrast to the traditional model of the publicly held corporation in law and economics, which says that corporate directors serve one constituency— their shareholders. As James J. Hanks, Jr. of Weinberg & Green said, it is "an idea whose time should never have come."[90]

The stakeholder theory is now being applied in at least three different contexts: state antitakeover legislation, public pension fund investment policy, and corporate policies in responding to takeovers.

Traditionally, one of the most important aspects of the corporate form was the directors' and officers' absolute fiduciary duty of loyalty to the shareholders. As Louis Lowenstein, head of Columbia University's Institutional Investor Project, has said, shareholders should come first, "Not because you like them or hold them in high esteem, but because if you don't, there is no bottom line, no way to measure efficiency. . . . The system collapses if shareholder interests are not primary"[91]

In the past couple of years, a number of states have adopted "stakeholder laws" to permit a board of directors to consider the impact of any proposed action on its employees, customers, suppliers, creditors, and communities, plus any other factors it deems pertinent, in addition to the impact on shareholders. Typically, these statutes "apply generally to decisions by the Board, including decisions with regard to tender offers, mergers, consolidations and other forms of business combinations."[92] The early state laws of this kind make this provision available for adoption by corporations, with shareholder approval. And most of them make it clear that the board's authority is completely discretionary, and no stakeholder constituency is entitled to be considered.

It has always been permissible, even required, for directors and managers to consider the interests of stakeholders, in the context of the interests of shareholders. Courts have upheld a corporation's right to donate corporate funds to charities, for example, as it was in the corporation's long-term interests. As the American Bar Association Committee on Corporate Laws pointed out, "[T]he Delaware courts have stated the prevailing corporate common law in this country: directors have fiduciary responsibilities to shareholders which, while allowing directors to give consideration to the interests of others, compel them to find some reasonable relationship to the long-term interests of shareholders."[93] The committee also noted that *Unocal*, which enabled directors to analyze the effects of a potential takeover on a variety of factors, including constituencies, does not suggest "that the court intended to authorize redress of an adverse impact on a non-shareholder constituency at the expense of shareholders."[94] Although it is useful (and cost-effective) to consider the best way to meet the admittedly competing needs of the company's diverse constituencies, it is an oversight to fail to make clear that the shareholders must have first priority.

No court, no legislature, and no shareholder has ever claimed that the duty of loyalty prevented consideration of other constituencies. Indeed, directors who fail to consider the interests of customers, employees, suppliers, and the community fail in their duty to shareholders; a company that neglects those interests will surely decline. In the past, these proposals have been occasionally submitted by shareholders, who want the board to undertake a more comprehensive analysis of proposed actions. But "stakeholder" language, in legislation or in corporate charters, can be camouflage for neglect, whether intentional or unintentional, of the rights of shareholders.

The danger is in allowing corporate managers to make policy trade-offs. That should be left to those who have another kind of accountability—through the political process.

F. A. Hayek posed the alternatives this way:

> So long as the management has the one overriding duty of administering the resources under its control as trustees for the shareholders and for their benefit, its hands are largely tied; and it will have no arbitrary power to benefit this or that particular interest. But once the management of a big enterprise is regarded as not only entitled but even obliged to consider in its decisions whatever is regarded as the public or social interest, or to support good causes and generally to act for the public benefit, it gains indeed an uncontrollable power—a power which could not long be left in the hands of private managers but would inevitably be made the subject of increasing public control.[95]

The Business Roundtable seems to agree. In its 1990 report, *Corporate Governance and American Competitiveness,* it contrasts political and "economic" organizations. "Legislative bodies . . . represent and give expression to a multiplicity of constituent interests. Our political system is designed to create compromises between competing interests, to seek the broad middle ground. . . . This system of governance would be fatal for an economic enterprise."[96] Yet that is just what the stakeholder initiatives it supports would require.

In 1990, Pennsylvania risked the consequences Hayek warned about when it adopted the notorious Act 36 of 1990, which went far beyond other stakeholder laws in moving beyond consideration—a rather benign concept—to one with more legal bite: Directors may consider "to the extent they deem appropriate" the impact of their decisions on *any* affected interest. They are not required "to regard any corporate interest or the interests of any particular group . . . as a dominant or controlling interest or factor" as long as the action is in the best interest of the corporation.[97] In the context of a potential or proposed change-of-control transaction, a determination made by disinterested directors (those not current or former employees) will be presumed to satisfy the standard-of-care requirement unless *clear and convincing* evidence proves that the determination was not made in good faith after reasonable investigation. This means, as a practical matter, that directors cannot be held liable for what they do, absent some element of self-dealing or fraud. This provision required no shareholder approval; it was immediately applicable to all companies incorporated in Pennsylvania, unless they opted out within 90 days.

The anti-shareholder bias of the bill was made clear during the campaign to pass the bill. In December 1989, a "fact sheet" sent to state legislators from the Pennsylvania Chamber of Commerce, which cosponsored the bill with the local AFL-CIO, contained the statement that the bill would "reaffirm and make more explicit the time-honored (and current) principle that directors owe their duties to the corporation, rather than to any specific group such as shareholders."[98] The new law does not say that directors are free to place greater importance on factors other than long-term profit maximization, but to give it any other interpretation is to violate the foremost principle of statutory construction and assume that the legislature intended its language to have no effect.

It did have an effect, though perhaps not what the legislature intended. By October 15, 1990, 99 companies—nearly 33 percent of the state's publicly traded companies—had opted out of at least some of the provisions of the bill. Over 61 percent of the Fortune 500 incorporated in Pennsylvania opted out, as did over 56 percent of those in the S&P 500.[99] So massive was the stampede out of Pennsylvania Act 36 that a *Philadelphia Inquirer* editorial noted: "These business decisions make it all the more clear that the law was crafted not in the best interest of the state's businesses, but to protect Armstrong World Industries Inc. and a few other companies facing takeover attempts."[100] A company spokesman for Franklin Electronics Publishers stated that its board "believes that the Pennsylvania legislation runs counter to basic American principles of corporate democracy and personal property rights."[101]

Apparently, the market agreed. Jonathan M. Karpoff and Paul M. Malatesta at the University of Washington School of Business found that from October 12, 1989 (the date of the first national newswire report of the bill), through January 2, 1990 (when the bill was introduced in the Pennsylvania House), the shares of firms incorporated in Pennsylvania underperformed the S&P 500 by an average of 6.9 percent.[102] Another study, by Wilshire Associates, linked enactment of the Pennsylvania antitakeover law with a 4 percent decline in stock prices of companies incorporated there. The study of Pennsylvania companies with a stock market capitalization greater than $5 million charted 63 companies from January 1, 1989, through August 15, 1990.[103]

One important question is how the "best interests of the corporation" differ from the "best interests of the shareholders." Scholars have debated for decades just what a corporation is, but whether it is a "bundle of contracts" or an "imaginary person," it seems fair to envision a hypothetical long-term shareholder, such as the beneficial owner of most institutional investor securities, as the ultimate party at interest. This allows all other interests to be factored in. But without a clear, direct, and enforceable fiduciary obligation to shareholders, the contract that justifies the corporate structure is irretrievably shattered.

4

The Scarecrow of the Law:
The Failure of Government

We are comfortable living in a society that includes powerful, large, profit-seeking corporations, because we believe that along with profit they are producing goods, services, and jobs in the public interest. The myth is that there is a system to limit the scope of their activities, to make sure corporations act in the public interest. In the next chapter, we discuss the inability of a profit maximization goal to provide those limits. In this chapter, we discuss the inability of the federal and state governments to prevent what we have been calling externalities, to keep corporations accountable. Indeed, corporate management has been very successful in using the law to neutralize the other mechanisms for accountability, from boards of directors to civil suits for damages to the market itself.

Corporations, as systems of power, work to expand and to compete with other institutions in the allocation of societal resources. This energy creates unexpected consequences, as shown by the experience of the automobile industry during the 1980s. There are a number of other examples of the failure of federal law—whether statute or regulation, civil or criminal—to prevent or even punish actions that externalize costs.

We will see how government unsuccessfully attempts to place limits on the unacceptable aspects of corporate behavior through laws relating to private wrongs (torts and punitive damages) and those concerning public wrongs (criminal law). But the law is another mechanism for accountability that corporate management has co-opted, a "scarecrow" that has become an extremely cozy perch.

The Scarecrow of the Law

We must not make a scarecrow of the law, setting it up to fear the birds of prey, and let it keep one shape, till custom make it their perch and not their terror.

William Shakespeare

Source: William Shakespeare, *Measure for Measure,* Act 2, Scene 1, Line 1.

Perhaps the most powerful myth about corporations is that they are ultimately held accountable by the marketplace and they therefore must maximize profits to compete for investors. The reality is that the "profit maximization" model does not provide an accurate explanation of the way in which large corporations function in our society. Essentially, modern corporations often use their power to reduce risks and transfer costs on to others, creating results that were not intended, that are not in the interests of society as a whole, and that have nothing to do with profit. In this chapter, we examine how that is done by influencing federal and state law; in the next chapter we examine how it is done through other means.

The Effect of PACs

PAC money is destroying the election process.

Senator Barry Goldwater (R Ariz.)

Because corporate power over government is so critical in directing the country's energies, it is important to look at the importance of corporate money in elections. This topic is worth a book in itself and has been ably covered in several, so we will just touch on it here to make two points. The first is that PAC money is a factor in neutralizing the federal government's ability to hold corporate management accountable—either directly or indirectly—through imposition of criminal or civil liability. As the forthcoming VRA and tobacco examples show, it is even a factor in the market's ability to evaluate products. The second point is that corporate influence on government, most recently through PAC contributions, is a nice paradigm for the topic of this chapter: how corporations have taken even those laws designed to restrain them and have transformed them into laws to protect them. These are the "scarecrows of the law."

Each effort to "reform" the federal election process's sensitivity to large financial influence seems, ironically, to result in increased importance of corporate involvement. The Watergate scandal led to great concerns about blatant efforts to circumvent the plainly understood prohibition against corporate contributions to federal elections. Such pardoned "felons" as Armand Hammer of Occidental Petroleum, George M. Steinbrenner III of American Ship Building, and Thomas V. Jones of Northrop were found to have funneled corporate funds illegally into the 1972 reelection campaign of Richard Nixon.

The resulting "reforms" permit the use of corporate personnel to organize, corporate resources to solicit, corporate professionals to ensure compliance with law–all so that corporate officers, shareholders, or constituents can make "personal" contributions net of overhead costs to a corporate PAC. Although the corporation can direct the PAC to make expenditures on behalf of candidates, the PAC can be funded only by contributions from shareholders, directors, officers, and managerial employees; it cannot receive corporate treasury funds. This involves high administrative expenses, which can legally be borne by the corporation, estimated to be up to 50 percent of the sums raised. The ability of PACs to commit money early is indispensable to success in federal elections, because these contributions can be used to "prime the pump"—to set up a professional money-raising operation.

PAC contributions to congressional candidates have risen in the election years from $34.1 million in 1978 to $150 million in 1988. Some 83 percent of the total went to incumbents. Says former Senator Barry Goldwater, "PACs set the country's political agenda and control nearly every candidate's position on the important issues of the day."[1] The power of such special-interest groups as the American Medical Association, the National Rifle Association, and the insurance industry is well known. The increasing reliance of congressional incumbents on PACs for financing their reelection campaigns suggests the capacity by those who control the flow of PAC funds—top management—to find willing listeners to their views on governance. One way to alleviate this problem in the future may be for institutional shareholders to organize their own PACs, although this kind of involvement presents the same problems related to collective choice as any other kind of activism.

What's Good for General Motors...

The automobile industry is a particularly appealing example of the use of the political process to protect industry from the marketplace. Cars symbolize America in a way no other consumer product ever has; it is no coincidence that Charlie Wilson equated General Motors with the United States. Cars are a metaphor for an area of traditional American excellence and domination, an area where recent concerns about safety, oil prices, and the environment have all focused, and where international competition has caused great change and has suggested the desirability of a great deal more.

Between 1980 and 1982, the "big three" automakers—General Motors, Ford, and Chrysler—lost $8 billion pretax, and their domestic market share sank to 71 percent,[2] from a high, in 1955, of 95 percent of the nation's sales.[3]

In 1980, the government "bailed out" Chrysler, saving it from almost certain bankruptcy. The vaunted discipline of the marketplace was overruled, establishing a basis for the belief that no corporation in America that is large and sufficiently well advised will be allowed to fail by a government unable to deny focused constituency pressures. It is well known how the most sophisticated of Washington lawyer-lobbyists choreographed the assault on elected officials by labor unions, suppliers, customers, dealers, and representatives of local communities where plants were located. The bailouts of Continental Illinois Bank, Lockheed, and Chrysler all prove that the government will not allow a company to fail, so long as it is of a critical size. Company management can successfully involve government; government will take the steps necessary to ensure survival; the interests of the constituency groups will be served in the short run. It has nothing to do with profit; it has to do with the continuance of a pattern of industrial functioning for which a politically effective coalition can be mobilized.

President Reagan, a free-market advocate, while campaigning in Detroit in 1980 addressed another "problem" of the automobile industry: "I think the government has a responsibility that it's shirked so far. And it's a place government can be legitimately involved, and that is to convince Japan that in one way or another, and for their own best interest, the deluge of their cars into the United States must be slowed while our industry gets back on its feet."[4] As we will see, Reagan delivered on his promise, illuminating how even the most ideologically opposed elected officials ultimately will serve as agents for the *status quo* rather than let their constituents (or their political fortunes) risk creative adjustment to change.

If You Can't Beat 'Em, Exclude 'Em: VRAs

Within three to four years, there came about such an explosive reversal in the fortunes of the Big Three auto manufacturers that all were reporting record profit levels and amassing huge cash reserves. For instance, in 1984 total net income from automotive operations was over $10 billion, cash flow from operating activities exceeded $20 billion, and cash on hand at the end of 1984 was over $16 billion. Market value soared to $37 billion, and market share was edging back to 74 percent.[5] A key reason for the strong financial performance of the Big Three was the Voluntary Restraint Agreement (VRA) with Japan, which was an early priority of the Reagan administration. This agreement limited car and truck imports from 1981 onward.

There are interesting implications: VRAs are increasingly being used (by the United States) as part of a web of devices to support domestic industry or improve its competitive position, without having to compete in the traditional sense. They form part of an unwritten industrial policy for which consumers pay the price.

The automobile industry was able to generate virtually unanimous political support for the government to intervene. The only real question was how. VRAs for the automobile industry constitute a particularly prominent and well-analyzed example of how corporations influence their regulatory environment, how wielding such influence can become a competitive weapon. Parenthetically, we may ask who benefits from this flexing of corporate muscle. We will see that, in the short term, all of the most affected constituencies benefited. The union workers were locked into their jobs with higher-than-competitive salaries for a few more years; the companies made profit and cash; shareholder values soared. Even the Japanese companies were happy: "[T]he quotas were a boon to the Japanese manufacturers, who did extremely well and greatly strengthened their position in the U.S. market. Thanks to the artificial hold-down of supply, they boosted their prices and profits....Buoyed by the profits from price premiums that often exceeded $2,000 per unit, the Japanese companies' U.S. dealer networks got bigger and stronger."[6]

VRAs are devices to limit foreign competitors in favor of domestic industry, based on the argument that because they do not play by the same rules, competition is unfair. The essence of the agreements is that they should be voluntary and temporary; in reality they are neither. The beauty of it, from the importing government's point of view, is that it shelters domestic industry without appearing protectionist, and it does not directly contravene the General Agreement on Tariffs and Trade (GATT) or domestic legislation. Because the arrangements are "informal," the traditional and expected legal protections against monopolistic behavior are simply suspended.

There is another beauty to VRAs that is more sinister. Powerful corporations can use VRAs to ensure their own "earnings" at the expense of other constituents—in this case the American consumers, "who paid over $5 billion a year in artificially elevated car prices and were deprived of product choices."[7]

There have been a number of studies of the impact of the VRA. One study estimated that the restraints produced an increase in cash flow estimated at some $6 billion. Accordingly, between 33 percent and 45 percent of the automobile industry cash flow for 1984–85 may be attributed to the restraints.[8] The premium for consumers has been estimated at between $500 and $2,000 per car and total consumer losses of up to $5.3 billion.[9] One study estimates that "by 1984 the restrictions led to an $8.9 billion increase in U.S. producers' profits, virtually all of the industry's record profits of that year."[10]

The VRA produced pricing increases typical of successful cartels. Consumers still purchased imported cars, but paid up to $2,000 more for them. Not surprisingly, having achieved protection from competition, the domestic manufacturers substantially increased the prices of their own cars. Profits for the automobile industry in the mid-1980s were, therefore, really a government-mandated transfer from the American customer to the Big Three (and, as we will see, to the Japanese manufacturer, the unintended beneficiary of the whole exercise).

The actual effect of the VRA was to boost short-term earnings and support wage levels (higher than those in Japan or those for other American manufacturing jobs). But it is another of the principal uses of the huge cash flows that deserves special attention. During this period the automakers repurchased upward of $10 billion of their own capital stock.

Issue (Repurchase) of Stock, Millions of Dollars			
	GM	Ford	Chrysler	Total

	GM	Ford	Chrysler	Total
1981	304			304
1982	354			354
1983	212		(254)	(42)
1984	(12)		(373)	(385)
1985	(128)	(449)	(843)	(1,420)
1986	(679)	(700)	(291)	(1,670)
1987	(730)	(1,342)	(391)	(2,463)
1988	(534)	(816)	(27)	(1,377)
1989	(1,482)	(894)	(214)	(2,590)

Total $9.289 Billion

In our continuing efforts to understand the driving forces behind large American companies, the fact that $10 billion was allocated to the repurchase of stock rather than research and development, new facilities, or any other corporate purpose, is of seminal importance. The automobile manufacturers effectively exerted extensive political pressure to induce the federal government to adopt VRAs, which increased profits for the automobile companies by increasing prices for the American consumer. Approximately the same dollar amount as was extracted from the customer was used to reduce the capital of the corporations, or, in other words, to partially liquidate them.

This analysis is intended not to demonstrate causality, but rather to identify certain phenomena. Regardless of what else happened in the U.S. automobile industry in the 1980s, consumers paid approximately $10 billion more for their cars than they would have, had the auto industry not been successful in having the VRAs imposed. At the same time, the automobile industry used approximately the same amount of money to buy back its own stock. This is not a long-term plan for value enhancement.

Taking It Twice

The auto industry took money from the consumers and then took it again from the shareholders by failing to use the windfall for long-term growth. Apparently, management of the Big Three could not identify investment opportunities for their extra cash. Thus, the hugely publicized government intervention and the extortion from American customers in the form of higher prices did not provide money that was used in any meaningful way by the industry. By the end of the decade, market share for the Big Three had declined from 77 percent to 69 percent, accounted for by a 10-point decline for General Motors, to 36 percent.

It is difficult to correlate the operations of the American automobile system over the last decade with a dynamic of profit maximization for shareholders. Indeed, the only constituency that seems well served by these events is top management, whose reward is calculated not by market values but by the manipulable intricacies of accounting.

The statement that the eventual consequences of the VRA will be beneficial to the U.S. auto industry is rather ironic, depending on one's perspective. In campaigning for the VRA, management spoke of "profit maximization," meaning that by protecting their oligopoly and creating an excess demand they could achieve a short-term boost in earnings. The United Auto Workers was concerned with preserving premium-wage jobs. Some public officials may have believed that the VRA would provide the "breathing space" necessary to invest, remodel, retool, retrain, automate, and introduce new management techniques in order to compete successfully with Japanese manufacturers. What actually happened, in addition to the short-term wage support and earnings boosts, was acceleration in setting up "transplant" factories and new capacities in the United States, as well as an increased number of joint ventures between U.S. and Japanese companies.

This acceleration was not entirely due to the VRA. Yen/dollar exchange rates have had some impact, although Japanese decision making is so long-term that these fluctuations are not as significant as some have claimed. The VRA creates an immediate incentive to obviate the quota by producing within the United States. An industry that expends its energies to secure a VRA is likely to be a vulnerable one. The protectionism prolongs the distortions and the inefficient allocations in the economy that gave foreigners an advantage in the first place. This, in turn, makes direct investment in the United States very attractive, as the domestic industry has failed to take the essential reforming steps to make itself competitive.

The huge presence of Japanese manufacturers in the United States has continued to erode the market share of the Big Three. In fact, with Honda and Toyota capturing as much of the market as Chrysler, it is no longer the Big Three. For American companies, it is the Big Two. Counting all comers, it is the Big Five. The irony is that the VRA may have cut short the breathing space and made a much more competitive environment than those who fought for it intended. Reports that "transplants" and imports combined will shortly achieve up to 40 percent of the U.S. market suggest that the consumer may well, at last, get a better product at a lower cost.

With the benefits of hindsight, let's contrast the automobile industry's recourse to its political power and the "protection" of the VRAs with a genuinely competitive industrial strategy.[11] We have seen that the artificial VRA profits in effect were applied to partially liquidate all of the Big Three. Suppose that U.S. automakers had lowered their prices and reduced their margins and earnings. This means that they would probably have sold more cars and would have been more successful in preserving their market share.

On the other hand, the course of action they took resulted in a 10 percent *direct* loss of market share, and the indirect loss through the transplants is substantially higher. Even with $10 billion of reduced earnings, they would have ended the decade in the same financial position they were in following the repurchases of their own stock. From this we understand that the dominant trend in the principal American industry is to use its power over government for short-term protection rather than in trying to compete in international markets. It is impossible to correlate this behavior with the profit maximization model.

From this experience, we will try to identify some of the characteristics of modern-day American business. The interrelationship of business with government, both national and local, creates the structure against which commercial activity takes place. The automobile industry, through the Chrysler bailout and the VRAs, together with a decades-long negotiation on pollution and energy efficiency standards, illustrates graphically some of the direct ways in which corporations extract preferential treatment from government. At the same time, in a more subtle way, business attempts to influence the "rules" so as to permit the appropriation of profit from commerce while externalizing—placing on society as a whole—as much as possible of the related costs.

Turning Scarecrows into Support Systems

The process of transforming a scarecrow into a perch is standard by now but is still a fascinating exercise in misdirection. First, corporate management denies that a problem exists. Second, they loudly claim that government involvement is unjustified and will cause the involved industry to become non-competitive, with according loss of jobs. Then, quietly, an utterly practical judgment is made as to which level of government is preferred. The ultimate commercial accomplishment is to achieve regulation under law that is purported to be comprehensive and preempting and is administered by an agency that is in fact captive to the industry.

This is not as hard as it sounds. Regulatory agencies are well-known "scarecrows of the law" that follow set patterns. First, the system is set up to protect against some harm, such as predatory pricing or unsafe food. Who is selected to staff the agency? Almost inevitably, an "expert" from the regulated community. Even the most vigorous opponent of the industry, however, soon becomes co-opted, for a variety of reasons. Perhaps he wants to expand the agency's jurisdiction or budget, for which he needs industry support. Perhaps he just wants a job with industry when the administration ends. Possibly an influential senator has an influential constituent. Or maybe all of the information coming into the agency is prepared by the industry itself.

For all of these reasons and many others, government regulation turns scarecrows not just into perches, but into props on which the industry is dependent. When Nell and I worked with the Presidential Task Force on Regulatory Relief, during the Reagan administration, we found that business representatives continually sought more rather than less regulation, particularly when it would limit their liability or protect them from competition.

A good example of an industry that is utterly dependent on government "props" is the tobacco industry. This might make sense if it were an industry that provided a benefit of any kind to anyone (other than the corporations that manufacture tobacco). On the contrary, of course, the tobacco industry has the distinction of selling the single legal product most injurious to health. As an economic matter, its only advantage is that it keeps the Social Security system's books balanced by killing people before they can begin to collect.

The tobacco grower enjoys an extensive system of subsidies. Costs for the tobacco industry are reduced by placing the costs of smoking on users, their families, medical service providers, and society as a whole.

The federal government's minor attempts at reducing smoking (dwarfed in cost by the amount spent indirectly encouraging it) have, not surprisingly, failed. The requirement that a warning be prominently printed on each pack of cigarettes has given the industry an effective defense in lawsuits where smokers claim damages for wrongful death. The companies simply argue that the federal government has, through its notice requirements, evaluated the risk and prescribed measures appropriate. And the ban on broadcast advertising was seen by some in industry as a benefit, because radio and television were most effective at introducing new brands; thus, the old, established (high-tar and high-nicotine) brands were made even safer from competition.

Suppose that the real costs of smoking were charged to the cigarette manufacturers. Add back growing and other subsidies, calculate and charge medical and workplace costs, and impose liability for shortened life. Would there still be a tobacco industry? Experience in Europe with a drastically increased cigarette tax indicates that cost significantly reduces consumption. Arguably, this is an industry that would not exist were it not for the variety of societal subsidies that its effective use of power has managed to command. The business logic would be to reduce or eliminate investment in cigarette manufacturing, were the industry not so successful in dumping a substantial portion of the external costs on society. Society is a double loser, first in paying the various subsidies and second in fostering a reduced standard of living.

Liability: Heads Business Wins, Tails Consumers Lose

The ubiquitous sign "You break it, you bought it" makes it clear that a customer who jostles a knickknack is accountable for the consequences of his carelessness. But no such standard applies to business, not when it can get the equivalent of a "Get out of jail free" card from the government. The theory of the market is that a company will not sell a product that may be harmful because it does not want to be liable for any damages it may cause. Under this system, a company has two choices: to test its products carefully or to limit its liability. The government has gone overboard in imposing liability in some cases, mostly environmental cases, by making purchasers liable for the violations of the companies they buy. But in other cases, it has allowed corporations to avoid a true market test by limiting liability. This perspective is reflected in the comment attributed to GM's famous long-time chief executive Alfred Sloan that he did not use more expensive safety glass in autos because his obligation as a businessman was to make money. If GM were liable

for damages caused by the failure to use safety glass, Sloan would realize
that the cheaper glass was, in fact, more expensive.

Don't Do the Crime If You Can't Do the Time

Government attempts to address externalities by creating penalties, often
through the criminal law. In theory, by defining an activity as "criminal,"
government is making the determination that it should not occur; and in
theory, penalties are designed to make it more expensive to violate the
law than to abide by it. By allowing "punitive damages," a fine greater
than the amount of damage caused, the government is trying to protect
citizens against corporate misconduct in extreme situations. Antitrust law,
for example, allows for fines triple the amount of damage inflicted. And
some statutes allow litigants to collect attorney's fees, to encourage those
who would otherwise not be able to afford to bring the suits.

But it is shareholders who pay the cost of criminal activity by corporations; and they pay for it three times. First they pay as members of a
society with polluted water or rigged markets or dangerous products or
workplaces. Then they pay the costs of both the prosecution (as taxpayers) and defense (as shareholders) when charges are filed. Then they pay
again, for the fine comes not from the bank accounts of the men and
women who participated in the criminal activity, but from the corporate
coffers.

Criminal convictions, *nolo* pleas, and routine involvement in illegal
activity by all of the largest and most respected American corporations
have become commonplace. Such conduct both trivializes the relevance
of society's determinations of what constitutes unacceptable activity and
demoralizes the citizenry in the face of continued inability to hold corporations meaningfully accountable to societal standards.

Why do corporations engage in criminal behavior? It has to be because, at some level, they find that the benefits outweigh the costs. Or,
more likely, management finds that the benefits accrue to the corporation while the costs are borne elsewhere—the externalizing machine
at work. This question becomes increasingly pressing as Congress in-
vestigates the defense procurement scandals, as hospital refuse washes
up on beaches, and as Wall Street brokers are led away in handcuffs. These events have shown that companies do not have adequate

incentives to obey the law and that shareholders can play a constructive and important role in creating appropriate incentives.

It is important to emphasize here that some infractions are inevitable. Laws and regulations are complex, and their interpretation and enforcement vary enormously from one administration to another. Shareholders do not want companies to be so risk-averse that they always adopt the most conservative interpretation possible; sometimes it is worthwhile to challenge the law. And Congress has a tendency to react to a problem by criminalizing it; Congress tries to appear to be cracking down on defense contractors and polluters and does so by characterizing relatively minor violations as criminal. But directors must take the responsibility for setting some standards for the company.

Morton M. Lapides of Alleco was convicted of a price-fixing scheme that resulted in record-breaking fines. The judge found the facts of this case so disturbing that he took the unprecedented step of issuing a prison sentence for *the corporation.* Four of its top managers were directed to spend up to two years performing community service. The judge said, "I cannot imagine any company being more tied up with illegal activity." This is simply and clearly unacceptable in corporate leadership. Yet, despite a challenge in court, Lapides was permitted to take the company private.

The president and vice president of Beech-Nut admitted that they knowingly permitted sugar water to be sold as apple juice for consumption by babies. The company pled guilty to 215 counts of violating federal food and drug laws and paid a $2 million fine. This severely damaged its credibility. According to the *New York Times,* its market share has dropped 15 percent.[12] It is reasonable for the shareholders to expect the directors to make sure that this kind of thing does not happen again. Did the directors of Nestle, the parent company, fire these men? On the contrary. They paid all of their legal fees and continued to pay their salaries during the prosecution.

Shareholders can reasonably conclude that by providing such assistance the directors have made it clear to the company's employees, its customers, and the community that it will tolerate—even support—the knowing sale of colored sugar water as apple juice, to be fed to babies, who cannot complain about it. The directors have made it clear that they will tolerate—even support—actions that result in record-breaking criminal penalties. Shareholders can reasonably conclude that the directors have made it clear that they do not deserve the shareholders' support. And the shareholders should not give it.

From the point of view of the institutional investor—particularly the pension funds, who are the epitome of the long-term investor, acting as proxy for millions of working Americans who want to retire in a country that is, among other things, law-abiding—there is no issue more important than their capacity to require that corporations comply with the standards of criminal behavior established by society. Owners must insist that their managers run their businesses in compliance with the laws of the country in which they operate.

Although there is great public concern over the existence and extent of corporate crime, there is remarkably little baseline scholarship—virtually no centralized sources of information, no agreement on terminology, and only the slightest sense that we are even now grasping the extent of the problem. The "scholarship" boils down to two studies: Sutherland's *White Collar Crime,* first published in 1949,[13] and the various collaborative works of Marshall Clinard and Peter Yeager, sponsored by the U.S. Department of Justice, including *Illegal Corporate Behavior* (1979)[14] and *Corporate Crime* (1980).[15] *Illegal Corporate Behavior* confirmed Sutherland's principal finding: corporations violate the law with great frequency. "The 582 Corporations surveyed by Clinard and Yeager racked up a total of 1,554 crimes, with at least one sanction imposed against 371 corporations (63.7 percent) of the sample. And although 40 percent of the sample had no actions initiated against them, a mere 38 parent manufacturing corporations out of a total of 477—less than 10 percent—had ten or more actions instituted against them. These 38 recidivist corporations accounted for 740, or 48.2 percent, of all sanctions imposed against all the parent manufacturing firms surveyed."[16] In 1980, *Fortune* magazine surveyed 1,043 large companies and concluded that a "startling" number of them had been involved in "blatant illegalities." "Almost two years after the *Fortune* story, *U.S. News & World Report* conducted a survey of America's 500 largest corporations and found that '115 have been convicted in the last decade of at least one major crime or have paid civil penalties for serious misbehavior,' " defined as criminal convictions, civil penalties, or settlements in excess of $50,000.[17] Recent concern over the extent of criminal activity by defense contractors has attracted wide attention.

The problems presented by corporate criminal activity leave one with a sense of resignation. While almost no one condones it, no one seems to know what to do about it, raising the worry that corporate criminality may be part of the inevitable price for the undoubted benefits derived from large business organizations.

The applicability of criminal law constraints to corporations has been mired in an apparent effort to treat artificial entities as if they were natural persons. One of the most astute current observers concluded, "At first glance, the problem of corporate punishment seems perversely insoluble: moderate fines do not deter, while severe penalties flow through the corporate shell and fall on the relatively blameless."[18] It is worth noting that the United States Sentencing Commission concluded its multiyear study in 1990 with sentencing recommendations for corporate crime, but Bush administration support for them was withdrawn weeks later, after some discreet lobbying by business leaders and a phone call from the office of the White House Counsel.

State Legislatures:
The Home Court Advantage

One of the most cherished prerogatives of corporate management is the preeminence of state law. A corporation may have customers, suppliers, employees, and shareholders in all 50 states, but for many important purposes its activities will be determined by the state in which it chooses to be incorporated. The state of incorporation may have no other connection to the company. Most companies, including all those I have established or run, are incorporated in Delaware, the second smallest state. Although only six of the S&P 500 are located there, 256 are incorporated there, and 17 percent of the state's income is from their tax revenues and fees.[19] This does not even include the enormous industry created by Delaware's friendliness to corporations, from the law firms to the "Incorporate while you wait" offices.

California, on the other hand, with a GNP that would be the world's ninth largest if it were a separate country, is the physical location of many of the nation's largest company headquarters. If there is such a thing as a "race to the top," California is in it alone. The state legislature has a real commitment to the notion that accountability to shareholders is the best guarantee of productivity and competitiveness. The result? While 56 of the S&P 500 are located in California, only seven of the S&P 500 are incorporated there. Times Mirror, Occidental Petroleum, Wells Fargo, and Disney are among those who left California for Delaware during the 1980s. The state senate's Committee on Corporate Governance, Shareholder Rights, and Securities Transactions, on which I serve, has recommended federal preemption of corporate law in utter frustration. At the federal level, California has 2 senators and 45 representatives in Congress. However, under the current system, laws governing California corporations, and other corporations invested in by California shareholders, are enacted by the Delaware state legislature, where California has no representation at all. Massachusetts, concluding a long, thoughtful study of its takeover laws, came to a similar conclusion.

No one thinks any more that state control of corporate law is useful because it has some connection with local interests, but there are still those who think it is a good idea because it encourages diversity and innovation—the "states as laboratories" theory. This theory holds that states will compete with each other for corporations by enacting better laws. But, as former SEC chairman William Cary has memorably noted, what we have is a "race to the bottom."[20] Management picks the state of incorporation, and, to the extent that there is competition, the result is a contest to see who can treat management the best. So far, Delaware has been the clear winner. A state cannot give a CEO a higher salary, but it can give him a more secure job. When Nell and I testified before the Delaware legislature, in opposition to its antitakeover law, every single representative of shareholders, every scholar, every economist, every representative of the U.S. government was on our side. But when the CEOs suggested that they might have to consider reincorporation elsewhere, there wasn't a chance that our side would prevail. How many shareholders vote in Delaware? And if they don't like the outcome, what can they do about it?

Not much. Although the state of incorporation must be approved by shareholders, there has never been a case where the vote has even been close. And shareholders do not have a meaningful right to change a company's state of incorporation; this is typically a prerogative of the board of directors. Indeed, as a technical matter, a company does not "change" its state of incorporation; it ceases to exist in one state and is recreated in another.

The "Race to the Bottom"

Delaware has been the clear "mother of corporations" for quite a long time, but recently some other states, most notably Pennsylvania, have tried to give Delaware a literal run for the money, each with a comprehensively revised corporate code that has everything but a welcome mat. Why not? It's an ideal way for a state to make money. Not many other enterprises provide so much employment that is utterly recession-proof (in good times and bad, there are always deals) and have no problems of pollution, occupational safety, tort claims, or politics.

The first state antitakeover law, enacted in Virginia in 1968, inspired 36 states to pass similar laws over the next 13 years. In 1982, the U.S. Supreme Court ruled in *Edgar v. MITE*[21] that the Illinois takeover law was invalid due to interference with interstate commerce, in effect canceling the majority of existing laws.

The states then devised another method of corporate protection: regulating business combinations and shareholder rights. This time the Supreme Court upheld the state laws. With the landmark 1987 decision, *CTS Corp. v. Dynamics Corp. of America,*[22] the Supreme Court ruled that the Indiana control share antitakeover law was constitutional, opening the floodgates for more antitakeover legislation that used this tactic.

The issue in that case was an Indiana statute that limits takeovers of Indiana corporations by requiring shareholder approval beyond the requirements in federal law. The Indiana statute provides that the shareholders of the company have the opportunity to decide whether a would-be acquirer obtains voting rights along with the shares if the shareholders' company is chartered under Indiana law, and there are a significant number of shareholders in the state. This type of statute is called a control share statute. Its effect is to make taking over an Indiana corporation very difficult.

The Court found that the Indiana control share statute was valid, even if its effect was to decrease the number of successful tender offers for Indiana corporations, because it treated in-state and out-of-state corporations equally. The Court also found that the Indiana act served a legitimate purpose.

This decision led to a real scramble as states moved quickly to protect local companies. Since the *CTS* decision, over 40 states have successfully enacted antitakeover laws, including Delaware, despite the fact that studies have consistently shown that they depress share value.

The *CTS* Decision

It thus is an accepted part of the business landscape in this country for States to create corporations, to prescribe their powers, and to define the rights that are acquired by purchasing their shares. A State has an interest in promoting stable relationships among parties involved in the corporations it charters, as well as in ensuring that investors in such corporations have an effective voice in corporate affairs.

There can be no doubt that the Act reflects these concerns. The primary purpose of the Act is to protect the shareholders of Indiana corporations. It does this by affording shareholders, when a takeover offer is made, an opportunity to decide collectively whether the resulting change in voting control of the corporation, as they perceive it, would be desirable. A change of management may have important effects on the shareholders' interests; it is well within the State's role as overseer of corporate governance to offer this opportunity. The autonomy provided by allowing shareholders collectively to determine whether the takeover is advantageous to their interests may be especially beneficial where a hostile tender offer may coerce shareholders into tendering their shares...the possibility of coercion in some takeover bids offers additional justification for Indiana's decision to promote the autonomy of independent shareholders.

Source: 481 U.S. 69, 91, 92 (1987).

The Benefits of Protecting Entrenched Management

Nothing in the Constitution says that the protection of entrenched management is any less important a "putative local benefit" than the protection of entrenched shareholders.

Justice Antonin Scalia

Source: 481 U.S. 69, 95 (1987).

One of the first states to pass a post-*CTS* antitakeover bill was Washington, to protect Boeing from a possible 15 percent acquisition by T. Boone Pickens. The only problem was that Boeing was incorporated in Delaware—not Washington, where it was physically located. But Boeing accounted for an estimated 8 percent of Washington employment. A special clause was therefore included to cover out-of-state companies, narrowly drafted so that, in effect, the only company it applied to was

Boeing. Thus, Boeing is doubly entrenched: it receives not only the protections of the state where it is chartered, but those of the state where it is located. Needless to say, its shareholders get no protection from anyone.

The traditional justification behind such laws, that worthwhile experimentation is incubated by competition among the states, simply makes no sense any longer, if it ever did. Competition works only if the states must bear the costs of the benefits they provide to entice corporations. State corporation law is just another opportunity to impose externalities on others—in this case, shareholders. Delaware can make its laws as liberal as it wants because it bears such a tiny proportion of the consequences, with that proportion vastly outweighed by the benefits of the tax revenue, and the people adversely affected are almost all outside the state. The Delaware state pension fund, probably the largest shareholder in the state, was prepared to testify against the same antitakeover law we opposed, but it was rolled at the last minute by the governor.

When lobbying for or against such legislation, managers use corporate funds, whereas stockholders, who are dispersed geographically and unable to identify each other without great expense, are not as able to pool resources. Thus, shareholders are again faced with the problems of collective choice; those who would oppose such legislation would likely incur individual costs greater than the individual benefits.

As of 1988, some 17 states had passed statutes for the specific purpose of protecting a specific local company from a specific pending takeover. Another study concluded that, in the vast majority of cases (28 out of 40), state antitakeover legislation was introduced on behalf of at least one large firm headquartered and/or incorporated in the state. In 1990 alone, there were three more statutes, all worth examining for the process that produced them and the impact they had: Pennsylvania, for Armstrong World Industries, Inc.; Massachusetts, for Norton; and Indiana, for Cummins Engine. Interestingly, all three states had recent antitakeover provisions on the books; the Indiana law was the one upheld in *CTS,* and the other two states made comprehensive revisions, Massachusetts' enacted after thoughtful review by a special commission and legislative hearings, and Pennsylvania's based on a proposal developed over more than a decade by the Pennsylvania Bar Association.

The earlier revision to the Pennsylvania law included what is called a stakeholder statute, discussed in Chapter 3. It gave directors the authority to "consider" the views of employees, customers, suppliers, the community, and other concerned parties in evaluating various options. This apparently was not enough, and when local company Armstrong World Industries was a takeover target, the law was amended to make it clear that directors owed no special duty to *any* one corporate constituency, including shareholders.[24] In other words, under Pennsylvania law, it is apparently now permissible to say that a takeover would have been good for shareholders, but the directors voted against it because of some speculative concern about its impact on any segment of any group having any connection to any aspect of the company. In order to exempt directors from any possibility of liability if they "just say no" to potential acquirers, irrespective of price and term, this statute was passed, destroying the basis of corporate legitimacy by eliminating any enforceable obligation of competence or loyalty by management to ownership.

In effect, Pennsylvania rendered common stock obsolete for those companies that chose to be covered by Act 36. It eliminated the guarantees that are an essential part of the contract with stockholders: the duty of loyalty that ensures that their interests are paramount in the directors' minds and the ownership rights that enable them to make changes if management fails to act responsibly.

The new Pennsylvania law also included a control share provision and a few new twists.[25] Anyone who unsuccessfully tries to take control of a company incorporated in Pennsylvania may have to "disgorge" the profits, that is, pay them back to the corporation. In addition, it provides for tin parachutes for employees who lose their jobs following a change in control and prevents abrogation of labor contracts for up to five years following a change in control.

Possibly no investment group in the Western Hemisphere had acquired such a reputation for the successful extraction of greenmail as the Canadian Belzberg family. When they acquired significant minority interest in Armstrong, the legislature, acutely aware that 1990 was an election year, came to Armstrong's aid.

The New York Times editorial section called Act 36 "the sorriest example of state intervention. . . . Pennsylvania's gain is the nation's loss. By protecting poor managers, the law perpetuates inefficiency. There will be more jobs in Pennsylvania, fewer elsewhere . . . the effect would be to absolve management of accountability for the property they manage."[26] *Forbes* wrote that if managers of "underperforming companies catch on, Pennsylvania—long the legal residence of some of this country's greatest

4 4 4

4 4 4 4 4

4 4 4

4 4 4 4

4 4

companies—could end up as the last refuge of corporate laggards."[27] And a *Wall Street Journal* editorial simply said, "It is indeed an awful piece of legislation."[28]

As noted in Chapter 3, two studies—one by Wilshire Associates and one by Karpoff and Malatesta—have concluded that the adoption of the law caused a significant drop in Pennsylvania stock values. Karpoff and Malatesta estimate that the economic loss to shareholders of firms affected by state antitakeover laws passed before 1988 is at least $6 billion.[29]

These studies provide such strong evidence of an adverse impact on share value that they provide a strong basis for other kinds of shareholder action. A fiduciary will find it hard to support change of the state of incorporation to Pennsylvania. There may even be sufficient basis to encourage, even require, a fiduciary to initiate action to encourage a company to opt out of one or more provisions of the law, or to incorporate in another state.

"The British Are Coming!"

In Massachusetts, the company at issue was Norton, a Worcester grinding wheel and abrasives company with about 3,000 employees in the state. The Norton Company "rescue" illuminates the careless destruction of value. To escape the combination tender offer and proxy contest threat of a British company called BTR, Norton strong-armed the legislature to pass a law requiring that all Massachusetts corporations have three-year staggered terms for boards of directors. Not since the ride of Paul Revere has Massachusetts responded with such alarm to the prospect of a British arrival. One official claimed, "A British company called BTR is reaching across the Atlantic to rip the heart out of Worcester, Massachusetts."

It is important to note that any Massachusetts corporation could, at any time, have adopted this provision (with shareholder approval). Every such proposal has been approved by shareholders, except for Honeywell (discussed in Chapter 6). There was something sadly ironic in watching the state legislators *voting* as *elected* officials to disenfranchise shareholders.

Legislators, in fact, unanimously supported the bill. James Segal, who was BTR's counsel at the time, believes that legislators felt there was "no clear political advantage in opposing the bill...BTR didn't have any constituencies in Massachusetts. People just don't think of themselves as shareholders, for the most part. They think of themselves as employees, or they think of themselves as managers, or they think of themselves as neighbors, but certainly not as shareholders."[30]

The result of the new law is that no matter how large a percentage of the company's stock is acquired, the shareholders can elect only one-third of the directors and will not be able to dismantle the various antitakeover provisions in effect—principally the poison pill. In turn, this means that the tender offer cannot be consummated, so the vote cannot be cast, and thus the effort is stillborn before it can begin. Within a week of the effective date of the new statute, Norton management concluded an arrangement with St. Gobain on terms more satisfactory to themselves—and, it should be said, to the shareholders. (Another irony: one of Norton's objections to BTR was that it was foreign—apparently not a problem with the French St. Gobain.) The result is that the Massachusetts legislature has permitted its corporations, *for no reason,* to sever the accountability of management to ownership that existed through the annual election of directors, and they. have left nothing in its place.

Ambrose Bierce:
"A Man Is Known by the Company He Organizes"

Earning the Right to Corporate Existence

No corporation has an inherent right to exist. It wins its right by producing needed goods and services within the parameters set by law and acceptable conduct. In industry we have long accepted the fact that if a corporation cannot compete effectively in the marketplace, it will fail; we are less ready to accept the fact that the justification for our existence depends also on meeting the requirements set by the societies in which we operate.

Henry B. Schacht and Charles W. Powers

Source: Henry B. Schacht and Charles W. Powers, "Business Responsibility and the Public Policy Process," in David Vogel and Thornton Bradshaw (eds.), *Corporations and Their Critics: Issues and Answers to the Problems of Corporate Social Responsibility,* McGraw-Hill, New York, 1981, pp. 27–28.

But the story of Cummins Engine outdoes them all. Like GAF, Cummins is worth looking at because it is a good company with a good record of commitment to shareholder value. Yet Cummins galvanized

all of its corporate resources and political power over a two-year period to successfully repel *two* uninvited shareholders and recapitalized
the company on terms that specifically entrenched current management.
It might fairly be said that Cummins represents the state of the art in
corporate governance in the 1990s, demonstrating the ultimate external-
ization of costs and the subordination of all other concerns to establishing
the absolute "right" of current management to direct a public company's
affairs, with no accountability to anyone, public or private, shareholder
or government.

Cummins is one of the crown jewels of the American industrial establishment. Its longtime chief executive officer and founding family
member J. Irwin Miller, now 81 years old, is the archetype of a business
statesman. National finance chairman for Nelson Rockefeller's political
efforts and midwestern Medici in bringing the world's best architects to
Columbus, Indiana, Miller also developed what was probably the only
fully staffed corporate "ethics" office inside a major company. *Esquire*
once picked him as presidential material. In short, Miller is an authentic
culture hero.

Henry Brewer ("Hank") Schacht, of Yale and the Harvard Business
School, was widely applauded for turning down "a relatively glamorous
opportunity on Wall Street to work in the boondocks."[31] His resume
reads like the dream of every young MBA. A director of CBS, Inc., the
American Telephone & Telegraph Company, and the Chase Manhattan
Bank, a trustee of the Yale Corporation, the Brookings Institute, the Conference Board, and the Ford Foundation, and a member of the Business
Council and the Council on Foreign Relations, Schacht became CEO of
Cummins at a relatively young age and has presided for more than a
decade over a company that, until the most recent times, was widely
admired.

No corporate cast of characters would be complete without the board,
and this one glitters. Cummins's outside directors include former cabi-
net officers and chief executive officers, a university president, and the
chairman of the Ford Foundation. They sit on each other's boards in an
interweaving that might be considered the summit of America's business
establishment.

As a company, Cummins long epitomized the paternalist corporation of the post–World War II years. It paid its workers handsomely,
it poured millions of dollars into its home town, it expanded rapidly, and
it produced products—engines for the heavy truck market—of the highest
quality. But in the 1970s, demand for heavy truck engines declined. To

make matters worse, Cummins's Japanese licensee, Komatsu, bolstered by a 30 percent cost advantage due to its extraordinary efficiency, began producing a replica of the Cummins engine. Cummins's response was much admired. In contrast to virtually all other sectors of the economy who were clamoring for government protection—notably the automobile industry, as we discussed above—Cummins made the brave and virtually unprecedented decision simply to cut engine prices to whatever level was necessary to maintain market share. That price was below cost, forcing Cummins to lose money on every engine sold. This, of course, guaranteed a period of losses and cash drain.[32]

Year after year, Schacht predicted that the bottom had been reached and that a return to profitability was in sight. But despite improvements in quality and delivery time, and savings in production costs, the company's performance did not improve. Part of that could be attributed to overall market conditions, but not all; Cummins lost market share not just to the Japanese, but to a U.S. competitor as well. Management set a target of a 5 percent return on sales as the chief measure of its performance, a standard met only twice in the past 11 years and not at all since 1985. Cummins's losses and declining management credibility have caused stock losses of nearly half the market value since 1983, during a period when the Dow Jones Industrial Average has doubled. In the past two years Cummins has fallen from first place to seventh (out of 10) in its industrial category in *Fortune*'s annual survey of America's most respected companies.

This low stock price and the company's historic reputation caught the attention of two prominent foreign industrial groups. First, Hanson from Great Britain bought a 9.9 percent stake, which was purchased by the Miller family in July 1989. In that same month, New Zealand's Sir Ronald Brierley of Industrial Equity (Pacific), Limited (IEP) first disclosed his accumulation of stock, which ultimately rose to 14.9 percent.

Cummins's reaction to these investments by large foreign industrial groups exemplifies the conflicting considerations underlying corporate governance. Simply put, Cummins, the essence of what is best about American industry, with a combination of leaders who define the establishment, has failed the test of the marketplace. In theory, then, there should be some kind of correction. The ultimate discipline of corporate managements, the structure that legitimates their exercise of power, is the accountability that should provide this correction. The only thing that prevents them from being dictatorships (even, as might be the case with Cummins, benevolent ones) is the capacity of shareholders to change the board of directors. In this case, it didn't happen, because Cummins changed the rules. Accountability to shareholders is no longer convenient—management develops strategies for whose ultimate success or failure it is not accountable to anyone.

Cummins management developed a full panoply of antitakeover devices to shield itself, and to protect the company (to the extent that the two are different), from the impact of declining earnings. They were legitimately concerned that the institutional shareholders who held a majority of their stock would jump at any offer over the depressed trading price. In 1986, the board enacted a poison pill that prevented any person from acquiring more than 25 percent of the outstanding common stock without board approval.

Incorporated in Indiana, Cummins then lobbied the Indiana state legislature to rid its corporation statutes of a provision requiring a company to allow any shareholders owning 25 percent or more of a company to call a special meeting. The legislature was more than happy to oblige. It is interesting to note that even Delaware, the most popular state for incorporations, does not alter its laws so blatantly for corporate interests. In Delaware, corporations instituting antitakeover measures generally make changes to their charter and bylaws. In Indiana, like Massachusetts and Pennsylvania, corporations seem to make changes to state statutes as well. In January 1989, the board amended the bylaws accordingly, eliminating shareholders' ability to call a special meeting or to put particular items on the agenda. None of the Cummins changes was submitted to shareholders for their consideration or approval. In its most recent financings, the 1987 series A preferred stock and two debt issues, Cummins inserted so-called poison puts. In the event of any change of control that is not approved by the board of directors, each holder has the right to require Cummins to repurchase the security. The stock option and bonus plans provide for vesting and extraordinary payouts in the event of a change of control. Cummins had circled its wagons to fend off any form of unwanted involvement.

An Offer They Could Refuse

This was the background in late 1988, when the U.S. subsidiary of Hanson made its initial purchase of 8.3 percent of the outstanding shares of Cummins, making it the largest shareholder. Hanson never indicated any interest in obtaining control of the company, but Cummins was deeply concerned. Hanson agreed to sell the shares back—with a premium. But

Cummins refused. The Miller family, now the second largest holder, rose to the occasion in a tripartite transaction on July 14, 1989. The family purchased the Hanson holdings at some $5 million over the market—a transaction that would have been called greenmail if paid directly by the company. The Millers then transferred their preexisting holdings plus the newly acquired Hanson shares back to the company in exchange for a new class of preferred stock. Cummins paid them a "conversion premium" for the transaction.

It was represented widely that the Millers had actually lost money in these transactions, and that this was really the ultimate act of corporate statemanship, the ultimate statement of the Cummins culture. It showed the willingness of the principal owners to incur personal loss to remove any distraction from their ability to continue to conduct the business in the long-term direction they were convinced was ultimately of maximum benefit.

Also in July 1989, the board established a leveraged ESOP, holding approximately 11.5 percent of the shares outstanding.[33] As we earlier learned, ESOPs, with the unexceptionable purpose of increasing employee ownership, can be used as a defense against takeovers, because they put a large block of the company's stock under management control—enough to prevent a takeover under Delaware and some other state laws. The Cummins ESOP provides a formula for voting the shares. Most of the shares will not be allocated for some time, and they are to be voted in proportion to the directions received from the participants with respect to the allocated shares.[34] Allocation will initially be made to those employees, including officers and directors, with the longest service and the highest pay. They might be willing to vote against management; but this would be not only highly unlikely, it would be unprecedented. The ESOP is therefore the greatest rabbit management ever pulled out of a hat; it is a way for management to get control over sufficient stock to stand off just about any would-be acquirer, absolutely free.

This scheme to increase incumbent management's voting control was underscored with a provision in the preferred stock issued to the Millers in July 1989. The Millers gave up voting rights for both the stock they bought from Hanson as well as the stock they held before.

An Offer They Could Fight

You would think this would leave Cummins management feeling pretty secure. But there's more. The Brierley group made a filing on July 26,

1989, reporting to the SEC that it had acquired a 9.9 percent ownership position in Cummins and indicating its intention to seek approval
under antitrust laws of authority to acquire up to 25 percent. The Cummins board, at its next meeting on August 8, amended the poison pill
by lowering the threshold to 15 percent, thus prohibiting as a practical
matter Brierley's acquisition of 15 percent or more. In September, Brierley bought 14.9 percent of the stock, right up to the limit, triggering an
Indiana state freeze-out provision preventing an investor from engaging
in any business combination for five years following the purchase of 10
percent or more of a company's stock. Thus, even assuming Brierley
wished to take over the company, there was no real threat for five years.
Cummins seems to have acted on nothing more than the unshakable belief that a significant position of this kind, a significant *minority* position
held by an uninvited shareholder, had to be bad.

Certainly, lawyers have found takeovers to be an unmitigated bonanza.
As with most of these cases, litigation, countersuits, and federal and state
investigations ensued, all focused on one specific aspect of the subsequent discussion between Brierley and Cummins. The facts are clear, at
least in their broadest outline: First quarter bullishness about Cummins's
earnings prospects was succeeded by the September 21 announcement
that there would be a substantial third-quarter loss, with the outlook
for the fourth quarter uncertain. This announcement caused the price of
Cummins stock to fall by more than $5 per share. Brierley (this part
depends on whose filings you believe) either merely requested a board
seat or threatened to wage a proxy fight against Cummins if he didn't get
a board seat. The various legal challenges center on whether IEP made
appropriate public disclosure of its intentions.

Although there is some question as to the tenor of the request, there
is no question that Brierley asked for—demanded, if you will—only a
single representative on the board of Cummins. Why, one might ask, is it
not utterly reasonable for the holder of approximately one-seventh of the
corporation's equity to have representation on a board of more than 10
directors? In a state like California, which until 1990 required cumulative
voting in the election of directors, Brierley's ownership could, as a matter
of right and mathematics, require Cummins to give it a board seat. What
was Cummins so afraid of? One director can, at most, make motions.
He is not even guaranteed that anyone will second his motions, to allow
them to be discussed, much less that they will be adopted.

Management firmly controls the process of nominating directors,
notwithstanding many bylaw provisions and public statements purport-

ing to encourage nomination by shareholders. At Cummins, directors are nominated by the board's nominating committee, which has turned down some management suggestions, but has not generated any of its own candidates. We have been unable to find a single instance of any company accepting a director candidate nominated by shareholders; the closest a company has come was when Texaco selected New York University president and former congressman John Brademas from a list provided by the California Public Employees' Retirement System.

The suggestion that an investor with more than $90 million invested in the company should be permitted to have representation on the board was such a threat to Cummins management that they engaged in defensive maneuvers that set a new standard for energy and scope. As we have already noted, Brierley had 14.9 percent of Cummins stock, had triggered the Indiana freeze-out provision, and could not buy more without triggering the poison pill. If he did go on the board, he would be subject to restrictions on insider trading, further limiting his ability to buy or sell this stock. Thus, Cummins was protected against any threat to control for at least five years. Nevertheless, the presence of an outside shareholder with a major financial interest in the company initiated a commitment of corporate resources virtually without precedent in its ferocity.

Indiana to the Rescue

Cummins contacted every Indiana representative to the U.S. Congress, all of whom signed a letter to John Dingell, chairman of the House Energy and Commerce Committee, informing him of the Cummins situation and urging him to "stand up to the tactics employed by the corporate raiders of the 1980s." Dingell, in turn, pressed the Federal Trade Commission and the SEC to investigate, which they did. Simultaneously, Cummins filed suit in the federal court in Indiana, where Cummins might expect a home court advantage. The governor of Indiana, Evan Bayh, was moved to write a letter to Joseph Hogsett, Indiana's secretary of state and Mark E. Maddox, commissioner of the Indiana Securities Commission, alerting them to the Indiana suit and stating that "although the lawsuit is a dispute between private parties, I am sure you will recognize its significance for the State...Cummins has been an important foundation for the State's economy and prosperity." Local law firms were even pressured by their Indiana corporate clients to decline representation of Brierley. So far, this is no more than standard corporate hardball.

But the ball got a bit harder with the involvement of the Indiana Securities Commission (ISC). As background, we note that the commission has been known to be friendly to local businesses. In an unusual suggestion of bias by an administrative agency, federal Seventh Circuit Court Judge Richard D. Cudahy said in an earlier case, "Without trying to anticipate the conclusion of the Indiana courts, to us Coons' [the Indiana Securities Commission's executive officer] construction of the Act has all the earmarks of a 'hometown call.' Indeed, were his interpretation to be sustained by the Indiana courts, the conflict with the Williams Act might well prove irreconcilable."[35]

The ISC initiated formal proceedings without conducting any preliminary investigation or demonstrating any Indiana jurisdiction. The staff attorney at the ISC originally in charge of the case was removed, according to some sources, because she tried to coordinate with the federal investigation.[36] In essence, she agreed not to take action unless the federal court turned up something tangible. Ultimately, the ISC spent a day at Cummins and a total of approximately four hours in the office of IEP's counsel reviewing the extensive discovery materials—examining only 2 of the 25 depositions taken for the case—and set a hearing date without advance notice to Brierley. "A reasonable observer," said one source close to the case, "could conclude that what the Commissioner did was in line with what the Commissioner had done for the past 20 years: when faced with the possibility of a hostile takeover of an Indiana company, they've done everything they can to aid management."

Brierley's representative was served with an ISC subpoena while in Indiana attending the Cummins annual shareholders' meeting on April 3. To the Brierley representatives from New Zealand, it seemed clear that the home court advantage was insurmountable. Although they believed they would continue to prevail in the federal challenges to the truth of their filings with the SEC, it seemed impossible to overcome the state's protection for local interests. The ISC hearing was scheduled to commence on May 10. On May 7, the ISC agreed to drop its claim that Brierley did not properly disclose the intent of their investment in Cummins. The next day, Brierley signed a standstill agreement with Cummins. The single essential provision from Brierley's point of view was the termination of the Indiana Securities Commission proceeding; Cummins was able to deliver freedom from the ISC without any need for Brierley or its counsel to so much as answer a letter or speak by phone with the ISC ever again. In our view, a state agency was acting as a subsidiary to a local corporation.

Secretary of State Hogsett's press release of May 10, 1990, sounds like a Cummins press release: "Without the aggressive enforcement of our state's Securities' Laws, this dispute may have still been unresolved. With this dispute behind it, Cummins may once again focus on its long-term plans, the long-term interests of its employees and suppliers, and its future as an important part of the Indiana economy." The *Indianapolis Business Journal* noted, in a classic understatement, that "Indiana Securities Commissioner Mark Maddox thinks pressure from his office may have speeded up the [Brierley/Cummins] settlement."[37]

Brierley surrendered by agreeing not to increase its holding, not to seek representation on Cummins board, not to attempt to acquire the company, not to make any shareholder proposals, and not to seek control of the management or policies of the diesel engine maker. Furthermore, for five years, Brierley is required to vote for management nominees for director in the same proportion as shares voted by disinterested stockholders.

Schacht had long proclaimed his interest in outside capital. His struggle to obstruct uninvited industrial groups made clear that he wanted to choose the investors. By early summer, he found some—three companies with close business ties to Cummins. Ford, Kubota, and Tenneco invested $250 million in exchange for a 27 percent stake in the company at a price highly favorable to the company and its shareholders. Like the IEP stock, after the standstill agreement, this stock also carries voting restrictions: "The Investor will vote (whether by proxy or otherwise) all Voting Securities then beneficially owned by the Investor for the election of all nominees included in the Company's slate of directors at each shareholders' meeting of the Company." Management now controls the new 27 percent, the ESOP (now slightly under 11 percent), and the Millers' 5 percent; moreover, Cummins placed significant restrictions on Brierley's 14.9 percent. Furthermore, under the company's financing arrangements, if there is a change in control of the company, the debts become due.

What this means is that a majority of the vote is guaranteed to be for management nominees—no matter what—for the foreseeable future. They still have the right to vote on other proxy issues, but not on the most important issue, selection of the board. This would be like a hostile takeover from the inside, except that the shareholders never got paid for what was taken from them. The company has taken a lot of the value out of the common stock; it will be interesting to see how this is reflected in the market's valuation.[38]

The Cummins saga raises squarely the question of whether the chief executive officer acts properly when he acts as a "benevolent dictator," the modern incarnation of Plato's philosopher/king. Cummins deserves praise for adopting a competitive industrial strategy. This is not "entrenchment" in the usual sense. Schacht has no employment contract and no salary increase since 1985. He is utterly devoted to Cummins and its constituents, including shareholders. His strategic plan is courageous. But we can admire the strategy without giving up the right to evaluate its implementation. Schacht has arrogated to himself the choice of suitable shareholders, a class composed of people who are prepared to confer their voting rights to the incumbent management. He has thus also arrogated to himself the choice of suitable directors. There is a sort of implicit bargain: management says that they will take chances and compete aggressively, but only on the condition that they foreclose involvement by owners who might have an independent opinion in the governance of the corporation. In sum, having wrapped themselves in the American flag, are Cummins management entitled to claim that industrial virtue exempts them from the obligation to be accountable to anyone?

One final note. In July 1990, Hank Schacht agreed to serve as a director of United Airlines if the employee-led leveraged buyout was successful. Why not? He has plenty of time to devote to directing a new company, because no amount of outside commitments can get him removed from Cummins.

5

Performance Anxiety

The notion that the marketplace imposes meaningful restraint on corporations boils down to the question of profit. And yet, for most large American corporations, any meaningful financial accountability can be deferred for a long time, certainly beyond the retirement date of any current senior executives. The conventional wisdom is that profit is an indispensable key to new capital. The model of profit maximization has been a convenient formulation, particularly for scholars, because it supposedly provides "a single, objective, easily monitored [residual] goal."[1] Nothing could be more misleading.

What Is Profit?

First, the pursuit of profit is not the pursuit of a single goal, but involves decisions and actions in furtherance of numerous goals. Second, it is not objective. What costs and benefits, for example, are to be included in the calculation of profits? If social costs are to be included, how are various social costs and benefits to be valued? How are potential future economic benefits and costs to be quantified given the uncertainty of future markets? Third, it is not an easily monitored goal. How can decision-makers be made accountable on the basis of profit when their decisions involve making predictions of future returns from uncertain markets?

Lynne Dallas

Source: "Two Models of Corporate Governance: Beyond Berle and Means," *University of Michigan Journal of Law Reform*, 22(1), 1988, p. 104.

Profit is part of any definition of a private corporation. The incentive to invest comes from the expectation of profit. This core dynamic is essential for two reasons. First, the motivation for profit is what keeps companies competitive. Second, an important justification for the legitimacy of corporate power derives from the limits imposed on activity by its need to be profit-related.

When corporate management is confronted with the failure of other mechanisms of accountability, it unfailingly points to the marketplace as the ultimate means of accountability.[2] That makes sense, at least to the true believers in efficient markets, who argue that the corporation must be efficiently organized or it would go out of business. Corporations exist to maximize profits, according to those theorists, and that is the definitive accountability.

The problem with that approach is that it neglects the impact of the corporation as externalizing machine. Imagine that a management is presented with two options—one that increases profits, with some risk, through marketplace competition, and the other offering less profit but more certainty in the short run. Without meaningful accountability to shareholders and independent boards of directors, management will go for the second option. That has often been the case, as the examples in this chapter demonstrate.

Profit maximization is an ideal, but there is no formula to achieve it—indeed, no way to know for sure if you have. In 1982, a best-selling book called *In Search of Excellence* told stories of glorious success and wonderful profits at companies selected for their superb performance. The authors distilled what they learned from observing these corporations into a list of recommendations, and the book was as wildly successful as the companies it described. Yet, only a few years later, *Business Week* noted that at least 14 of the 43 companies touted as excellent in the book had "lost their luster."[3] And other companies who tried to adopt the strategies outlined in the book learned that it wasn't so easy. The volumes written on the subject of maximizing profits are as abundant in number and varied in approach as the volumes on how to lose weight—and they are about as effective. In Chapter 2 we talked about fads such as conglomeration and leveraged buyouts. They and many other corporate strategies are all attempts to maximize profits over the long term. As with fad diets, any results may be temporary.

The GAAP Gap

As the lawsuit Art Buchwald brought against Paramount made clear, profits for one purpose are losses for another, and generally accepted accounting principles (GAAP) are infinitely flexible. In his lawsuit, Buchwald charged that Eddie Murphy's 1988 movie *Coming to America* had been plagiarized in part from an original story by Buchwald, and that he was thus entitled to a share of the profits. What appeared to be a hit—grossing about $300 million—was shown on the books of Paramount as losing $18 million as of December 1989.[4] The economics of movies has been changed to defy traditional methods. Increasingly, stars and directors get a percentage of the gross. The studio—the traditional owner—makes its profit by charging the largest possible fees for use of facilities, distribution costs, interest on loans to the film, and other expenses. Thus, with "Hollywood accounting," it no longer matters if the movie makes a profit or not; everyone has taken his piece of the pie beforehand. Ultimately, a California state court appointed an accountant to examine Paramount's books to see if Buchwald can receive a percentage of the "profits." (I am a director of a company that acquired a division from another company, and I learned that the entire deal had been restructured to make sure that the CEO of the seller would qualify for his maximum bonus.)

There are many levels on which to try to understand profit, and a lot depends on which level you start from. Both management and shareholders claim to be interested in long-term profits and accuse each other of focusing on the short term. On close examination, both are right, and both are wrong.

All of the wisdom of the ages can be employed in the effort to achieve long-term profit, and yet the effort can fail for reasons beyond anyone's power of contemplation. Adam Smith (the contemporary business writer, not the eighteenth-century economist) quotes a memorable report: "The light we saw at the end of the tunnel . . . was a freight train coming the other way."[5] Business school case studies are filled with examples of companies that snatched defeat from the jaws of victory, such as Bendix fighting for Martin Marrietta, only to lose itself to Allied. These were companies that were doing well until they embarked on an overly ambitious and faulty plan. Short-term profit, on the other hand, is usually a course of action that someone else takes. The only self-admitted short-termers are the arbitrageurs, whose involvement in the takeover process is so critical and accordingly so subject to criticism.

Short term denotes profit you can take today; *long term* is what you hope to get tomorrow. At the end of one of his bravura performances at a Polaroid annual meeting during the 1960s, Dr. Edwin Land, following hours of impassioned involvement with an audience of several thousand across the extraordinary range of his vision, was brought up a little short by a question from a financial type asking about the "bottom line." The great man was a little taken aback by this plunge into the mundane but managed to compose the ultimate formulation. "The bottom line," he said, "is in heaven."

Buffett on the GAAP

. . . auditors annually certify the numbers given them by management and in their opinion unqualifiedly state that these figures "present fairly" the financial position of their clients. The auditors use this reassuring language even though they know from long and painful experience that the numbers so certified are likely to differ dramatically from the true earnings of the period. Despite this history of error, investors understandably rely on auditor's opinions. After all, a declaration saying that "the statements present fairly" hardly sounds equivocal to the non-accountant . . . .

Our approach to this accounting schizophrenia is to ignore GAAP figures and to focus solely on the future earning power of both our controlled and non-controlled businesses. Using this approach, we establish our own ideas of business value, keeping these independent from both the accounting values shown on our books for controlled companies and the values placed by a sometimes foolish market on our partially owned companies. It is this business value that we hope to increase at a reasonable (or preferably unreasonable) rate in the years ahead.

Warren Buffett

Source: Berkshire Hathaway, Inc., Annual Report to the Shareholders, 1985, pp. 13–17.

There is a reason that accounting principles are called "generally accepted" and not "certifiably accurate." GAAP represents a generally good-faith effort to delineate a language of numbers that will consistently apply comprehensible standards. It doesn't purport to deliver truth, only some kind of consistency. As with most codes, what turns out to be important is not what is intended but what was unintended. Accounting conventions can create an environment that compels particular business conclusions. For example, the treatment for "good will" in an acquisition—amortization over a relatively short period—creates such pressure on earnings for so long that public acquirers with sensitivity to reported earnings per share are put at a disadvantage in competition with private groups. This simple convention, as much as any other factor, may account for the widely proclaimed "death of the public company."

Accounting methods have proven so manipulable that a company such as Prime Motor Inns can celebrate net income of $77 million one year and go bankrupt the next. *Forbes* notes that Prime Motor Inns is by no means an unusual case; W.T. Grant, Penn Central, Crazy Eddie, Miniscribe, and many savings and loans all reported impressive earnings and still went bankrupt.[6]

If leases are "off balance sheet," corporations lease their executive jets. If they must be recorded, usually the company will buy the airplane; why give a profit to the leasing company? Often, the most valuable assets of a company are not recordable on the financial statements under GAAP—for example, the creativity of Dr. Land in the early days of Polaroid, the "rights" of the major oil companies with respect to reserves in other countries, franchises or licenses, or brand names (the critical asset in the huge RJR transaction).

Profits calculated according to GAAP should not be confused with the myth of value maximization. The current practice of "big bath" accounting has considerably diminished the credibility of annual numbers. A sort of "ooops!" by the accountants, this is a practice increasingly resorted to across the board in American industry. At intervals of 5 to 10 years, an enormous "one-time" charge is made, usually attributable to prior operations and often, as with Honeywell, when a new head of the company comes in. This is the treatment used when a company makes a mistake with respect to the acceptability of a new product. All of the costs are written off at one time. The effect is to change previously reported earnings retroactively (without changing bonuses based on them) and, by the establishment of reserves, to "hard-wire" earnings levels for the succeeding several accounting periods. There is therefore no real time in which management has to live with the consequences of the mistake. During the period of time when, for example, the new product bombs, earnings are being reported normally. All of the ultimate adjustments for writing off development costs, prepaid selling expense, inventory adjustments, and the like are wrapped up in the one huge "big bath." At the time of the "big bath," prior-period earnings may be reduced, but there is no adverse impact on current or future reported results. Indeed, the opportunities for anticipating future costs in the "big bath" are irresistible. This does not seem to be the basis for a "discipline" imposed by the marketplace. You can believe neither the past nor the future. The figures are virtually meaningless.

Discipline of the Capital Markets?

The Business Roundtable spoke in early 1990 of "the powerful accountability imposed by markets. . . . Financial markets also quickly reflect their evaluation of the quality of accountability through the price of equity and debt."[7] The theory is that companies will be disciplined by the marketplace when they need to raise new capital; the practice has been different.

An incidental consequence of the "hostile takeover" boom of the late 1980s was the revelation that large American companies were overcapitalized. The "raiders" demonstrated a capacity to pay a premium over market value, liquidate assets to pay down their acquisition cost, and still keep a fortune for themselves. Managements showed themselves to be true believers through MBOs. Company after company, year after year, bought back their own shares in large volumes. The chart in Figure 3 shows the staggering reduction of equity capital by America's principal companies. Merrill Lynch compiled the list shown in Figure 4 of the biggest stock buybacks over the last five years of the decade.

Large companies simply did not need new capital in the decade of the 1980s. They apparently had no use for it. It is difficult to speak of an effective discipline that is based on a demonstrated lack of need for access to the capital markets.

They did not need to go outside for investment capital because they could provide it themselves, through an ESOP. The tax-aided Employee Stock Ownership Plan (ESOP) not only provided a popular antitakeover function but became an important source of new financing that was essentially internally generated. "ESOPs are utilized in more than 11,000 U.S. corporations covering an estimated 11 million employees with a total stock value of approximately $70 billion."[8]

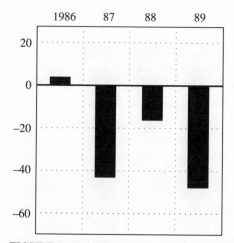

FIGURE 3 *New Stock Sales, Minus Shares Retired in Stock Buyback Programs (in Millions of Dollars).*

Issuer	Year	Shares (in millions)	Estimated Amount[1] (in millions)
1. General Electric Co.[2]	1989	173.9	$10,000
2. General Motors Corp.[3,4]	1987	74.0	5,125
3. IBM Corp.[2,3]	1989	50.1	5,000
4. Santa Fe Southern Pacific Corp.	1987	60.0	3.375
5. Union Carbide Corp.	1986	38.8	3,298
6. Goodyear Tire & Rubber Co.[3]	1986	60.0	2,985
7. Allegis Corp.	1988	35.5	2,840
8. General Motors[3,5]	1986	53.0	2,735
9. IBM[3]	1986	15.0	2,061
10. Ford Motor Co.[2]	1987	27.9	2,000
11. IBM[2]	1988	17.8	2,000
12. E.I. du Pont de Nemours & Co.	1989	20.0	1,928
13. CSX Corp.[3]	1988	60.0	1,858
14. Coca-Cola Co.	1987	40.0	1,800
15. Henley Group[3]	1987	64.5	1,756
16. Sears, Roebuck and Co.	1988	40.0	1,745
17. Norfolk Southern Corp.	1989	45.0	1,654
18. Gencorp	1987	12.5	1,625
19. IBM[2,3]	1987	12.9	1,574
20. Philip Morris Cos.[2]	1989	36.1	1,500

FIGURE 4 *The Biggest Buybacks of 1986–1989: Repurchase Announcements by U.S. Companies. (Source: Reprinted by permission of Merrill Lynch, Pierce, Fenner & Smith Incorporated © Copyright 1990.)*

[1] Estimated dollar amount equals (a) the number of shares announced multiplied by the prior-day closing price for open-market programs; (b) the actual dollar amount, if announced, for private transactions; (c) the number of shares announced multiplied by the tender-offer price for self-tenders (or the maximum price for Dutch-auction self-tenders); (d) the number of shares announced multiplied by the stated value of the cash plus debt or stock plus debt or stock equivalents of exchange offers.

[2] Announced as a dollar amount; number of shares equals the dollar amount divided by the prior-day closing price.

[3] Totals include more than one announcement.

[4] Totals include 64 million shares of common stock, 5 million shares of Class E common stock, and 5 million shares of Class H common stock.

[5] Totals include 10 million shares of common stock, 20.5 million shares of Class E common stock, and 22.5 million shares of Class H common stock.

The fascinating story of ESOPs starts in the creative mind of San Francisco lawyer Louis O. Kelso. Graduating from law school in Colorado in the 1930s, Kelso devoted a substantial amount of his energy to coming to grips with the failures of capitalism that were apparent on all sides. In 1958, in collaboration with Mortimer J. Adler, he published the book entitled *The Capitalist Manifesto* that set forth the theoretical bases of his theories of ownership. The title indicated the book's intent to be a direct refutation of Marx, whose *Communist Manifesto* purported to prove the intrinsic contradictions in capitalism.

Kelso argued simply that the traditional notion that net profit or value added in a corporation should accrue entirely to the benefit of the passive shareholders was arbitrary and undesirable. Although capital is entitled to rent, so is labor. Kelso urged that workers be entitled a portion of ownership as an incident to their labor. This is a practice that entrepreneurs have long styled as "sweat equity," but no one other than Kelso had theorized it as a normal practice involving the entire work force. Kelso is a determined and a persuasive man. Over decades his proselytizing was undiscouraged and little availing. In one of those coincidences that embellish history, he finally caught the ear of the one man in the United States able not only to understand but to convert single-handedly Kelso's ideas into law. Russell Long, son of the Kingfish, senator at age 30, and legendary chairman of the Senate Finance Committee, had the kind of power that accounted for the favorable tax treatment to ESOPs or TRASOPs (ultimately encompassing a veritable acronym zoo) in every tax bill passed over a decade. Even with this encouragement, Kelso's dream of employee ownership was slow to develop until, as for so many other corporate devices, the unmistakable pressure of hostile takeovers in the 1980s alerted creative minds to previously unsuspected possibilities.

Kelso and Russell Long ultimately created the so-called leveraged ESOP. This is a device whereby a newly formed ESOP acquires a substantial stock position with borrowed money. The loan from a bank is guaranteed by the employing corporation, with payback over a period of years as shares are allocated to eligible employees. The company contractually commits to provide sufficient funds to pay all debt service, regardless of the company's earnings and profits. Favorable federal income tax treatment is accorded to virtually all stages of the transaction, with the intention of creating a competitive new source for corporate finance that will result in employee ownership.

ESOPs solve three problems. First, they are a convenient place for overcapitalized corporations to put their money. Second, they are tax-aided sources of new capital. Third, they provide protection against hostile takeovers.

In addition, world capital markets have become increasingly liquid and fungible at the same time, as the Securities and Exchange Commission has deregulated the sale of new securities to financially sophisticated buyers.[9] The traditional shareholders' protection of preemptive rights (very much insisted on by British institutions) is only a memory in the United States, so managements are able to pick and choose their shareholders among countries and categories to minimize the possibility of their acting collectively in the future. (We earlier discussed the almost *keiretsu*-like financing by Cummins from its customers in the summer of 1990.)

In sum, although the argument of "the discipline of the financial marketplace" continues to be the favorite myth of those who argue that existing systems of accountability are functional, the reality is plain that companies demonstrate little, if any, need for access to the marketplace to fulfill their requirements for new capital.

The Market versus the Externalizing Machine

Consider the use of nuclear power by public utilities. For years, the low cost of nuclear power convinced companies, customers, and voters of the efficiency of this fuel and technology. Did cost include amortization of the developmental technology? Did it include the cost of manufacturing the processed fuel? Did it include insurance costs? All of these costs were, in fact, funded by the federal government. Not only did citizens underwrite these projects with their tax dollars, but the government also passed on additional costs to society as a whole by limiting the amount of claims recoverable from a nuclear accident. We still have no idea of what the cost will be of decommissioning the plants themselves or of the ultimate disposal of spent fuel. Because of the extent and the changing nature of government involvement in nuclear power, it is virtually impossible to determine whether many private utility companies are actually profitable.

Take a more prosaic example—coal mining in eastern states. For many years, public utilities burned so-called high-sulphur coal from Pennsylvania and West Virginia. Changing social standards regarding air pollution resulted in the closing of most of these mines, and yet nothing had changed respecting the underlying economic logic of extracting and transporting the coal, burning it in boilers, and converting the steam to electrical energy. What changed was that society was no longer willing to bear the cost of a contaminated atmosphere, and industry was unable to develop cost-competitive techniques for clean burning. Should, and do, the costs charged to utilities and customers include the ultimate expense of retraining and relocating "obsolete" coal miners? Where does the cost fall for supporting those who either can't or won't relearn or move?

A further externality affecting the coal industry is seen in the capacity of government to affect markets. Politicians find it difficult to resist acting in the corporate interest. The increased revenue, jobs, and other benefits to a politician's region outweigh the cost to the nation as a whole. Corporate interests, for example, keep the Pentagon buying coal, even though it no longer wants or needs it. Congressmen from coal industry states, notably Pennsylvania, routinely include a requirement in spending bills that the Pentagon purchase $20 million of anthracite coal, even though the Department of Defense has enough to last for the next four years. Back in 1962, Representative Daniel Flood, a congressman from Pennsylvania, convinced the Kennedy administration to use U.S.-produced anthracite coal, rather than coke produced in Germany, to heat bases. When military bases began to phase out coal in favor of other fuels, coal state legislatures "delayed the conversion of coal furnaces, required the Pentagon to consume more coal, and for a time even required that U.S. coal be shipped to Germany for stockpiling."[10]

There is no general agreement as to what costs are appropriate in a given situation; there is instead a continuing effort by companies to incur as little of the costs as possible and to externalize them to society as a whole. Nuclear power and coal production are two examples of the way in which changing government and society priorities become controlling elements in determining the profitability of a particular industry. To the extent that the industry itself is a moving force in creating the government policies, it is important to note that what is profitable for the industry may well be hurtful to society as a whole.

Exclusive focus on the financial measure of corporate performance is a relatively recent and domestic practice. In the original concept of a corporation, charters were granted to meet a particular perceived need. Each company had an industrial purpose. Courts made sure that a corporation's activities were limited to those specifically authorized in its charter. Companies could be directly compared with their competitors on a variety of levels—technology, quality, range of products, as well as size and profitability. The corporation's mission was seen as providing goods and services that society had determined to be desirable. As the industrial rationale of corporations eroded, the objective of pure financial performance took its place. Reviewing the last 75 years, we can perceive the trend that brought us to where we are today.

Joseph Schumpeter, a leading philosopher on business organizations in the mid-twentieth century, considered a world in which companies competed; some survived, some failed. With the passage of time, some products became obsolete.[11] All of this was accompanied by uncertainty— closing of plants and loss of jobs. Schumpeter characterized the capitalist process as "creative destruction." Out of the ashes of the failed industries the phoenix of the new emerged. To his way of thinking, the "genius" of capitalism was in its giving outlet to human creativity to deal with the prevailing circumstances without the burden of the past.

The disinclination of the business community to continue a world of perpetual competition was apparent at the turn of the nineteenth century in the trend toward monopolies. In the twentieth century, companies have adopted different strategies to deal with the threat of competition. We have already noted the tendency to seek governmental protection.

The trend toward conglomeration severed the last ties to the corporation with an industrial rationale. The new companies would have a diversified capacity to survive. The brief claims that managerial genius enabled a few to run all manner of businesses better than anyone else were dashed in the stock market crashes of 1974 and 1975. Conglomerates became just a presence, an energy prepared to move in any direction but committed to none. These were companies of financiers, not researchers, not production men, and not industry specialists. Harold Sidney Geneen, not Henry Ford. The goals were survival, growth in size, and diversification of sources of revenue. As Louis Auchincloss said, "The age of the tycoon could only be followed by the age of the fine print."

Herbert Simon coined the term *satisficing* to characterize the conduct of large corporations in the 1960s. By this he meant that the energy and the sacrifices necessary to achieve optimal results had drained out of the enterprises, and the dynamic of "managed growth" had been substituted. The best manager is one who not only achieves this year a specified improvement over the last, but who also achieves the same next year. The corporation, a creature of risk and change, was converted into something resembling a public utility with an "acceptable" rate of growth.

Early in the 1980s, another trend became pronounced. It was commonplace for a company to have assets that were worth vastly more than its value in the marketplace. A spectacular example is the Ford Motor Company, which sits on nearly $15 billion in cash and securities in an industry that has excess capacity. The company already has significant positions in defense and finance. And yet the management is reluctant to give the cash to its shareholders.

We believe that profit maximization means that managers must avoid practices that are irrelevant to or inconsistent with ultimate profit. This might include charitable contributions unrelated to any of the corporation's constituencies, compensation policy unrelated to profit, and acquisitions that add size and not profit—most generally any allocation of corporate resources that promotes some objective other than profit maximization.

As we discussed in Chapter 3, the new "stakeholder" statutes explicitly authorize directors to prefer the claims of nonshareholder constituencies, thus endorsing non–profit maximization goals. Like "prudence," "profit maximization" is a process, not a guarantee of results.

There is no way to ensure that a particular decision is "profit maximizing," but two axioms should be observed. First, as the Business Roundtable has urged, it is absolutely essential that the business judgment rule be interpreted liberally to permit management that level of risk taking essential to the healthy future of business enterprises. The only limit we would add is that it should not protect officers or directors when they are acting in the context of a conflict between their interests and the interests of shareholders. Second, in the absence of a quantifiable standard of performance, managements *must* be meaningfully accountable to *someone*. If there is no self-executing mechanism for determining that management in a given company is bad and should be changed, the health of the system requires that there be a structure of accountability. Those who can keep power without being accountable are tyrants, whether in a political or a business mode.

The Babe: "I Had a Better Year"

In 1930, Babe Ruth was asked to justify why his $80,000 salary was higher than the $60,000 that President Herbert Hoover received that year.

The Babe's unforgettable answer: "I had a better year." The unassailable logic of this response has never been persuasive in boardrooms, where directors routinely approve compensation plans with no more relation to performance than those for the kings who annually received their weight in gold.

The concern over compensation is nothing new. Alfred Conard reports that "for more than half a century, observers of the corporate scene have denounced excessive compensation of executives."[12] In fact, the question of compensation goes back even further. Plato thought that the perfect society would pay the top person no more than five times what it paid the average worker. Even a bona fide capitalist such as J.P. Morgan championed an equitable compensation system: each person was paid no more than 1.3 times the next lower rank.[13] Today CEO pay is 157 times that of the average worker.[14] It is increasingly harder even to identify the multiplier these days, because the compensation packages are so complicated.

Crawford H. Greenewalt, former president of Dupont, argued in 1959 that managers need to view their business with "the eye of the owner," and he believed that less cash and more company stock in the yearly package was the way to achieve this. Greenewalt went on to propose two systems: enough stock so that the dividends alone would at least equal the executive's retirement pay, and enough stock to equal five times the final salary.[15]

It was perhaps Michael Jensen and Kevin Murphy, however, who put it most eloquently: "The relentless focus on how much CEOs are paid diverts public attention from the real problem—how CEOs are paid. ... On average, corporate America pays its most important leaders like bureaucrats. Is it any wonder then that with so many CEOs acting like bureaucrats rather than the value-maximizing entrepreneurs, companies need to enhance their standing in world markets?"[16]

Jensen and Murphy are right. A $10 million compensation package may not be enough for a CEO who turned a failing company around, whereas a $1 million package is too much for a CEO who has presented shareholders with declining earnings. Disney chairman Michael Eisner is the best thing to happen to the company since Mickey Mouse. Shareholder returns at Disney have averaged over 60 percent per year for the last three years. Eisner deserves to be rewarded for this remarkable achievement, and he has: in fiscal 1989, Eisner received over $9 million in salary and cash bonus, and he exercised options that profited him $68 million. It was the billions that Eisner helped Disney to earn that brought him the millions in stock option profits.

I sit on the board of Tyco Labs, where a CEO made over $50 million for bringing the stock from $3 ½ to $65. You won't find a single director who will complain about it, and I imagine you won't find an unhappy shareholder, either. In exchange for executives taking cash salaries on the low end of the scale, the board authorized the grant of 3,400,000 shares to management in 1983. The grants would vest over a 10-year period, and the company would loan executives the cash sums necessary to pay taxes. Some 3,100,000 shares have been granted through May 31, 1990. Simultaneous with this program, the board also authorized repurchases of the company stock in the open market. Since 1983, some 8 million shares have been acquired at an average cost of pennies less than $10 per share. Although the granted shares have a market value (assuming $50 per share) of $150 million, it can be argued that the cost of this executive compensation system to the long-term Tyco shareholders is only the $30 million that the company spent to purchase the shares in the marketplace. This is as close to a win/win situation as you can find. Problems may be anticipated concerning the future motivation of rich managers, but the correlation of manager and shareholder wealth is an optimal result. On an ongoing basis, it is reassuring to consider that senior management owns a significant percentage of the total outstanding capital stock.

In 1989, the average CEO at the top 200 American companies received $2.8 million in salary and bonuses, in addition to lucrative pension and insurance packages. Towers Perrin reported that CEO salary rose 8 percent in 1989. But American business did not have a particularly "good year," to use the Babe Ruth standard. CEOs always manage to have better years in terms of compensation, but, as Figure 5 shows, profits and the wages of others don't always warrant it. Were CEOs requiring more pay for lackluster performance to keep pace with inflation? No, CEO pay also outpaces inflation. Were they covering for tax increases? Hardly. Graef Crystal, a compensation expert, surveyed 10 CEOs over the past decade and a half, with these results: Between 1973 and 1975, CEOs' after-tax pay averaged 24 times that of the average manufacturing worker. By 1987 to 1989, the differential was 157 times the average manufacturing worker. But taxes for CEOs declined from 50 percent to 28 percent, while worker taxes increased from 20 percent to 21 percent. [17]

American CEOs may be behind the Japanese and Europeans in competitiveness and productivity, but we sure have outpaced them in com-

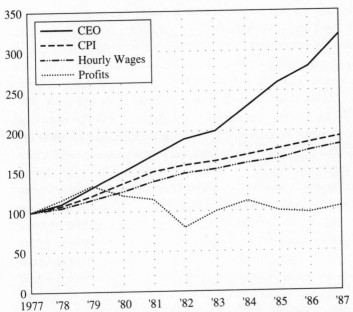

FIGURE 5   *CEO Compensation Rate Compared with Inflation, Wage, and Profit Rates, 1977–1987 (1977 = 100). (Source: Sibson & Co., used by permission)*

pensation. Pay packages of American CEOs at billion-dollar companies are two to three times greater than their equals in Japan, France, Britain, Germany, and the Netherlands.[18] In Japan, performance compensation takes another twist: CEOs who "disturb society"—by polluting the environment or being responsible for some public disaster, for example—often take pay cuts as a way of expiation.[19] Following a Japan Air Lines crash in 1985 that claimed 520 lives, the president of JAL made personal visits to the families of the victims. In 1981, after a series of leakages from a power station owned and operated by the Japan Atomic Power Company, the chairman and the president of the company resigned, in the hope that trust in nuclear stations would be restored under new leadership.[20] Other CEOs resign after poor performance. American CEOs just figure they are not being paid enough. At companies such as Manufacturers Hanover Trust, Borden, Phillips Petroleum, General Dynamics, Tenneco, Amoco, and Caterpillar, CEOs took home fatter paychecks in 1989 than they did the previous year, despite a drop in each company's return on equity.[21]

Compensation at the top levels of management has become so outrageous that even the bastions of capitalism—*Business Week, Forbes,* and *Fortune*—decry it with yearly cover stories that have become the business press equivalent of the "swimsuit issue"—the one everyone waits for. Intended to provide information for the marketplace, such coverage should permit "consumers"—in this case, shareholders—to have some kind of impact. In practice, however, management reads the compensation issues only to make sure that it is in the top group and, if not, to justify getting there. These stories have become an important factor in the spiraling increases.

Overcompensation is another example of externalizing costs through neutralizing mechanisms for accountability. Who is there to say no when the CEO asks for a raise? Shareholders are pretty much locked out of the process. Directors are picked by the CEO and are unlikely to oppose him; after all, he sets their pay. The system has no checks. Alfred Conard wrote:

> Overcompensation is particularly immune to correction by existing mechanisms of corporate governance. The "independent directors" who predominate on corporate boards are doubly biased; most of them owe their jobs to the executives whose compensation they must determine and are themselves executives of other corporations, where they hope for the reciprocal favor. . . . When levels of compensation are reviewed in derivative suits, judges can only compare compensation in the case before them with compensation in other enterprises that are subject to the same biases.[22]

Also encouraging overcompensation is the fact that compensation experts, brought in to devise pay packages, usually are selected by—and report to—the CEO, not outside directors.

Shareholders represent the only group—unlike directors, officers, or government—whose self-interest dictates approval only of compensation packages that are in the best interests of the corporation. They have every incentive to award lucrative contracts to attract the best minds to the corporation and to make sure that payment does not cripple the cost of operating the company. Shareholders can judge, for example, what sort of base pay will keep a corporation competitive within its industry, whether there is reason to limit top management's pay to a certain ratio of employee wages, and how much compensation should be provided through stock-based plans.

But shareholder involvement in the compensation issue is almost nonexistent. Under state law, shareholders have no direct voice in compensation decisions: the power to determine types and levels of executive compensation rests solely with the board of directors they elect. Most state corporation statutes also allow the board to determine its own compensation.

Under federal law, shareholder involvement is still limited. The SEC does not permit shareholders to file proxy proposals dealing with compensation, on the grounds that compensation constitutes ordinary business of the corporation. In 1990, the SEC made a significant reversal of its earlier policies and permitted the first shareholder resolution on a compensation matter, concerning golden parachutes, because of the role parachutes play in corporate takeovers. If they were purely a question of compensation, they would not have passed the SEC. On the other hand, it also proposed rules seriously limiting even further the required disclosures about compensation that companies must make.

State and federal rules thus preclude virtually any direct involvement by shareholders in matters concerning compensation. The presumption is that the board of directors will represent the shareholders' interests in executive compensation and other corporate policy matters, so all shareholders have to do is elect qualified representatives. The SEC's proxy disclosure rules require detailed descriptions of management compensation before each annual meeting. By requiring extensive disclosure, the SEC clearly intends for shareholders to have information with which to exercise broad oversight over the entire executive compensation program, not just those few items that must be submitted for shareholder approval. But, in most cases, shareholders who object to a company's compensation program have no way to demonstrate their objections other than to withhold votes for management nominees or to write a note on the back of the proxy card—both symbolic gestures at best.

There is one exception—almost an afterthought—one area where compensation issues are put to a shareholder vote. It is found in the Internal Revenue Code's requirements for eligible stock option plans and the SEC's proxy disclosure and short-swing profit rules. The federal tax code requires that, to qualify for preferential tax treatment, a stock option plan must be submitted for shareholder approval within a year before or after its adoption.[23] The Code also requires that employee stock purchase plans be submitted for shareholder approval within a year.[24] Thus, through the

Code, shareholders "creep" into the decision making process for at least some types of compensation plans.

The SEC's short-swing profit rule, meant to prevent the unfair use of inside information by corporate officers and directors, prevents insiders from trading company stock for a period of six months after the purchase date. There are a number of exceptions to this rule, many of which depend on shareholder approval of compensation plans that include company stock subject to the short-swing profit rule.[25] Just like the Internal Revenue Code, this rule gives shareholders an indirect entree into the compensation decision making process.

"Secondary Control" of Compensation

Technically speaking, the compensation of management falls partly within and partly without the purview of stockholder decision. However, since all elements of compensation are required to be disclosed in proxy statements relating to the election of directors, it seems to be the intention of our present laws that stockholders should exercise at least *secondary control* over the entire field. (Emphasis added.)

Benjamin Graham, David L. Dodd, and Sidney Cottle

Source: Security Analysis: Principles and Techniques, 4th ed., McGraw-Hill, New York, 1962, p. 672.

Overcompensation has many ill effects. One is the negative effect on employee morale. The Pittston workers on strike saw the management that was opposing their requests raise its own pay 61 percent. Imagine the feelings of the General Motors workers when, after massive layoffs of middle managers and operatives in 1987, the company proposed to pay executives large cash bonuses. Only the intervention of board member Ross Perot in conjunction with several key institutional investors stopped the management proposal. The impact on shareholder morale can also be devastating.

At Coca-Cola Bottling, J. Frank Harrison III was granted an option to purchase 150,000 shares of common stock—nearly 2 percent of the company. Harrison happened to be the son of the chairman of the board, J. Frank Harrison, and together the father-and-son team already held 9 percent of outstanding common stock. But the worst offense was that

Harrison III was also chairman of the compensation committee, giving him the unique privilege of presiding over the body that decided to reward him. What shareholder would want to invest in the company after that?

But the most serious problem is the morale of the CEO. What contact with overall commercial reality or the specific commercial reality of his own company does such a person have? The only other people in that pay range represent the ultimate in pay for performance: investment bankers, entertainers, and sports figures. No one else gets so much for so long without somehow, somewhere, sometime having to deliver.

In the worst cases, lucrative packages are granted to CEOs whose companies are sliding into oblivion. Instead of paying the captain to go down with the ship he wrecked, the board should find a new captain. ICN Pharmaceutical gave top officers raises as high as 91 percent in 1989, despite ICN's $82 million loss that year. The CEO, Milan Panic, received a 39.6 percent pay hike, bringing his salary to $574,050, not including $71,390 in legal, accounting, and insurance fees provided by the company. The reason? ICN wanted to "ensure his retention." But Panic founded ICN in 1960, and founders rarely leave their companies.

"Retention" is an empty catchword used to justify the unjustifiable. Says Michael Halloran of Towers Perrin: "It is rare that the CEO of one company leaves to become CEO of another. Retention is only an issue for employees below that level."[26] Retention could not have been a factor when First Interstate Bancorp gave CEO Joseph J. Pinola a 12.4 percent raise in 1989 for presiding over a $124 million net loss that year. Pinola retired that year, making the raise look more like a golden parachute than compensation for good work.

At its 1989 annual meeting, Toys "R" Us asked shareholders to approve a grant of 500,000 stock options, roughly 0.4 percent of current outstanding shares, for CEO Charles Lazarus. Lazarus, however, had already made a profit of over $72 million over the last three years on his stock options and was taking home another $4.4 million a year in base salary and "incentive compensation." How much more of an incentive did Lazarus need? Furthermore, under the plan, Lazarus was borrowing money from the company to purchase the stock, then selling the stock to realize a profit. One could hardly claim the CEO was investing in the company.

The most disturbing trend in compensation is its ability to change with the times, always appearing to be designed to reward management for performance, but rarely actually doing so. Stock options emerged as the dominant form of performance-tied compensation, curbed somewhat by tax reform and depressed P/E ratios in the 1970s.[27] But these plans could just as easily be designed to shield the executive from risk. Executives seemed to have no qualms with developing compensation packages that were apparently tied to performance but in fact were rigged with safety nets that ensured a hefty minimum amount of compensation. The

---

Buffett on Options

Of course, stock options often go to talented, value-adding managers and sometimes deliver them rewards that are perfectly appropriate. (Indeed, managers who are really exceptional almost always get far less than they should.) But when the result is equitable, it is accidental. Once granted, the option is blind to individual performance. Because it is irrevocable and unconditional (so long as a manager stays in the company), the sluggard receives rewards from his options precisely as does the star. A managerial Rip Van Winkle, ready to doze for ten years, could not wish for a better "incentive" system.

(I can't resist commenting on one long-term option given an "outsider": that granted the U.S. government on Chrysler shares as partial consideration for the government's guarantee of some life-saving loans. When these options worked out well for the government, Chrysler sought to modify the payoff, arguing that the rewards to the government were both far greater than intended and outsize in relation to its contribution to Chrysler's recovery. . . . [T]o my knowledge, no managers—anywhere—have been similarly offended by unwarranted payoffs arising from options granted to themselves or their colleagues.)

Ironically, the rhetoric about options frequently describes them as desirable because they put owners and managers in the same financial boat. In reality, the boats are far different. No owner has ever escaped the burden of capital costs, whereas a holder of a fixed-price option bears no capital costs at all. An owner must weigh upside potential against downside risk; an option holder has no downside. In fact, the business project in which you wish to have an option frequently is a project in which you would reject ownership. (I'll be happy to accept a lottery ticket as a gift —but I'll never buy one.)

Warren Buffett

Source: Berkshire Hathaway, Inc., Annual Report to the Shareholders, 1985, p. 12.

obscurity of compensation write-ups was best described by Graef Crystal, who awarded his 1988 Proxy Obfuscation Award to Citicorp "for strewing [CEO John] Reed's pay information across some 20 pages of numbing text."[28]

When a company grants options to a manager, the incentive comes from the fact that the executive knows he will not make money unless the stock goes up from the date of the grant. The executive has the right to purchase a certain amount of options at a certain price, called the "strike price," which is usually the market price of the stock on the day of the grant. He can hold on to the option for a certain amount of time, usually between 5 and 10 years. If he exercises that option 5 years later and the stock price has climbed 50 percent, he buys the stock at the option price, sells at the present market price, and keeps the 50 percent difference as his compensation, or he just uses a stock appreciation right (SAR) to cash in on the profit. If the stock depreciates in those five years, his options will be worth substantially less. If he is caught holding them at the end of their term and they are below the strike price, they are useless, because exercising them means he actually loses money. The theory of options is that they spur the director to drive his stock price up for 5 to 10 years; he then exercises his options just before they expire, for a maximum profit.

Executives, needless to say, did not like the degree of risk brought by options. So, as documented by Crystal in his bimonthly *Crystal Report on Executive Compensation*, the compensation industry has invented a number of tactics to ensure that executives will still profit even if their options are losing money. One of the first innovations was "underwater" repricing, which came of age after the stock market crash of 1987 left many executives holding options with market values less than the strike price. At Northrop in 1989, CEO Thomas Jones was able to swap 1.2 million options with a $45.88 strike price for 1.2 million options with a $29.88 strike price because Northrop stock had declined since his first option grant. In effect, Jones's options were "repriced." Thus, even though the company lost market value, Jones was rewarded with repriced options worth up to $4.5 million more than his old ones.[29]

AMR gave its executives floor protection: a cash make-up payment would be made to its CEO if the free shares they gave him dropped below the market price.[30] And at Bally, restricted stock grants are designed to cover any increase in the tax rates automatically. With packages like these, there is no way an executive can lose.

Sears, Roebuck & Co. came up with the most innovative compensation scheme to increase compensation without appearing to do so at the expense of shareholders. The Tax-Benefit Right entitles the executive to a cash payment equal to the company's tax deduction on the compensation payment. Thus, the executive gets his options' profit or bonus, plus the tax dollars that the company saved. Shareholders dish out the compensation, then lose the tax break they would have received, forfeiting that to the executive as well over the vesting period. There is little risk when executives can keep exercising options for every little jump in price, without having to worry if they missed the most opportune time to exercise.

If shareholders are able to increase their influence and vigilance in the area of compensation, the obscene payment amounts and fraudulent pay packages may abate. Already, thanks to increasing pressure by the public and institutional investors, many corporations are tying compensation to performance. At Reebok and Jefferies, the boards actually reduced the compensation packages of their CEOs to reflect slowdowns in performance. A Reebok spokesman stated that "directors believed that it was particularly appropriate to tie [Reebok CEO Paul] Fireman's long-term compensation directly to increases in value for Reebok's stock."[31] Jefferies CEO Frank Baxter was even more direct: "We feel we have to perform to get paid. We don't want to get paid for showing up." Although Chrysler is no paragon of virtue in the executive compensation department, the corporation did take the unprecedented step of asking its top 100 executives to own stock equal to a certain percentage of their salaries.[32] And in 1990, Bear Stearns introduced a new compensation package, approved by shareholders, allowing officials to acquire shares of company stock by deferring part of their cash compensation for a minimum of five years. "While participation in the new deferred compensation plan is voluntary," noted Bear Stearns president James E. Cayne, "initial indications are that nearly all eligible employees will participate."

At the heart of all of this is director compensation. On one hand, directors get paid too little for what we ask them to do. On the other hand, they get paid far too much for what they actually do. Directors have an extremely important job, but, for the most part, they spend a very small amount of time doing it while getting paid a very large amount of money. According to Spencer Stuart, the average "total" 1990 compensation for outside directors at 100 major corporations was $45,650.[33] According to a 1989 Korn/Ferry study, fully one-fourth of the outside directors received an average of $60,609 a year[34] while serving at companies with over $1 billion in sales. Like officers' plans, these plans are often designed to appear to bear a relationship to performance; and, like the officers' plans, they more often do not.

Most directors receive an annual retainer and a board meeting fee. At Boeing, for example, a director earns $26,000 a year and receives $2,000 at the end of each board meeting. Usually, such compensation is exchange for attending about 10 meetings a year. In 1988, CEOs estimated their directors spent about 108 hours on board-related business, which included reviewing and preparing for meetings, as well as attending and traveling to them.[35] This amounts to less than three weeks' work a year.

But this does not take into account the fringe benefits. If, for example, a director serves on a committee, his compensation increases. In 1988, the average director who also served on the audit committee for a Fortune 100 company received a total of $37,761 for board service. In exchange, he had to attend an average of four extra meetings a year.

Other fringe benefits include accident insurance, travel expenses for spouses of directors, and life insurance. Over 90 percent of the Fortune 100 reimburse travel expenses, and 51 percent grant matching education gifts. Sixty-seven percent of the Fortune 100 offer retirement plans. Medical and dental coverage, travel accident plans, and accidental death coverage are also available at some companies.

Thus, even a $50,000/year package is misleading. If you sit on the board of Texas Instruments, you receive $40,000 as an annual retainer. If you sit on the audit, corporate objectives, or finance committee, the retainer increases to $50,000. If you chair one of those committees, add another $2,500; and if you serve on a subsidiary of Texas Instruments, add an additional $2,500. Every year, Texas Instruments holds a strategic planning conference. If you attend, you get $5,000. If you attend any special company events, you get another $1,000 per day. If you serve on the board for five years, you get a retirement package worth 60 percent of your retainer at the time of retirement for the number of years served as a director, up to 10 years. You also get life and travel accident insurance, as well as medical and dental coverage. Thus, you could receive in excess of $60,000 a year plus benefits and, upon retirement, receive roughly $24,000 a year.

At Allied-Signal, a director immediately receives $24,000 a year. Every meeting brings in another $1,500. Each committee membership is worth an extra $5,400, and chairmanship of the audit or compensation

---

The Components of Director Compensation

Annual retainer
Regular board meeting fee
Committee meeting fee
Special position fee (e.g., chairman)
Stock grants
Pension plan
Life insurance
Travel accident insurance
Medical/dental coverage
Perks from company's product line
Gifts to charity (matching and insured)

---

committee carries a $4,000 bonus. The director receives restricted stock, $350,000 worth of business travel insurance, $100,000 in life insurance, and medical and dental coverage for himself and his dependents. The director also gets a retirement package equal to the annual board retainer for the rest of his life if he retires at age 70 or later. If he retires between the ages of 60 and 70, the director receives a retirement package for the number of months served on the board. If he dies before this is fully paid, his spouse will receive the payments until the package is fully vested or at the end of 120 months, whichever is earlier.

Many corporations also grant golden parachutes for directors so they will be compensated in the event of a change in control. Pension funding is also available in limited cases. A Sears director is eligible for a full pension from the first day he is on board. Directors also get company products. GM directors often get free cars, and airline directors get free travel for themselves and their families.

Charitable contributions are the newest form of compensation. Several companies have decided to pay their directors, in part, by making contributions to their directors' favorite charities through purchase of insurance policies that name the charity as beneficiary. General Electric, PPG Industries, Westinghouse, General Mills, and Waste Management, Inc. all have such charitable packages in place, although only Waste Management notes the package's existence in its proxy. Companies like them because they can deduct the cost of premiums as an expense and deduct the benefit as a gift. Directors like them because they provide a way for them to give their favorite charity $500,000–$2 million without actually spending any money—quite a nice payment for their services as a director, and one utterly unrelated to their performance. The only people who don't like them are the people who don't get to vote on them—the shareholders—who ultimately pay for the annual premiums, which run as high as $25,000 per director.

With directors setting management pay and managers setting director pay—and, often, with the two parties switching roles at another company's board meeting—it is a most friendly, congenial, and convenient arrangement. But it is shareholders who foot the bill, and it is clear that, too often, they do not get what they pay for.

We have found in Part II that much of big business in America at this time is not necessarily involved in profit. It is involved with ensuring an environment within which its prerogatives can be better preserved. It has lost an "industrial" purpose; it has not enough sense of the long term; it conforms to the pattern of other large institutions, without ideological base. It will have great difficulty in successfully competing with industries, which are driven by the goals of profit, quality, industrial purpose, and even national interest. There is need for a system of governance that will help to guide the genius and energy of business and bring it back to accountability to some entity, outside of itself. Owners must be involved. That is the subject of Part III.

PART III

The New Ownership Agenda

6

Slumbering Giants:
The Institutional Investors

Institutional shareholders now hold the majority of common stock. Pension plans alone will be the majority shareholders in most companies by the turn of this century, less than a decade away. This makes it possible to have in the United States what has been a key ingredient in Japanese and German competitiveness: a dominant class of corporate owners with a long-term orientation.

"We Have Met the Market and They Is Us"

Institutions own such a large percentage of the market that two of the elements driving short-term orientation—the need for liquidity and the competitive advantages of active fund management—are no longer important, or even prudent. As Assistant Secretary of Labor David Ball said, institutional investors can paraphrase Pogo: "We have met the market and they is us." Nonprofessional investors have become so scarce that it is no longer profitable for funds to expend resources necessary to beat them. The rewards are simply too low. While a target's shares go up in a takeover, the acquirer's shares go down, and institutional investors, who usually hold both companies' common stock and their bonds as well, are left with no net profit, even in the short term. The only way for them to enhance value is through effective involvement in the affairs of the portfolio companies they hold in virtual perpetuity. This is especially true for the indexed portfolios.

181

Much of the present concern with conflicting interests, takeovers, and social responsibility arises from the structural conflict between the corporation's continuing need for long-range commitment and the half-century-old pattern of short-term stockholder focus. The possibility of eliminating this conflict appears to offer a sound continuing basis for the legitimating of private power and for minimizing the adverse impact of large corporations on society without the need for increased government restrictions.

Institutional Investors: Who They Are and What They Want

Institutional investors are just beginning to discover and flex their ownership muscles. It's important to take a look at them, to understand who they are, what they are looking for, and where they are going.

The Institutional Investors

[I]nstitutional investors are by no means a monolithic group, since they have vastly different investment objectives, tolerance to risk, understanding of their fiduciary mandates, and perceptions of their appropriate role in corporate governance. Notwithstanding major differences among them, institutional investors as a group, have vastly expanded their economic sphere of influence in a number of important ways. Moreover, while they may be diverse, a high concentration of economic power resides among a relatively small and extraordinarily stable group of institutions.

Dr. Carolyn Kay Brancato

Source: *The Pivotal Role of Institutional Investors in Capital Markets: A Summary of Research at the Columbia Institutional Investor Project,* Center for Law and Economic Studies, Institutional Investor Project, Columbia University, New York, June 14, 1990, pp. 1–2.

Institutional investors are indeed a diverse crowd. They include pension funds, trusts, mutual funds, and endowments—all pools of money invested for different purposes and with different obligations. They have only one thing in common: They manage assets on behalf of someone else, someone to whom they owe a duty as fiduciaries. Institutional investors go back to the earliest development of property law. In the 1780s, for example, Benjamin Franklin established a trust fund out of his salary as Governor of Pennsylvania because he did not believe that public servants in a democracy should get paid. The £2,000 sterling he set aside vested in part 100 years after his death, in 1890, with the rest to be paid out in 1990. After 200 years, that portion was worth $16.5 million. The beneficiaries were citizens of Boston and Philadelphia, and politicians from both cities spent most of 1990 fighting over how to spend it.[1]

The five largest groups of institutional shareholders had the following equity holdings (in billions) in 1989:[2]

Private pension funds	$666.7
State/local pension funds	290.2
Open-end investment companies	239.2
Life insurance companies	116.7
Other insurance companies	94.3

The holdings were skewed toward the larger-capitalization companies, with the result that, by 1989, institutional ownership of the top 50 corporations had reached 50 percent.

The growth in the last 25 years has been encouraged by federal tax policies that give favorable treatment to funds committed for retirement and charitable purposes. To ensure that public policy is carried out, the tax law usually requires that the funds be held in the form of a trust. Thus, to adapt Gresham's well-known law, "tax-aided savings drives out all others." Increasingly, the savings of America are being held in institutional form, and the owners of corporations are becoming large and concentrated.

Majority ownership of our largest companies is managed by institutional investors. The question, then, is on whose behalf? And are the concerns of the beneficiaries being met?

A Federal Law of Ownership

All of the major institutions collectively estimated to own 45 percent of the total of all equity securities in publicly held U.S. companies are subject to the strictest standard developed by our legal system, the fiduciary standard, for the same reason it is imposed on corporate directors and officers: it's not their money they are handling. In this case, though, the fiduciary standard is more than myth; it is a very tangible reality. Almost every institutional investor is governed by existing federal regulation and supervision as to how they exercise their responsibility as owners of the portfolio companies. That makes it possible, through purely administrative action, to create a "federal law of ownership" right now.

The institutions have little in common beyond their trust structure. Although institutional investors may own, through their trustees, a majority of the equity of the principal companies in the country, it is virtually impossible in the case of mutual funds, insurance companies, universities, foundations, and banks to define either the beneficiary by name or to establish a constant set of values for governing the operation of the trust.

It makes no sense, then, to think of institutional investors as a class capable, without some outside stimulus, of formulating plans for extensive common action. Even if they wanted to, it would be impossible. They are all impeded not just by the endless litany of procedural obstacles to collective action by shareholders,[3] but, more important, by the "prisoner's dilemma" discussed in Chapter 2, which prevents shareholder action of any kind in most cases. This dilemma, also called the "collective choice" problem, means that any shareholder who wishes to act must underwrite all of the costs, for only a pro rata share of any returns, if there are any. Everyone else gets a free ride.

Economists have come up with a term for the individual investor's involvement that sounds almost oxymoronic: rational ignorance. Institutional investors have also been rationally ignorant; they have received no benefits from paying attention to voting. They face some of the same obstacles to collective action, but a more serious impediment is the extreme conflicts of interest, as noted in this book, along with their neglect and inefficiency—even abuse—of ownership rights.

Meanwhile, corporate management has no such barriers to action. They control the agenda, timing, and financing of corporate action. There has been little progress in developing structures for collective action by owners, possibly because the largest owners in today's society are the employee benefit plans of those companies most satisfied with the current governance system; the scope of shareholder decision making has been accurately described by one of the nation's finest scholars as nominal, tainted, coerced, or impoverished.[4] "Corporate democracy" became a vestigial notion, a polite fiction that remained a part of our vocabulary only because it underlies the exercise of private power.

Institutional investors collectively are large enough to make activism not just feasible, but prudent as well. As we noted earlier, a study showed that adoption of the 1990 Pennsylvania antitakeover law depressed share value of companies incorporated there by 4 percent; it is therefore reasonable to assume that shareholder action calling for reincorporation to another state with more favorable laws could increase share value.

But an initiative such as a shareholder proposal calling for reincorporation is expensive. Although it takes only a couple of hours of a lawyer's time to draft and submit such a resolution, it takes much more time for the lawyer to fight it out when the company tries to get permission from the SEC to exclude it from its proxy. There are additional necessary expenses: without a proxy solicitor—one of a handful of (primarily) New York City firms that have the practical knowledge of where proxy cards are physically located—it is virtually impossible to get majority support for a shareholder resolution. It can cost one-half million dollars to hire one (if you can get one; in one case, our client retained a proxy solicitor only to be told the next day that the solicitor had thought about his other relationships and decided it would be bad for business to do the job). Let's say the institution decides to proceed, spends the money, and gets a majority vote. It is still nonbinding. There has never been a shareholder resolution that was drafted to be anything more than advisory, although we believe it is possible to have one under some state laws, including Delaware's. How can a fiduciary, committed to prudence and diligence, justify proceeding on that basis, even if the institution in question has enough stock to be likely to make more than the cost of its effort if the company does reincorporate in another state?

Now let's make this example more realistic. Let's say that the institution in question also has a commercial relationship with the Pennsylvania company; let's say it is a bank that loans it money, or an insurance company that provides liability insurance, or a money manager who manages its pension fund, or a brokerage house that underwrites its securities. It's a lot easier just to accept the depressed stock because the alternative course would most likely mean a loss of business. Fiduciary obligation is nice, but commercial relationships are business, and every commercial institution and every private institution has relationships it does not want to discourage. As discussed below in this chapter, institutional investors are subjected to the most extreme conflict-of-interest pressures. Meanwhile, institutional fund managers do not get paid extra for voting; indeed, hardly anyone knows if they vote or not.

The public institutions, like the state pension funds, for example, have relationships, too. When the Wisconsin state pension fund wanted to object to General Motors' $742.8 million of greenmail to Ross Perot, it was stopped by the governor, who was trying to get General Motors to build some plants in his state.

Private Pension Funds: The 900-Pound Gorilla

Gordon Binns presides over a staff of 50 people managing some $35 billion in pension assets that General Motors has amassed in its pension system. There are over 848,000 participants and beneficiaries in the domestic plans. There may be some question as to the position of GM in the automobile world, but there is no question that Binns and his people have solid claim to preeminence in the world of pension investments.

I first met Gordon when I was the ERISA (Employee Retirement Income Security Act) administrator. He invited me to an informal dinner at the Harvard Club with the responsible officers of the large plan sponsors having principal offices in or near Manhattan. As I sat down with General Motors, Bethlehem Steel, AT&T, USX, IBM, General Electric, Dupont, and Exxon I was struck by the extraordinary concentration of investment capital in the private pension system. I have continued to feel that this base of resources and talent provides the best possibility for restoring a system of accountability to corporate governance in America.

General Motors hires about 65 "external" managers. The range of investments covers the spectrum of possibilities, from country funds, real estate, and oil and gas to ventures of all kinds. They have been adventuresome, and successfully so. The investment results have exceeded their actuarial projections by a wide margin over recent years. In fact, the success rate of the plan has encouraged GM to raise the assumed earnings rate several times, and the 11 percent rate currently being used is one of the most aggressive among funds. To the extent that the pension funds can continue to generate such returns, the size of the company's annual payments can be reduced. Also, it is possible to use these "excesses" to fund obligations for which there is no other source, such as inflation adjustments in the payments made to those already retired. Binns would certainly question whether these results could be achieved if GM were required to "index" the domestic equities portion of its portfolio, as is suggested later in this book.

Binns has been an industry leader and has testified for ERISA plans before Congress. He was the first chairman of the Committee on Investment of Employee Benefit Assets (CIEBA), a technical committee of the Financial Executives Institute. GM has been highly conscious of its responsibilities in the area of corporate governance. In keeping with its policy of delegating investment authority to "outside" managers, GM depends on these experts to function as responsible owners, but it insists that they demonstrate their commitment to thoughtful, prudent exercise of voting rights, and it monitors them to make sure that they are meeting their responsibilities.

Binns is the best example there is of the class of institutions that make up the largest pot of money in the world. These are, of course, the pension and welfare plans covered under ERISA, pension funds established by corporations on behalf of their employees. The Labor Department estimated ERISA funds to be worth $2 trillion in 1990. It took 11 years to pass federal legislation encouraging and regulating the creation of private pension funds, and during that time no one anticipated that the impact would be so dramatic. I once asked the chief sponsor of ERISA, the late senator Jacob Javits, whether he had any idea that the money gathered under this statute would reach such proportions, and he said, "I have never been accused of modesty, but I will tell you in all sincerity that it never occurred to me."

The statute was passed after years of testimony from employees who found themselves destitute upon retirement. There were several different drafts of the legislation, principally directed at state and local government employees. Effective lobbying of local interests resulted in the exemption of public plans, so that it was transformed into a program for private sector employees. The result was ERISA, which many people claim stands for "Every Rotten Idea Since Adam." The statute is incredibly complicated; having served as the political appointee charged with administering it, I admit that even I do not understand it all, and that, indeed, I have met only two men who do: Mort Klevan and Alan Lebowitz, both at the Department of Labor and both men of stunning intellect and integrity.

The idea behind ERISA is simple. Congress wanted to make it worthwhile for private companies to create pension plans for their employees, and then it wanted to protect the money after the plan had been created. The statute was designed to resolve questions of conflict of interest and liability that had left the private pension system uncertain, and, in some cases, chaotic. ERISA was designed to resolve them with one massive federal law, preempting all state law in this area. ERISA itself, however, still created the potential for abuse, and it raised questions that required volumes of regulations, guidelines, and advisory opinions.

ERISA pension funds are modeled on trust law. But trust law never contemplated a group of beneficiaries as large and diverse as pension plan participants. As we discussed in Chapter 2, in our description of Trip's investment in Boothbay Harbor, pension plan participants include those who just started work, those a few years from retirement, and those who are already retired. The common law of trusts also never contemplated a trustee like Widget Co., Trip's employer, one with not only a lot of other business concerns to occupy its attention, but with an inherent conflict of interest. The CEO's obligation as trustee of Trip's retirement money can conflict with his obligations in running Widget Co.

ERISA permits a "nonneutral fiduciary" in recognition of the fact that in pension plans, unlike traditional trusts, employers and employees are both settlors and beneficiaries.[5] This is also acknowledgment that the plan sponsor is the party at risk if the plan is poorly run. Employers would be understandably reluctant to establish a pension fund if they had no say in selecting those who manage the assets or deal with benefit claims. The statute makes it clear that, between those two obligations, that of fiduciary of the pension plan comes first. A fiduciary must act "for the exclusive benefit" of plan participants. In practice, this standard has been difficult to understand and enforce.

Today's ERISA funds include every possible kind of investment—not just in the domestic market, but, increasingly, in the global market. The global market is investing here, too. Pension funds and other institutional investors in Europe and Japan hold significant stakes in American companies.

ERISA requires that a "named fiduciary" with responsibility for the plan be designated by the company, called, in ERISA's myopic terms, the "plan sponsor." Typically, a major corporation designates a committee of the board of directors as the "named fiduciary." ERISA recognizes that these people are too busy and important to watch over the pension fund money, so it permits them to delegate authority (and responsibility and potential liability) to an investment manager. So long as the selection of the investment manager is prudent and the plan sponsor monitors its performance, the sponsor company will not be liable for the investment manager's mistakes. The standard is utterly process-oriented. As long as there is a reasonable process, and it is followed, the Labor Department will not second-guess the results.

ERISA might as well have been named the "consultant employment act." So much attention has been paid to ensure that selection of an investment manager is "prudent" that an entire industry of consultants has been created to provide the substantive and independent "proof" that a particular investment manager meets the standards necessary to justify selection. And another new species of expert has been generated to provide the most exhaustive analysis of the performance of the investment managers. Hiring these consultants is itself evidence of prudence and diligence and thus functions as sort of an insurance policy.

Corporate managements really have not decided what to do with their pension assets. For two reasons, their focus has been on the procedural aspects of ERISA. First, the issues raised are remote from whatever goods or services the company produces, so it is easier to file the pension fund away under "human resources." And the government seems to agree—administration of ERISA was given to the Labor Department, not the Treasury Department. Second, meaningful exercise of the ownership rights of the pension assets is worse than thankless. No investment manager, in-house or outside, ever got paid a dime for voting proxies especially well. On top of all of the practical and procedural obstacles listed in Chapter 2, it is a threat. ERISA funds face the same problem of collective choice that all shareholders do: can it be prudent to expend resources knowing that, without the ability to communicate with other shareholders, any positive results are unlikely? Even if the results are positive, any returns to the active shareholder will only be proportionate to its holdings, with all of the other shareholders getting a free ride. Furthermore, to the extent that Widget Co.'s pension department adopts an activist posture with respect to portfolio companies, it risks retribution—retaliation in the marketplace and an invitation to other pension professionals to take an equally aggressive view of their own functioning when they vote the shares they hold in Widget Co. From the point of view of all institutions, then, it is simplest to do nothing, to try to maximize value by trading, despite all evidence that the majority of those who do so fail to outperform the market.

Without any sense of irony, much less responsibility, the CEOs who condone this policy at the office condemn it when they are outside. The takeover hearings conducted on March 4, 1987, by the Senate Committee on Banking, Housing, and Urban Affairs included testimony by a panel of 16 chief executive officers. They all argued that institutional investors provide the momentum for violent and unchecked hostile takeovers, that they are rapacious and omnivorous, and that they have a short-sighted commitment to quarterly figures that skews the market and that can only be addressed through new federal legislation. None of them mentioned that they themselves controlled well over $18 billion through their corporate pension funds. None of them suggested that they themselves were taking any steps to direct their pension funds—through trading policy or proxy policy—according to the longer view.

Indeed, the top level of corporate management has paid relatively little attention to a program that, in a surprising number of cases, represents the company's greatest asset and its greatest liability. In the corporate hierarchy, the chief pension officers are like orphans. Most CEOs are interested in the company's core business, and all they want to know from the pension fund is whether it is adequately funded. They do not hesitate to terminate pension plans when it is expedient. In some corporations, pension officers are assistant secretaries, in others assistant treasurers, in some vice presidents—in none are they considered participants in the principal activity of the corporation. I don't know of a single large company's chief pension officer who is also a director of that company.

Although a pension officer may through a particular investment "make" more money for the company, in the sense of decreasing the amount it is obligated to contribute to the pension system in a given year, than the operations of a whole plant, he is not compensated in the same manner as an operations person who achieved the same dollar results. No one in 1974 thought that, within 20 years, one of the largest problems of the pension system would be what to do about the surpluses. Today, many of the largest companies have surpluses—that is, assets with a market value exceeding the actuarial amount of liabilities— in the billions. AT&T's is over $10 billion as of this writing.

The Inactive Institution:
The Raider's Best Friend

Because activism raises difficult questions, corporate plan sponsors have, until the most recent times, generally preferred to delegate the problems to their money managers. This inaction by the largest shareholder group has had the ironic effect of providing support for others whose interest, in many cases, is hostile to incumbent corporate management. The "raider" who acquires 4.9 percent of a corporation's stock has the additional leverage of "knowing" that the largest single class of shareholders—holding on average 20 percent, and in the case of large companies substantially more—will be on his side. Arguably, therefore, the passivity of the plan sponsors in developing policies for their pension plan holdings is, on the one hand, a major contributor to the success of the raiders and, on the other, a conspicuous loss of opportunity to maximize the value of their own holdings—the arbs got that money! Corporations, their shareholders, and their employees lose both ways.

The emerging importance of proxies, due to increased contests for control and public pension plan support for shareholder resolutions, has led corporate management to rediscover ERISA funds as another kind of asset. As documented in the Cohen committee report,[6] some officials pressured investment managers to support them, at the risk of losing business.

Returning to Trip's investment in Boothbay Harbor, this is what would happen: Boothbay is the target of a hostile takeover attempt, because the CEO has spent more time playing golf than watching the business, its facilities are out of date, and dividends are down. The group running against incumbent management has substantial credibility, and the investment manager handling Trip's pension fund, hired by Widget Co., Trip's employer, is inclined to vote for them.

But the investment manager handles pension money for 10 different companies, including, by coincidence, Boothbay Harbor itself. The manager gets a call from the CEO or CFO of Boothbay that goes something like this: "I see that you hold our stock, not only in our pension fund, but also in your nine other funds. You know, when we think about where to put our money, we think about the kind of judgment we look for in an investment manager. In my opinion, a vote for the other side shows bad judgment. We sure would like to keep paying you that nice management fee, and we're sure we can count on your support." Keeping in mind that Trip, on whose behalf this stock is being held, will never find out how the stock is voted, that Trip's employer will never ask, and that the CEO of Boothbay will know how the investment manager votes and will act on what he knows, would you vote for the opposing slate?

Or maybe the money is handled by a bank trust department, which goes ahead and votes for the takeover. This time, the CEO calls up his old friend, the head of the loan department at the bank, or maybe even the bank president, and politely reminds him that Boothbay is one of the bank's biggest loan customers (or is thinking of becoming one). It is the simplest thing in the world (and the hardest to trace) to call up the trust department and tell them to submit a new proxy card.

This friendly arrangement was the norm for some time, until 1987, when Avon, Rockwell, GTE, and International Paper took it one step further.

GTE's Request for Help from CEOs

December 12, 1986

I am writing to share my concern about the heightened unfriendly merger and acqusition activity, and related greenmail, and what I consider to be the increasingly unhealthy short-term speculative nature of the nation's financial markets. I also want to ask for your assistance with respect to a specific aspect of this problem related to GTE.

We both recognize the economic and social implications of what I believe to be an overemphasis on short-term financial performance. Both of us have spent many years building organizations which proudly serve the varied interests of our shareholders, employees, communities and customers.

The GTE Board of Directors has called for a special meeting of our shareholders because of its unanimous belief that prudent corporate stewardship dictates that we act decisively to enhance values for all shareholders while satisfying our responsibilities to other constituents. The proposals that our shareholders are being asked to approve undoubtedly have been discussed by most executives and their Boards and already have been adopted by shareholders of many public corporations. GTE's proxy statement is included for your information.

I am writing to you because I feel strongly about this subject and because your corporation has a very large pension fund. Accordingly, there is a good chance that your pension fund owns shares of GTE voting stock.

Because of the short-term orientation of certain money managers, absent specific voting instructions from plan sponsors, such money managers will vote against certain proposals similar to those proposed for adoption by GTE's Board. Consequently, some plan sponsors have instructed their money managers not to vote against such proposals without the sponsor's specific approval. If you have not taken this step—and if you agree that the proposals will benefit GTE's shareholders in the long term—I would greatly appreciate your providing specific voting instructions to your money managers to vote for the proposals adopted by GTE's Board.

Since the GTE special meeting of shareholders will be held on December 24th, time is of the essence. I would, therefore, very much appreciate your expedited action on this matter.

I welcome your thoughts and encourage your support in our joint goal to continue to improve the economic environment in which we all work and live. If you have any questions, please do not hesitate to telephone me at 203-965-2103.

Sincerely yours,
Theodore F. Brophy
Chairman of the Board

Source: James E. Heard and Howard D. Sherman, "Conflicts of Interest in the Proxy Voting System," Investor Responsibility Research Center, 1987, Washington, D.C., pp. 99–100.

Those companies responded to the first wave of corporate governance resolutions sponsored by institutional investors by putting pressure on someone higher than the money managers and bank trust departments; this time the pressure was put on their fellow CEOs. The shareholder resolutions that sparked this response concerned the adoption of poison pills; the resolutions either asked that they be rescinded or asked that they be put to a shareholder vote. Even if these resolutions received majority votes, they would still be nonbinding, and advisory only.

Nevertheless, some of the CEOs of companies that received these resolutions from shareholders wrote letters to other CEOs encouraging them to make sure their pension funds shares were voted against the resolution, suggesting something like: "You support me on this one, pal, and I'll support you when it gets to be your turn." Some of the letters included the implication that a vote against these proposals would be in the interest of shareholders/plan participants and therefore consistent with the fiduciary duty imposed by ERISA. International Paper's letter, however, did not even bother with that.

The Labor Department responded on February 23, 1988, with a widely released letter to Avon formally adopting what had been the consistent policy of the department since the passage of ERISA: ownership powers, including proxy voting, because they have economic value, are an asset of the plan and are therefore subject to the same standards as the other assets. This was followed by a series of increasingly focused statements and rulings by DOL that, along with the rising activism of public pension funds, provided the momentum for the seismic impact of institutional investors on corporate governance.

The simple statement that the right to vote must be exercised with as much "care, skill, prudence, and diligence" (ERISA's fiduciary standard) as the right to trade doesn't sound as if it could turn the world upside down, but, coupled with the Labor Department's promise to start enforcing that standard, it did, at least in that part of the world that votes proxies. The later rulings and releases, including the 1989 "Proxy Project Report," underscored the department's commitment to this issue.

A fiduciary who fails to vote, or casts a vote without considering the impact of the question, or votes blindly with management would appear to violate his duty to manage plan assets solely in the interests of the participants and beneficiaries of the plan. We will be vigilant in assuring that pension fund fiduciaries handle proxy voting as they handle any other corporate asset—namely not for the benefit of themselves or third parties, but for the benefit of participants and beneficiaries.[7]

Investment managers could no longer shrug off the responsibility; the Labor Department said they were stuck with it, and stuck with doing it right, unless the plan sponsor retained the voting authority itself, in which case *they* were stuck with the responsibility of doing it right.

This put corporate management in a catch-22. In the late 1980s, thousands of corporations urged their own shareholders to let them adopt various antitakeover devices. But is what you can adopt, with permission (however obtained) from your shareholders, different from what you can support, when you are acting "for the exclusive benefit" of pension plan participants?

For example, one popular item was "elimination of the right to act by written consent." Most states, including Delaware, permit shareholders to take any action they could take at an annual meeting at any other time, by "written consent"—something like a petition or referendum. Corporate management saw this as a threat, and why should they feel vulnerable 365 days a year, when they could bring it down to 1 (the day of the annual meeting) by eliminating that right? (The ever-ingenious Martin Lipton recently proposed to reduce this "feeling of vulnerability" even further by holding the "annual" meeting and election of directors only once every five years.) So, many boards then quietly did away with the right to act by written consent by asking shareholders to give it up, claiming that it promoted "instability." And in every case but one (Honeywell, to be discussed later), they did.

Now let's say that the management of one of these corporations is considering how to vote its proxies (or how to evaluate the way that their investment managers vote its proxies). Can they, acting as fiduciaries on behalf of their current and retired employees, find any way to justify relinquishing the right to act 364 days of the year? On the other hand, how could corporate management have one policy for the provisions they urged on their own shareholders and another for the provisions they evaluate when they themselves are shareholders, through their pension fund?

Elmer Johnson has a unique perspective on the private pension system in America today. He was one of the few individuals ever to be engaged by General Motors at the top level—general counsel and director—and then return to the private practice of law. He recently wrote a trenchant analysis of today's private pension system in the *Harvard Business Review,* urging corporations to become more involved in the administration of their pension funds, including their ownership rights.

> Ever since the creation of ERISA in 1974, boards of directors and their legal counsel have been driven chiefly by the fear of legal exposure. In establishing the apparatus for the administration of corporate pension plans, they were mainly concerned with how best to insulate directors and officers from fiduciary liability. As a result, boards abdicated even their ethically nondelegable role of establishing overall direction and purpose. That abdication can no longer be excused in light of the explosion in the size of pension assets and the failure of the investment community to provide a climate conducive to the building of long-term wealth-generating institutions. Legal counsel needs to become much more imaginative in protecting boards against undue risk of liability, while reasserting the board's oversight role.[8]

On the face of it, no one could have more interest in trying to develop a system of corporate governance based on ownership than the private companies whose pension plans are themselves the largest holders of equity. Elmer Johnson suggested a place to begin: "For example, large corporations might create a special top-level executive office to identify opportunities for long-term equity investments of very substantial size and voting influence."[9]

But many of the largest and most influential ERISA plans are run by the largest companies, such as AT&T and General Motors, which were considered takeover-proof and were therefore impervious to many of these problems. One of the most serious consequences of the failure to organize private plan ownership is that the agenda is being created without their input, which in some cases results in waste of effort and needless confrontation. For that reason, plus increased Labor Department scrutiny, and, not the least, because the best way to guarantee support for management is to let management make the decisions, corporations are taking an increased interest in the way they vote their pension plan proxies.

The Business Roundtable has encouraged its members to bring proxy voting inside the company, no longer leaving it to the money managers. A. Brewster Atwater, Jr., chairman and CEO of General Mills and chairman of the Business Roundtable's Task Force on Corporate Governance, proposed in a letter of January 17, 1990, that corporations consider taking back the voting authority customarily exercised by their investment managers. This is a step that could be either in the right or in the wrong direction. If it is simply a device to ensure that the process is carefully controlled to guarantee pro-management votes, the plan sponsors' take-back of the vote could involve serious violations of law and further destruction of trust. After all, this means that corporations will be voting the stock they hold in their customers, their suppliers, their competitors, possible players in a friendly or unfriendly business combination, and even in themselves. On the other hand, if the corporation is prepared to undertake the difficult problems of managing this asset in a structure protected from conflicts of interest, this could be the critical step in reestablishing the competitiveness and legitimacy of American corporations. Atwater's suggestion was pivotal for the development of governance. We believe, however, that it can be accomplished only by the creation of an entity within the corporation that is itself protected from conflicts of interest—probably a subsidiary organized under the Investment Advisor Act—and reporting directly to a committee of outside directors of the board.

Bank Trusts:
A Contradiction in Terms

Another large category of institutional investor is the banks, which act as trustees for everything from gigantic pension plans to the estate that rich Uncle Hubert left to Aunt Marie (who can't be bothered about the details of money and just needs to cash her dividend checks) and wayward son Richie, who can't be trusted with the principal. For the moment, though, we will concentrate on Aunt Marie and Richie, and other individual beneficiaries designated by the person establishing the trust. Trust administration is dominated by the complexities of federal income, gift, and estate taxes. Like other institutions, trusts have different classes of beneficiary with different kinds of interests. Aunt Marie may want to invest for income, whereas Richie might want to invest for growth or to persuade the trust to invest in one of his get-rich-quick schemes.

In most instances, the trust is irrevocable; unless there is fraud, which is almost impossible to discover or prove, the bank can continue to serve and collect fees as trustee, regardless of its investment performance. The security of the trust business may well be the reason for the traditional poor investment performance by banks. After all, in literal terms, they—unlike the beneficiaries—have nothing to lose. Again, the issue is "other people's money." What kind of theory will underlie the way the bank trustee votes proxies?

A bank trust officer is a very special kind of person. He derives his sense of accomplishment from being reliable and from being able to meet the needs of his clients, and he usually defines those needs as reliable payments. What you get with a bank trustee is a level of confidence that the trust assets will not be looted. Usually he exists outside of the main culture of the bank; he is not on the track to the CEO's office.

And this is just what the bank wants. Someone setting up a trust is entitled to believe that the U.S. Trust Company, for example, is going to maintain certain standards—and these do not include encouraging iconoclastic trust officers. Banks generally get the most profitable, and certainly the most interesting, portion of their business from prominent local corporations. The smaller the community in which the bank is located, the more its tone is apt to be dominated by the locally based businesses. There is no way that a bank executive is going to be promoted on account of courageous positions of any kind, especially with respect to positions contrary to management's recommendations on proxies. The mediocrity inherent in a lowest-common-denominator culture that applies to personnel as well as policies, added to a lack of incentive for risk taking, ensures that bank trusts will be administered in an atmosphere of establishment orthodoxy.

In the late 1980s, Karla Scherer watched the value of R.P. Scherer Corporation—a company her father had founded—deteriorate under her husband, the CEO. As a major shareholder and board member, Ms. Scherer soon realized that the inefficiently run company would be more valuable to shareholders if it was sold. However, the board repeatedly refused to consider this option, forcing her to take the matter to shareholders in the form of a proxy fight for board seats. She also ended up in court, challenging the way her trust shares were being voted.

Scherer recalls that the most devastating blow to the ultimately successful campaign to force a sale occurred when she had to deal with certain institutional investors.

> Manufacturers National Bank, the trustee of two trusts created by my father for my brother and me, indicated it would vote all 470,400 shares for management, in direct opposition to our wishes. Remember the bank's chairman sat on our [company's] board and collected director's fees as well as more than one-half million dollars in interest on loans to [R.P.] Scherer. During the trial, the then-head of the bank's trust department admitted under oath that he did not know what the "prudent man" rule was. He also stated that he had arrived at his decision to vote the stock for management in less than 10 minutes, without conferring with us and after affording management an opportunity to plead its case over lunch in a private dining room at the Detroit Club.[10]

Several years ago, the then-CEO of the U.S. Trust Company ran a series of advertisements in which he offered to resign as trustee of any trust at the request of a customer. On behalf of my wife, beneficiary of a trust established by her late grandfather, I decided to accept his offer before it was withdrawn. I began by asking a simple question: How was the trust doing? It turned out he couldn't tell me. His letter, written seven months later, is a miracle of polite obfuscation.

Daniel P. Davison to Robert A.G. Monks, October 15, 1986

Dear Mr. Monks:

I apologize that no one has replied to your letters of March 8 and March 31. There is no excuse for such lack of courtesy, but a reason may be that we cannot really be responsive to your request for a review of your trust to see how it has fared vis-à-vis inflation, nor are we prepared to resign. Let me explain.

As to the first, it would be doubtful if we could track back all the necessary transactions through the decades. We would be looking for some needles among literally billions of transactions. If we could perform the well nigh impossible, it would cost tens or possibly hundreds of thousands of dollars to do it.

Secondly, the information gathered would then have to be weighed against some background factors such as the constraints of the instruments and the intentions, oral and written, of the settlor, beneficiaries and remaindermen. Some of these might be quite subjective. We would then have to set up data bases and adopt inflation criteria, e.g., CPI regional, national or international or GNP deflator or whatever. Then we would have to agree on what method of performance measurement we should adopt—dollar weighted, time weighted, etc. etc.

To state the matter bluntly, we probably can't do it; if we could it would be horrendously expensive, and if we could and did the results would be hard to judge. U.S. Trust has a business of measuring the performance of others. We don't do it retrospectively. It makes some sense to do it when the results are read by sophisticated investors who understand the limitations of the process.

I believe the best reply to your query would be that the study of history is somewhat beside the point. Our joint interest is that future performance be up to snuff. Adequate compensation is no guarantee of this—but inadequate compensation almost certainly will result in inadequate performance.

You point to an accurate press quotation that I advocate provisions in trust instruments permitting a change in trustees. I think this provision is important from the Company's point of view. There is nothing more enervating than a customer that can be taken for granted. However, we cannot insist on this provision since settlors frequently do not want beneficiaries to have this kind of discretion and usually for some sound reason. If we agreed to resign upon request where the instrument has no specific provision we would almost certainly be hauled into court and charged as a faithless trustee.

I have a certain sympathy for persons who are charged higher rates and don't have the right to refuse them by walking. There is however real protection. The law requires us to charge uniform rates. About 50% of our business can be terminated at will by our clients; thus we must remain on the market or we will soon be out of business.

Pardon my prolixity, but I thought you should have as full an answer as possible, especially in view of our failure to reply to your first request.

Sincerely,
Daniel P. Davison

Translated into English, the letter says that he couldn't tell me how the trust was doing, because it would require separating transactions pertaining to her trust from thousands of others undertaken by the trust department. Imagine getting the same response if you asked the bank for a record of your checking account. Could they possibly respond that it would be too difficult to separate your checks from those of all their other customers?

He then goes on to say something that boils down to this: We do actually look at performance of accounts managed by other people, as one of the services we make available to people, unlike me, "sophisticated" enough to understand it. (Too bad they don't use that service themselves.) Anyway, we don't really look to the past in figuring out performance; we look to the future. In other words, forget what we have done so far, and listen to how well we will do someday.

Finally, he says that, despite the apparent claims in his ad, the bank just could not step down as trustee, no matter who asked for it. Not a bad deal. The guy who set up the trust and appointed him trustee is dead, and the trustee is therefore set for as long as the trust exists.

I was in that business myself in the late 1970s, as chairman of the board of the Boston Safe Deposit and Trust Company, and I was astounded to find a generally low level of service and minimal fiduciary concern for beneficiaries throughout the industry. One example of this was the practice, virtually universal until recent times, of administering trusts as if they had uninvested cash balances, attributable to delays in settlement and the like. In fact, the banks had very sophisticated "clearing" capabilities, required by their corporate pension clients, which permitted the daily retrieval of all cash entitlements. These differences between collected and reported cash were invested for the bank's own account and represented a significant share of the bank's total profits. This is what lack of accountability to beneficiaries produces.

Bank trusts are established with money made by some ancestor who at some time in the past successfully invested in a business. Tradition has it that few of the heirs inherit the ancestor's appetite or business acumen. That may or may not be true, but it is certainly true that most inherit the belief that a system that made them rich is not all bad. They can't even get reports on how the trust is doing; even if they want to know how the proxies are voted, why would the bank tell them? Aunt Marie and Richie won't notice whether the ownership rights are being exercised, much less encourage their trustees to assert them. A bank trust department has nothing to lose from voting with management on every proxy, and a lot to gain in commercial relationships. Therefore, there is little support anywhere in the banking system for trust officers to take on themselves responsibility as owners of portfolio companies.

But, like corporate pension funds, bank trusts are beginning to recognize that they have an obligation to take on that responsibility. The reason is the same: a strong interest from the federal government. Institutional Shareholder Services wrote to the office of the Comptroller of the Currency, asking what its policy was on voting proxies, and we got a letter saying that it generally endorsed the standard set forth by the Labor Department in the Avon letter. The Federal Reserve Board has proxy voting on its audit checklist.

Largely because of the role banks play in voting ERISA securities, they are becoming more sensitive to these issues, but because they are risk-averse and conformist by nature and practice, banks will respond to regulation and to conventional wisdom established by others. They will not be pioneers.

Mutual Funds:
One-Night Stands

Mutual funds are trusts, according to the terms of the Investment Company Act of 1940, which governs them. Otherwise, they bear little resemblance to the other institutional investors because of one important difference: they are designed for total liquidity. The "one-night stands" of institutional investment, they are designed for investors who come in and out on a daily basis, or those who just want to be able to.

Congress wrote a law distinguishing two kinds of pooled investment vehicles for public shareholders—good ones, which are called "diversified," and bad ones, which are the rest. Diversification is required for entitlement to the favorable tax treatment of Internal Revenue Code Subchapter M, which alone makes mutual funds a competitive mode of investment. In general terms, it requires that mutual funds act as passive participants and not as owners of the companies in which they put their money.

Although the aggregate shareholdings of the mutual fund industry are large, they are scattered over a large number of individual funds. Each represents a specific investment objective. If you want to invest in a mutual fund, you can pick one that focuses on high-tech companies, on "socially correct" companies, or on whatever companies are likely to produce quick profits. You can invest for income or for growth. The fund is more liquid than a piggy bank. The investors are entitled to take their money out at any time, at whatever the rate is that day. The investment manager has no control over what will be paid out or when a holding will have to be liquidated. The fund manager thus must view investments as collateral to the promise to shareholders to redeem their shares at any time. This is not the kind of relationship that encourages a long-term attitude toward a company the fund happens to invest in, and if there is a tender offer at any premium over the trading price, they have to grab it.

Mutual funds perform an astonishingly difficult task in providing to potential investors a hybrid investment alternative. Each fund proclaims its own objectives, its own balance of risk and reward, of current and deferred income. There is no one corporation that embodies the precise promise made in a mutual fund prospectus. That promise is realized only by the blend of holdings that the fund manager picks. In the face of the real need to attract new money and to retain investors in a world of perpetual competition, the mutual fund manager cannot be concerned with the long term; his investors may all show up today, and he has to be prepared to deliver.

Edward C. "Ned" Johnson III is the archetype of an entrepreneur and a proprietor. He is the controlling shareholder of Fidelity, the largest privately held money management group in the world, and he can be considered the founder of the modern mutual fund industry. When you walk up Park Avenue in New York north of Grand Central Station, you may wonder what happened to all of the street-level bank offices that were once on every corner. Indeed, in this 10-block span, there is only one walk-in office in the financial services industry; it is Fidelity, on the northwest corner of 51st and Park. Johnson has outbanked the banks.

Fidelity has the customers and the money. It loans money to banks. This revolution in the American financial industry is substantially attributable to the vision, the persistence, and the genius of Ned Johnson. When Johnson started with Fidelity, there really was no "industry." Investing was an art; in good times people bought shares, and in bad times the managers held on. The problem was sales. A direct sales force cost too much, and the brokerage community was always uneasy about using its salespeople to distribute someone else's product. Johnson began a direct sales campaign that, over a period of several decades, has resulted in an estimated four million customers. To accomplish this, he had to think in the longest possible terms and defer Fidelity's earnings for years at a time. He revolutionized sales, customer service, computerization, product design, and diversification. Johnson's own commitment goes beyond money. There was a time not long ago when American Express was prepared to talk in terms of 10 figures for the purchase of Fidelity. It was both meaningless and unthinkable for Johnson. His commitment is one of personal creativity, of using money, people, and determination to keep creating better and more useful products.

Johnson is himself an excellent investor. A footnote in the history of Fidelity is that while Gerald Tsai's highly publicized fund was the group's second best performer, Johnson's was number one. Fidelity owns some stock in virtually every publicly owned company. There are few people alive who have a keener sense of the responsibilities (and opportunities) of ownership and of the managerial ethic than Ned Johnson.

Johnson on the Managerial Ethic

There is another challenge, one that has been written about piece-meal in the press and has received none of the fanfare that is reserved for tax reform. It has to do with the diminishing rights of the individual shareholder in the American corporation and the heretofore passive role of mutual fund and pension fund managers.

As corporate managements have attempted to thwart hostile mergers and takeovers, with various devices—staggered board of director terms, golden parachutes, golden handcuffs—they have, in the process, erected impenetrable barriers between themselves and their shareholders. The situation can be compared to the declaration of war by a faltering democracy. *American corporate management is declaring martial law*. And although they succeed in defending themselves in the short run, they have sacrificed the rights of the individual corporate shareholder in the long run. Their actions may also be demoralizing to employees and may affect the performance of every part of the corporation.

There are no easy responses to this phenomenon, but I am certain that we will see a time when shareholders and government regulators step in and call "time out." And it will become extremely difficult for mutual fund managers and pension fund managers to maintain the totally passive role of dormant shareholder. As individuals, we must consider responding when corporate managements demonstrate overreach, as in the recent merger of two industrial companies, Allied and Signal, to cite but one example.

To exercise our rights as shareholders is only sound business practice. If the companies whose actions we ignore should fall on hard times because of highly questionable management decisions, then *our investments* lose their value.

Edward C. Johnson, speaking at the Annual Meeting of the Investment Company Institute, May 21, 1986.

Fidelity has played a powerful behind-the-scenes role in many corporate dramas. One might well ask why Ned Johnson is not the shareholders' champion. It is not that Johnson lacks tenacity, is unaware of the problem, or, like other investment managers, is cowed by commercial relationships—quite the contrary. In selected situations, he has been the model of a concerned, involved shareholder, even when it has cost him clients. The problem is that the stewardship of a business such as Fidelity requires a sense of priorities. No matter how Johnson feels about the problems of a particular corporate management, he must recognize Fidelity's principal mission. His overall goal—and his obligation as a fiduciary—is to make money for his own investors. He does not want his analysts to be at a disadvantage in talking with company managements. And although he is willing to lose a client or two in a given situation, he does not want to be "blackballed" in every competition to manage corporate pension funds.[11] He is also restricted by the limits of his funds, which are designed to meet the needs of people who want constant access to their money. In short, he is restricted by the same problem of collective choice that restricts any shareholder, of any size: how can he underwrite all of the costs of activism for only a pro rata share of the profits, if there are any?

Institutional Investors and Shareholders

[O]wning stock and not being able to assert your ownership rights is like owning a piece of land over which you have little control. If you can't walk on it, garden it, put a fence around it, or build on it, it isn't worth much. If American corporations are owned by stockholders who can't assert their ownership rights eventually the ownership may not be worth much either. ... I believe that a number of steps must be taken to reinforce the rights of shareholders or they will be completely disenfranchised.

First, institutions must act like the permanent owners of the businesses in which they have invested and exercise their shareholder rights. Institutional investors, especially those who are investing other people's money, have an obligation to be intelligent shareholders. They must read and vote proxies, understand the factors affecting a company's business, and make their views on important issues known to managers and directors.

Second, institutional investors should put pressure on directors to be more responsive to shareholder concerns about long-term strategies and the productive use of corporate assets. If directors are consistently unresponsive to shareholders, they should be voted against when they are up for election or reelection to the board of directors of any publicly held company.

Source: Letter to shareholders from Edward C. Johnson, April 3, 1990.

But he has removed some restrictions. In 1990, he announced some changes to the charters governing his funds, putting his investors and the companies he invests in on notice that he understands the value of involvement in corporate governance. Fidelity is founded on the notion that equity securities represent valuable merchandise. As it becomes clearer that courts, legislatures, and lobbyists have changed the nature of the tens of billions of dollars of common stock held by the various Fidelity funds, Fidelity and Johnson may have no choice but to move governance up to their highest priority.

Dean LeBaron, trustee and sole owner of Batterymarch, may well be the most innovative and creative professional money manager presently active. He developed index funds before there was such a thing. To list some of his many initiatives—copra plantations in New Guinea, farmland in the American middle west, British Commonwealth Funds, Brazil Funds, and innovation in developing computerized trading—is like describing the visible part of the iceberg. Most recently, he developed the fund allowing American companies access to technology developed by the Russians. It is virtually impossible to reflect on any aspect of the modern money management business without following the intellectual or professional path of Dean LeBaron.

The son of a Boston doctor, LeBaron managed to survive prep school and Harvard's college and business school with his enthusiasm and creativity undampened. His brief apprenticeship as respected research director of a nationally renowned brokerage firm led, seemingly inexorably, to his self-employment as the principal of Batterymarch, one of the largest and most successful money management firms in the country. LeBaron has been uniquely willing to speak out about what he sees as management abuse of owners. It is certain that this concern has cost him the opportunity to manage the pension funds of companies, whose executives consider "ownership activists" the enemy. It has cost him a great deal of money. He has been so successful that the loss of some business does not matter to him. But that is not the point. The point is that only the rare person who is accountable, from a business point of view, only to himself *can* articulate concern over the governance of corporations. For LeBaron to do so means commercial loss; for others it means slow death.

Confronted by the indifference of fiduciaries to the value of their voting rights on the one hand and by the volume and ingenuity of the proposals he was receiving for the use of his voting position on the other, Dean LeBaron developed a typically imaginative proposal. He advocated separating the vote from shares and establishing a separate trading market for each—a market for voiceless shares and a market for voice. This would demonstrate the "dirty little secret" that everyone was trying so hard to ignore: that votes have value, and the value belongs to the owners of the shares. No longer would trustees, out of desire to avoid work, expense, and possible confrontation, be able simply to decline the responsibility for voting portfolio holdings.

LeBaron is an energetic and charming advocate. He made an unforgettable appearance on a forum with T. Boone Pickens. Pickens expressed his outrage with the notion of "vote selling," calling it "un-American"—even "prostitution." Dean coolly replied that if "you are going to use it, you had best be paid for it." In many ways, Dean's memorable demonstration that votes have value may be considered the beginning of the modern period of shareholder activism.

Insurance Companies:
The Untouchables

Insurance is the only major industry that has successfully avoided any significant federal regulation, although life insurers' "separate accounts" and money-management subsidiaries often invest ERISA fund assets and are subject to ERISA and other federal rules when they do. Life and casualty insurance companies prefer to deal with state legislatures, with whom they have historically had a close relationship. As chairman of the Finance Committee of the Republican party in Massachusetts, I listened to the chief executive officer of one of the largest mutual insurance companies explain why it would not buy a book I had published, as a means to enable corporations to support us without making a direct political contribution. "You don't understand, Bob. We have already purchased both parties in the legislature through directing agency commissions, and buying your book would just make us do something extra for the Democrats."

State law has, until most recent times, severely circumscribed the extent to which insurers are allowed to invest their own funds in equities. Even today, only 14 percent of insurance fund assets are invested in common stocks. The current limit on stock is 20 percent of a life insurer's assets, or one-half of its surplus. But insurers still cannot take influential blocks; life insurers cannot put more than 2 percent of the company's general account assets into the stock of any single issuer, and property and casualty insurers cannot control a non-insurance company.[12]

The insurance industry has been able to dominate state legislatures. Even though they are clearly in the mainstream of interstate (and often foreign) commerce, they have successfully and assiduously avoided general regulatory supervision by the federal government. However, this did not prevent the industry from arguing vociferously before the United States Supreme Court, in the fall of 1990, that the federal Constitution should be applied so as to limit "punitive damages" awarded under state law. The insurance industry really is best thought of as a foreign country with interests that are not always congruent with those of the general public.

The insurance companies, perhaps more than any other class of institutional investor, have a symbiosis with the companies in which they invest. First, they are usually holders of debt securities of any company in which they have an equity investment; debt instruments are very compatible with their needs because they have a reliable, set payout. Second, either they have a commercial relationship with the company by selling it insurance against a variety of risks, or they would like to. Third, they certainly want to sell the company insurance company products to meet its pension obligations. Finally, like other institutional shareholders, they are under no obligation to report to their non-ERISA customers on their proxy voting (but the companies whose proxies they vote—and with whom they do business—do know), and, like all other shareholders, the collective choice problem makes any form of activism uneconomic. Therefore, it is not surprising that the insurance industry consistently votes with management, regardless of the impact on share value. A major IRRC report recently stated:

> A major insurance company that had established a policy of voting proxies against "fair price" provisions reversed itself under pressure from several of its largest corporate clients.
>
> Another insurance company, owned by a large industrial company, had a similar, tough policy but is now being advised by its parent company on how to vote on antitakeover amendments—in most cases based solely on the parent's relationships with its client.[13]

A considerable exception is the Teachers' Insurance and Annuity Association and the College Retirement Equity Fund (known universally as TIAA-CREF), the retirement fund for college professors and administrators and other employees of nonprofit institutions. With over $80 billion in assets invested in virtually all sectors of the U.S. economy and in the economies of 26 foreign countries, TIAA-CREF is a prominent presence in the financial arena. It includes both insurance and mutual fund components. TIAA-CREF is the institution that most closely approximates the ideal institutional shareholder, as is clear from a few introductory words from its own 1990 publication, *TIAA-CREF: A Concerned Investor:*

> TIAA-CREF management and trustees have always emphasized the need for careful examination of the pension system's investments and their relationship to various shareholder issues, both social and economic. As a shareholder in some 2,400 companies, CREF exercises both a right and a responsibility in voting shareholder proxies, since the outcome of such votes can affect investment values. Concern with, and participation in, issues affecting its operating environment is consistent with TIAA- CREF's own corporate mission, which stems from Andrew Carnegie's recognition that retirement security for educators is important public policy.[14]

As you would expect from an institution having notably educated and concerned individuals as a constituency, TIAA-CREF has exemplified thoughtful presentation of both the financial and the social issues of concern to shareholders. Over 20 years ago, TIAA-CREF decided that the time had arrived to challenge the "Wall Street Rule" of sell or vote with management with respect to its 608,700 shares of General Motors.

In explaining CREF's new policy, Chairman William Greenough wrote GM CEO James Roche:

> Much is said of maximization of profits as if it is a concept incompatible with improvements in the quality of life. Not at all—especially not in the long run. . . . We want and expect the companies in which TIAA and CREF invest to take leading roles in solving economic and social problems related to the products these companies produce. We are confident that this will be the only way to maximize the long-range profitability of those companies and justify our continuing investment in them as a means of enhancing retirement security of college teachers.[15]

In the years since, TIAA-CREF has been innovative and imaginative—but always low-key—in exercising its ownership responsibilities. Dr. Clifford Wharton, the highly respected chief executive of TIAA-CREF, told a distinguished audience at Northwestern University in November 1990 that the existing legal and regulatory structure does not at all accommodate the needs of owners and managers. If a legitimate and effective institutional presence can emerge as an essential long-term element in the governance of American corporations, certainly TIAA-CREF—on account of its tradition, its leadership, and its constituencies—will play a leading role. Otherwise, the prospects for constructive involvement by the insurance industry are poor.

Universities and Foundations:
The Ivory Tower

Universities and foundations are institutional shareholders because they are usually funded through endowments. People contribute to a fund, and the interest that fund generates is used for whatever charitable or educational purpose the endowment permits. The J. Paul Getty Trust has $3.98 billion. The Ford Foundation has $5.83 billion, and the MacArthur Foundation (the one that gives out the "genius grants") has $3.13 billion. This money is put into widely diversified investments, including common stock. Nonprofit institutions are as rigorous as any other investor in making sure their investments produce high returns. But they have not been rigorous about exercise of ownership rights.

Universities teach ethics, and charities fund efforts to promote a higher level of conduct, including ethical conduct. Both groups spend a lot of time thinking about the best ways to use the income generated from their endowments to achieve these goals. But it is rare for them to consider their own ethical responsibilities in connection with the governance of the companies they invest in. Sometimes the universities taught better than they knew; student protests in the 1970s over endowment investment in companies doing business in South Africa led Harvard and a group of others to found the Investor Responsibility Research Center (IRRC), a nonprofit charitable group, to research the issue.

Foundations and universities are no less subject to commercial pressures than banks and insurance companies. After all, their money comes from alumni, who are often business executives, and from businesses themselves. One study reported that in 1985 corporate contributions to American universities and colleges "surpassed donations from alumni for the first time."[16] Indeed, nonprofits are "selling" a much less tangible product, so they must be extra diplomatic. Foundation and university trustees are usually drawn from the business community. The trustees of the Ford Foundation, of Harvard, of any museum or symphony, and of the New York Public Library are usually drawn from the same list as the directors of the S&P 500. In Chapter 3 we mentioned the college whose president served as head of the compensation committee of the company headed by his chairman of the board and large contributor.

Possibly the most poignant anecdote illuminating this trend concerns the premature resignation of Henry Ford II from the Ford Foundation, of which he was a founding trustee and his family were the sole contributors. He made it clear that the policies and grants of the foundation were fundamentally so antithetical to his sensibilities that resignation was the only honorable course. Sic transit gloria $3 billion.

Employees are beneficiaries of the pension funds. Investors are the beneficiaries of mutual funds. Who are the beneficiaries of charities and endowments? At Boston University, no one seems to know. The university sunk nearly one-third of its endowment in a risky biotechnology venture, and none of the beneficiaries has standing to sue for any eventual loss to the endowment. In 1987, Boston University president John Silber—who is largely credited with turning the university into one of the best in the country academically—persuaded his board to invest $35 million in Seragen, a small biotechnology firm organized around the work of a scientist at a BU-affiliated hospital. The investment was a $25 million stake, giving BU 70 percent of the company and a $10 million loan guarantee. Since then, the university has sunk $50 million in the firm, and discussions were under way for an additional $100 million investment in the spring of 1989.

Since the 1987 investment, Seragen has produced no product and no revenues, and plans for a public offering—which would give BU some of its investment back—fizzled in the wake of the October 1987 crash. Seragen's product, a toxin to cure leukemia—and possibly AIDS and cancer—can take up to 10 years to test, and only 1 in 10 such drugs receives FDA approval. Meanwhile, BU has assumed the full cost of Seragen's day-to-day operations.[17] One BU official told *Forbes:* "It comes down to this: We've got a $1.25 million-a-month biotech habit, and there's no way we can kick it."[18]

Then, in late 1990, as Silber was running what looked like an unbeatable campaign for the governorship, Boston's public TV station revealed that nine BU trustees and two BU officers were indirect investors in a Seragen subsidiary. The subsidiary had been sold off at a huge profit, while the parent company's future continues to be uncertain. At a minimum, this raises questions of conflicts of interest.

Whoever the beneficiaries of Boston University's endowment are— whether the students, the faculty, or the administration—management of the Seragen situation does not appear to be in their interests. Nor is it in the interests of the people who contributed to the endowment in the expectation that its dividends would be used to benefit the university. One in three of the endowment's dollars is in a firm whose survival is entirely dependent on the university's continuing support, a firm that will not turn a profit until 1993 at the earliest. Yet beneficiaries are captives of the university's investment scheme; none of them has the right to sue. Apparently, the only person who might have the right to sue is the state attorney general, who could claim that the rights of the public as a whole have been violated.

In the case of Harvard College, the trustees are the self-perpetuating members of the corporation. But for whom do they act as trustees? Current students? Current faculty? Future students and faculty? The long and the short of it is that one cannot really identify any individual or class as the object of fiduciary responsibility in the context of universities. In the case of foundations, it is even more difficult, and the only obligation that can be articulated is a generalized one of concern for the human race in the long run.

Derek Bok, the conscientious and insightful president of Harvard University, has over many years deplored efforts by military and intelligence agencies and businesses to use universities for purposes of their own choosing: "Social activists press the university to use its stock...to fight against apartheid and other evils and injustices." He most eloquently stated his view of "institutional integrity" on the occasion of Harvard's 350th birthday in September 1986, objecting to those who ask the university to "risk its independence by entering into political battles or ask it to act in ways that compromise the openness and freedom that characterize a healthy research environment. In all such cases, the problem is not that people seek the university's help to solve a social problem but that they urge it to act in ways that contradict its proper nature and threaten its most essential functions."

Bok expressed similar views on the university's responsibilities as owners of stock in a letter of May 2, 1979, to me.

> If Harvard undertakes to move affirmatively to police the social and ethical practices of corporations, we cannot deny the rights of others to exercise similar responsibilities vis-à-vis our own academic activities. I do not wish to encourage this process, not because I have anything to hide, but simply because I have come to distrust the competence and objectivity of many who would be likely to undertake this work and because I cannot afford to cooperate with any more investigations than are already thrust upon us by government agencies, accrediting bodies, visiting committees and the like.

Bok's vision is of a world where the laudable objectives of education can be pursued without peripheral distraction. To be sure, American universities are not well equipped to be the leaders of activism. Whether this serves the beneficiaries of the endowment, present and future students, faculty, administration, and the community at large is one question. Whether it is necessary or merely convenient is another question. Perhaps the most important question, though, is whether society at large has any alternative better than the universities.

The Public Pension Plans: Big Daddy's Legacy

It all began on a morning in 1984, when Jesse Unruh, then the treasurer of California, read in the morning newspaper that Texaco had repurchased from the Bass brothers their 9.9 percent shareholding for $1.3 billion, a $137 million premium over the market price. He picked up the phone, called the chief investment officer of CalPERS, and asked, "Say, do we own any of that Texaco stock?"

The answer was startling: "Own any? We are one of their largest shareholders."

"Do you mean these people can elect to buy out one class of share-holder at $55 and leave the rest of us in at $35?" Unruh asked the CalPERS staff. Yes, they can, they told him. "Like hell!" said Unruh.[19]

As state treasurer, Unruh was trustee of the huge California public employees' retirement system (PERS) and the state teachers retirement system (STERS). The treasurer job was almost an afterthought in a po-litical career that spanned being JFK's "man in California" at the 1960 Democratic convention to achieving the best results of any of Ronald Reagan's four electoral opponents. In the early days of his speakership of the California House, his larger-than-life presence—both physical and political—made "Big Daddy" a natural sobriquet. The man who once said "money is the mother's milk of politics" ended his career as a trustee for the largest agglomeration of institutional assets in the world. Unruh had a world-class personality, a world-class mind, and a world-class political sense. Although he was never particularly interested in business, there seemed to him something so fundamentally wrong with Texaco "green-mailing" the Basses that his formidable creative energies began to grope for an appropriate response.

There is a reason "greenmail" sounds like "blackmail," although it is really more like extortion. Someone buys a large stake in a company and begins to make his presence known, perhaps by making noises about trying to take over the company. Management does not want him, so they offer to buy him out, at a substantial bonus over what he paid and what the stock is now trading for. But the trick is that management does not make this same offer to the other shareholders. They are stuck with what they can get in the market, which will almost certainly be less, as a result of this large cash payment being made to silence a potential dissenting voice.

This kind of payment is not in the interests of the shareholders. If someone wants to try to take over a company, there is always some value in seeing what he has to offer. How can derailing such an effort possibly be consistent with management's duties of care and loyalty? Nevertheless, greenmail was widespread during the 1980s.

Someone once said that true change comes about when what has been seen as misfortune becomes seen as injustice. Greenmail was just the right issue to drive that home. Unruh quickly perceived that greenmail was an issue that, in political terms, could be sold in Pasadena. He got in touch with the trustees of other large public funds, which are less susceptible to commercial pressure than private plans. At this time,

I was serving as the principal federal official in charge of the private pension system under ERISA and had begun to speak about the need for pension trustees to act like owners. Unruh and I met in Chicago on an August night when the temperature never got below 100 degrees. He described his notion of an association of institutional owners that would meet periodically to develop an ownership agenda and to provide a forum for learning about ownership issues. And so, the very Republican federal pension official and the very Democratic state treasurer agreed that the interests of fiduciary owners transcended partisan politics, and we worked together to promote these issues until Unruh's death a few years ago.

This was the beginning of the Council of Institutional Investors. At one of the first meetings of the council, cochairman Roland Machold, the executive director of the New Jersey funds, presented the Shareholder Bill of Rights, a comprehensive statement of the core beliefs of the ownership group.

The Shareholder Bill of Rights

Preamble

American corporations are the cornerstones of the free enterprise system, and as such must be governed by the principles of accountability and fairness inherent in our democratic system. The shareholders of American corporations are the owners of such corporations, and the directors elected by the shareholders are accountable to the shareholders. Furthermore, the shareholders of American corporations are entitled to participate in the fundamental financial decisions which could affect corporate performance and growth and the long range viability and competitiveness of corporations. This Shareholder Bill of Rights insures such participation and provides protection against any disenfranchisement of American shareholders.

I. One Share—One Vote

Each share of common stock, regardless of its class, shall be entitled to vote in proportion to its relative share in the total common stock equity of the corporation. The right to vote is inviolate and may not be abridged by any circumstance or by any action of any person.

II. Equal and Fair Treatment for All Shareholders

Each share of common stock, regardless of its class, shall be treated equally in proportion to its relative share in the total common stock equity of the corporation, with respect to any dividend, distribution, redemption, tender or exchange offer. In matters reserved for shareholder action, procedural fairness and full disclosure is required.

III. Shareholder Approval of Certain Corporate Decisions

A vote of the holders of a majority of the outstanding shares of common stock, regardless of class, shall be required to approve any corporate decision related to the finances of a company which will have a material effect upon the financial position of the company and the position of the company's shareholders; specifically, decisions which would:

A. Result in the acquisition of 5 percent or more of the shares of common stock by the corporation at a price in excess of the prevailing market price of such stock, other than pursuant to a tender offer made to all shareholders;

B. Result in, or is contingent upon, an acquisition other than by the corporation of shares of stock of the corporation having, on a pro-forma basis, 20 percent or more of the combined voting power of the outstanding common shares or a change in the ownership of 20 percent or more of the assets of the corporation;

C. Abridge or limit the rights of the holders of common shares to:
  1. Consider and vote on the election or removal of directors or the timing or length of their term of office or;
  2. Make nominations for directors or propose other action to be voted upon by shareholders or;
  3. Call special meetings of shareholders to take action by written consent or;

D. Permit any executive officer or employee of the corporation to receive, upon termination of employment, any amount in excess of two times that person's average annual compensation for the previous three years, if such payment is contingent upon an acquisition of shares of stock of the corporation or a change in the ownership of the assets of the corporation;

E. Permit the sale or pledge of corporate assets which would have a material effect on shareholder values;

F. Result in the issuance of debt to a degree which would leverage a company and imperil the long-term viability of the corporation.

IV. Independent Approval of Executive Compensation and Auditors

The approval of at least a majority of independent directors (or if there are fewer than three such directors, the unanimous approval of all such outside directors) shall be required to approve, on an annual basis:

A. The compensation to be provided to each executive officer of the corporation, including the right to receive any bonus, severance or other extraordinary payment to be received by such executive officer; and

B. The selection of independent auditors.

It all came down to one principle: that informed shareholders should, proportional to their invested capital at risk, have the right to approve fundamental corporate actions.

Unruh's greatest legacy was his articulation of ownership responsibility as something our nation desperately needed. It seems particularly appropriate that leadership has been exercised by those following him at CalPERS. Significant change is apt to involve a very few key individuals. The chief executive officer of PERS, Dale Hanson, and its general counsel, Rich Koppes, are perhaps the most important. The affable Hanson had spent his entire career in the Wisconsin retirement system before being chosen by the PERS trustees in 1987; Koppes' service was in the health care sector of California state government.

The public servant against the corporate executive has a "David and Goliath" air about it. Few state governments have the staying power to challenge a major local corporation. We have already discussed in Chapter 4, the number of states that enacted special legislation to protect a particular company. But California is larger than any single corporation. So Hanson was able, for example, to ask for a change in the board of directors of Lockheed, an important California corporation. Hanson and Koppes routinely press the ownership agenda in conferences with executives and lawyers who earn as much in a month (in some cases, in a week) as they do in a year. Their strength is not in how much money they make, but in how much they manage and—even more important—in the patient, credible, and effective presentation of their agenda. This explains why they are the leaders in a cause that is of equal interest to all other owners.

It is fitting that the people most outspoken on the issue of accountability are themselves supremely accountable. Hanson is very conscious of the fact that he works for the 13 trustees of CalPERS, and Koppes is equally conscious of the fact that he works for the same trustees, as well as for Hanson. The PERS board meets monthly in sessions that can last three or four days. Trustees are hardworking and unpaid. The board includes a majority who are appointed—nominees of the governor and representatives of other elected officials, the state treasurer, and the controller, totaling seven. The other six are elected representatives of the active and retired participants in the system.

The critical element in the board's capacity to represent long-term membership interest is exemplified by the current president, Bill Ellis, a member for 15 years. Not only does he provide needed continuity, but his personal commitment that "the members' interest takes precedence" is reflected in every aspect of the process and substance of the board's activities. Ellis is always aware that he represents real people in contrast to abstract legal principles.

During a meeting in February 1990 at the Treasury Department in Washington, Hanson was asked by undersecretary Bob Glauber, "What is the secret? How can we create other boards like CalPERS?" At its core, the PERS board is grounded in the societal consciousness that ensures the compatibility of private power and the public good. The weight and tenacity of the PERS board is a reflection of the combination of constituencies representing current political concerns and the focused interest of the public employees, the character of the trustees, the willingness to commit long hours to a vast agenda, relative immunity from commercial pressures, and a competent and well-led professional staff.

CalPERS has $58 billion and expects to have more than $200 billion by the year 2000. Most of its equity securities are invested in index funds, as close to a permanent investment in the 1,500 largest American corporations as there is. This kind of trustee is a long-term owner of corporate America, who can be relied on to exercise the "legendary supervisory role" of the shareholder that James Willard Hurst talked about.

Dale Hanson was a compromise choice of a badly split board; it is testament to his skill and his collegial sensitivity that he has been able to get virtually unanimous support from the board for a careful but far-reaching agenda of corporate governance. Once a year, PERS adopts a corporate governance plan. The current plan identifies three major goals: to ensure that shareholders have the ability to select freely the best directors; to ensure that a company's directors have the ability to fully and competently supervise the managers; and to promote shareholder participation in those areas that represent a potential conflict between the interests of directors and managers and the interests of shareholders.

PERS pursues these goals, in part, by submitting shareholder resolutions to companies of particular concern, to be included on the company's proxy material. Some submitted in the past and expected this year include confidential voting of proxies, submitting poison pills to shareholders for their approval, and creation of shareholder advisory committees, the better to permit ownership-coordinated action. CalPERS works hard to be cooperative. The letters accompanying its proposals invite each company's chief executive officer to meet with them to discuss ways in which PERS's concerns could be met without the need to pursue the shareholder proposal. Hanson's style is patient and direct. PERS withdrew proposals to create a shareholder advisory committee at TRW and Occidental Petroleum because management promised to provide an improved level of communication. "To the extent that PERS' goal is to improve the responsiveness of company management to shareholder concerns, a corporate willingness to compromise represents an even greater indicator of 'success.' The vote results with respect to those shareholder proposals in which the companies were unwilling to compromise . . . create pressure for the companies to recognize the large number of shareholders who share a common concern."[20]

Hanson and Koppes have a good perspective. Between the two of them, they participate in almost all of the academic projects targeting governance; they are the prime movers in institutions such as the Council of Institutional Investors; and they encourage, support, and cajole the energies of other funds and activists in the area. Above all else, they are thoughtful and professional in dealing with company managements. They do not want to run the companies; they are attempting to restore some level of monitoring to the corporate system.

PERS is only one of hundreds of public pension plans serving employees of states and cities, including everyone from the public school teachers and the librarians to the firefighters, police officers, dog catchers, state legislators, mayors, and governors. Each one is different. Hanson was selected by trustees, themselves selected by elected officials and by the beneficiaries of the system. New York's Edward Regan is elected, one of only four statewide office holders.

As the elected candidate of the State of New York, Ned Regan is in the extraordinary position of being the sole trustee for the state's common retirement fund. He also is a fiduciary for the state teacher's pension plan. There have been repeated proposals in the legislature in recent years—Ned Regan's among them—to create a more traditionally composed board. This "power" of Ned Regan drew a hostile reaction in the 1990 elections when his Democratic opponent Carol Bellamy revealed that Carl Icahn was a huge contributor and fund raiser for her campaign. Icahn was openly angry that Regan had voted against him and with Texaco management in the 1988 proxy contest. The comptroller is a thoughtful expert in governance matters and has authored several well-received articles on the subject. Regan has been so prudent in the exercise of his authority that there seems little public interest in taking it away.

New Jersey's Roland Machold is a bureaucrat, a civil servant, and an important contributor to the development of the Council of Institutional Investors. New York City's pension plan, for a long time under the jurisdiction of Harrison J. Goldin, a brilliant finance expert, is now run by former congresswoman Elizabeth Holtzman, who was also elected to the office and has brought her own perspective, with more emphasis on corporate performance. Each system produces different perspectives and priorities, yet there has been remarkable consistency in vision and goals in governance matters.

The 1,000-Pound Gorilla:
The Federal Employees' Retirement System

Until 1986, employees of the U.S. government did not have a funded pension plan. The money would go in today, deducted from the paychecks of current employees, and it would go out tomorrow, to current retirees. The passage of the Federal Employees' Retirement System Act of 1986 (FERSA)[21] was, according to *Newsweek,* the biggest unreported story of the year. The reason it was unreported is obvious. The title alone contains at least three words that put people to sleep faster than Mandrake the Magician. And its purpose—creation of a funded retirement plan for federal employees—seemed unobjectionable in purpose and irrelevant to anything outside of Washington. But the statute is of unparalleled importance as a legislative accomplishment and for its inevitable impact on the stock market and the economy. As *Newsweek* said, the fund created by the statute may become "the largest lump of investment capital ever known, a wad that—if its managers so desire—has the clout to make or break huge companies, even national economies."[22] The *Washington Post* called it "a leap into the unknown," adding: "At once it creates a new source of investment capital and a new benefit for federal workers, while at least holding the potential to become an administrative nightmare, a political football, a way of cheating on deficit reduction or a temptation for Congress to play the stock market."[23]

This legislation was fueled by hopes of reducing the deficit. The total pension payout to nonmilitary employees was $26.7 billion annually.[24] More than 25 percent of the federal payroll was going to pay people who were retired. The new statute reduced the federal cost to 22 percent of payroll.[25] More important, it funneled a substantial portion of the outlay into government securities and changed part of the plan from defined benefit (like Social Security, where the benefit is established without referring to how much the employee put into the fund) to defined contribution (where the return on the employer's and employee's contributions to the plan determine the payout). The system is set up so that in its first few years, the investments mostly go into government securities, but as time goes by, more and more of them will go into common stock.

In a world of 900-pound gorillas, where a small pension fund controls $100 million and the top 20 pension funds control $621.8 billion,[26] the FERS fund will soon be a 1,000-pound gorilla. The provision for lending the funds to employees for home purchase, education, or emergency may turn this program into one of the largest lending institutions in the country.

The federal government has thus had to consider in careful detail the question of its involvement as shareholder in private companies. During the legislative proceedings, concerns were raised about either Congress or the President being able to bring political influence to bear on large pools of thrift plan money.[27] The system was designed to prevent this kind of manipulation by use of an index fund. The government therefore established the unmistakable policy that pension funds for the benefit of federal employees may be administered only for the interest of participants and that equity investments will be made only by formula, to eliminate entirely the possibility of discretionary involvement by federal officials.[28]

The federal government carried over this policy of disinvolvement into the area of appropriate shareholder conduct. The statute prohibits the board from exercising voting rights associated with ownership of securities in the thrift fund, finding: "It is inappropriate for the federal government or its employees to vote these securities."[29] Who should do it, then? Former Social Security commissioner Stanford G. Ross squarely raised this question in his testimony before the Senate committee considering the legislation.[30] The conference rejected the proposal in the Senate draft for a specially elected employee advisory committee to vote the fund's shares and otherwise act as owner, and just said that it shouldn't be a federal employee.

Social Investing, Part I:
"But the Pension Fund Was Just Sitting There!"

It is a truth universally acknowledged that a large pot of money set aside and dubbed inviolate will immediately be subject to all kinds of assaults. A pot of money the size of the pension funds could not escape notice. As *Doonesbury*'s Uncle Duke put it, "But the pension fund was just sitting there!" Although the laws creating public and private pension funds speak in traditional trust law terms of singleness of purpose in protecting and enhancing the value of the fund, that pot of money has been an irresistible target for policy initiatives. The traditional trust concept of an undivided duty of loyalty may not be possible in the context of pension funds, where both fiduciaries and beneficiaries are so divided in needs, priorities, and responsibilities.

Social investing is the term most often used for these activities, which cover a wide range of issues and methods. As we use it, *social investing* means making investment decisions, and other decisions relating to the exercise of stock ownership rights, on grounds that are unrelated to or in addition to the traditional investment concerns of minimizing risk and maximizing return. These investments are made because they are thought to provide intangible "quality of life" benefits to the pension plan participants and the community as a whole.

Social investing thus includes divestment from companies (otherwise investment-worthy) doing business in or with South Africa, for example. It also includes sponsoring or supporting shareholder resolutions opposing the sale of baby formula in third-world countries, the manufacture of materials for the Strategic Defense Initiative, or loans to Chile, or resolutions supporting the adoption of the Sullivan principles (equal rights in South Africa), the MacBride principles (equal rights for Protestants and Catholics in Northern Ireland), or company-specific initiatives on comparable worth and equal employment. And it includes investment in securities that might otherwise not meet investment criteria for risk and return, such as city employees' pension fund investments in the city's municipal bonds. Jesse Jackson's economic recovery program, widely distributed during his presidential campaign, was founded on the use of public pension plan funds for programs such as low-income housing, the investments to be federally guaranteed.

Social investing usually involves selling off stock in a company to protest specific activities, such as doing business in South Africa, or buying securities that would otherwise not meet standards for risk and return, such as local municipal bonds. Sometimes social investing involves exercise of ownership rights, like submitting shareholder resolutions. An unusual example of social policy–related financial management was the State of Pennsylvania's boycott of Shearson Lehman Hutton in 1988. Shearson was assisting in the takeover of the Pittsburgh company Koppers, a takeover many people feared would lead to huge layoffs. Shearson was not only acting as investment banker for the acquiring firm, but had loaned it $500 million and had agreed to acquire 46 percent of Koppers for itself if the takeover was successful.

Although the state had invested in Koppers common stock, it did not have enough to stop the takeover, so the state did what it could to influence the deal. State treasurer G. Davis Greene, Jr. suspended all state business activities (including bond business) with Shearson and its subsidiaries. Although this did not include any state pension fund investment business, a newspaper article reported that three subsidiaries of Shearson were eliminated from consideration for management of state pension fund assets.[31] One state official was quoted as saying that Shearson managers could submit bids, "but they would have a hard row to hoe." The takeover was ultimately completed in a manner that satisfied the state's concerns, and the suspension was removed.

Social investing is the result of the clash of two competing policies. We want to guarantee workers a retirement income, and to do that the laws speak the language of trust law. But employees want to retire into a world free from pollution and injustice. And why should their money be used to support something they oppose?

As already noted, trust law did not contemplate a group of beneficiaries as large and diverse as ERISA plan participants. The interests of young workers, workers nearing retirement, and retirees are quite different— even in conflict. A young worker might consider that social investing that ensures his continued employment is in his best interest. A retiree is looking for benefits right now. Some beneficiaries may consider it worthwhile to limit their returns and support divestment from companies doing business with South Africa. Others may feel that, for them, that trade-off is not justified, but other kinds of social investments are.

For defined contribution plans, where the workers put in a set amount and get back whatever the returns add up to, there is a stronger argument for allowing beneficiaries to make social investing decisions. Indeed, some pension funds give employees a choice among various investments, including one that is South Africa–free. The problem here is one of logistics—how do you select and present the choices? Social investing is based on the most personal moral priorities. If there is a way for an individual to make the decision, with the resulting investment still likely to produce a reasonable return relative to the other options, it should be permitted.

A defined benefit plan presents more problems. Under such plans, the company promises to pay a certain benefit. It may not be possible to allow individual plan participants to make social investing decisions because they are not the ones who will feel the consequences. The only option here is to choose between what some commentators refer to as "two prudent investments of equal financial merit." A typical suggestion is that, in deciding between two such investments, "trustees should be able to choose the investment offering the more desirable indirect benefits to the pension fund or the greater benefit to its participants' community."[32] But is there such a thing as "two prudent investments of equal financial merit"? Even if there is, it is more prudent per se to spread the risk by dividing the investment between the two. Divestment requirements limit the fund's ability to diversify, however, and they may skew the investments away from particular categories of investments, such as large capitalization companies, which because of their size are more likely to do business internationally. Defined benefit plans do not permit the key element necessary for social investing: a way for the people who pay the price to make the decision.

Public plans, more in the political spotlight and more accessible to political maneuvering than private plans, have been more aggressive at pursuing social goals through the use of pension fund assets. Public funds are confronted with the same issues that government agencies face in any commercial endeavor. The government is not just a party to a contract, even one as much a part of the ordinary course of business as the purchase of supplies or the managing of pension fund assets. The federal government puts dozens of restrictions on grant money that have nothing to do with the purpose of the grant but promote other policy initiatives. Anyone building a highway with federal funds, for example, must certify that the construction company does not discriminate on the basis of race, sex, age, religion, national origin, or handicap, and that it meets certain other standards with regard to, for example, wages and environmental impact. The theory is that the government should not be promoting policy goals with one effort and subverting them with another. Despite the fact that compliance with each of these restrictions imposes costs (in addition to the costs of certifying compliance), there is some finding, through the political process, that the trade-off is worth it.

The same thinking has led to decisions—some legislative, some not—that public pension funds should not, for example, invest in companies doing business in South Africa. Such policies are likely to limit the return to the fund (and the payout to retirees, and the risk to taxpayers, who must take up the slack if the fund falls short of its obligations). Some of these policies speak in terms of "two prudent investments of equal financial merit," a standard whose problems we have already addressed. Others are designed to disregard or supersede the risk and return considerations. At some level, a trade-off is made.

The question is whether it is made by the right person, at the right level. By that, we again mean those who pay the price—the pension plan beneficiaries themselves, either directly or through agents with some accountability. Legislators are the only people in a position to amend a statutory mandate to maximize returns, and they may not be reelected if their social policy initiatives are inconsistent with the social goals of the electorate. From that perspective, they are in the best position to make the trade-offs.

But other aspects of their special role with regard to pension funds make them less suitable. The prospect of taking political action with no quantifiable, short-term budgetary impact is just too tempting. And because the expenses are off-budget, at least when they are made, there is a real risk of action being taken without careful thought.

The clearest example of this is the differing policies of the New Jersey, New York City, and New York State pension funds. The New Jersey fund, required by state law to divest, ended up selling out of two New Jersey pharmaceutical companies whose only dealing with South Africa was the sale of medicine used exclusively by blacks. This policy fails on moral grounds, by any standard. It fails on fiscal grounds, too. The *Wall Street Journal* estimated that the divestment policy has cost the plan \$330–\$515 million in two years.[33] This is no different from taking as much as \$515 million out of the state budget and spending it on a program that at least in this case, cannot be said to be successful. This should be seen as an expenditure, subject to the same procedural protections and deliberations as other expenditures of public funds.

Divestment can also interfere with the pursuit of other important goals. The California Public Employees' Retirement System and Texaco have worked together to achieve unprecedented progress in achieving corporate governance goals, which benefit all shareholders. CalPERS is obligated by state law to sell out of Texaco, however, cutting short an effort that has been immensely productive. Pennsylvania PSERS, which worked with CalPERS on the Texaco bankruptcy committee and supported Texaco management during Carl Icahn's proxy contest, was also required to divest its Texaco stock. The divestiture requirement is limiting the pension fund's ability to work for goals that protect and enhance the value of its shares.

The city of New York, on the other hand, adopted a more flexible policy on South Africa. It began by writing letters to express its concerns and then sponsored and supported a number of shareholder resolutions calling for companies to adopt the Sullivan principles, a commitment to providing equal opportunity in their South African facilities. They sold out of a limited number of companies that they determined had business dealings that promoted apartheid, like those who do business with the police and military there. This more flexible approach is clearly the better way to promote the two social goals of protection of pension benefits and protection of human rights.

The New York State and Local Retirement Systems take a third approach to this issue. Confronted each year with a legislative proposal that would require it to divest its portfolio of stock in companies doing business in South Africa, valued between \$3.9 and \$9.2 billion, Edward V. Regan, the Systems' sole fiduciary, formulated an alternative plan. Rather than selling their shares, the Systems used them to commence a massive program of shareholder resolutions calling for divestment from South Africa. Regan's view is that mandated sale of stocks (for any reason) would impose unreasonable financial costs on the portfolio and force higher contributions from the taxpayers. By use of the shareholder franchise, he has negotiated results with the companies, thus meeting the objectives of divestment legislation without incurring the significant financial losses of such a program.

Social policy initiatives from pension funds have clearly been based on special-interest politics. This is not to suggest that the interests have been illegitimate; certainly, opposition to apartheid is an essential moral obligation of our time. However, the intersection of pensions and politics has led to peculiar consequences. There are countries with worse human rights abuses than South Africa, and yet we do not see them as targets of these initiatives.[34] There is no reason to believe that divestment is a more effective means of stopping apartheid than other avenues. Many thoughtful people, inside South Africa and outside, have argued that staying in the companies and working through them to improve the opportunities for black South Africans is more worthwhile.[35]

And there have been challenges to social investing. An important distinction in deciding these cases seems to be whether the challenged provision permits or requires the investment. A New York State pension fund invested in Municipal Assistance Corporation bonds, which were issued by New York City to protect itself from bankruptcy. This investment, legislatively mandated, was invalidated on the grounds that it violated the state constitution's prohibition against "impairing" the benefits of pension plan participants.[36] On the other hand, the New York City teachers fund's challenge to the law permitting their fund to invest in the MAC securities was not successful: "Under the unique circumstances presented—in which the survival of 'the fund as an entity' necessarily achieved prominence—the trustees' investment decision was such as to fulfill their fiduciary obligations to the [retirement system]."[37]

A Michigan state law requiring state-run colleges to divest from companies doing business in South Africa was also struck down because it encroached on investment decisions that were the sole province of the school's regents.[38]

Public plans also risk losing their tax-exempt status by making investments on other than strict financial grounds. Several proposals for a public-plan version of ERISA have been introduced, but state and local governments have been successful so far in keeping control over the public plans. These plans are subject to some federal standards, however: to maintain their tax-exempt status, they must comply with IRS requirements that have come to be known as "creeping ERISA" because of their reference to ERISA language on fiduciary obligation.[39]

As a practical matter, public funds advocating social policies will find themselves in opposition not only to private investors but also to the fiduciaries of the private pension system, who are obligated under ERISA to consider exclusively the interests of plan participants and beneficiaries in their management of plan assets. The question, then, might be posed this way: Is there a useful purpose in having public plans propose a social agenda when it appears clear that a substantially larger shareholder block will be obligated to oppose it?

Those who hope to use pension fund assets to promote social policies have one important commitment and two important opportunities. Their commitment is to the funds themselves and to the beneficiaries whose investment they manage. They must therefore be utterly scrupulous in making sure that their investments provide the greatest possible protection for retirement income. But this does not mean that they have to ignore social concerns. Social goals can pay off. There is some evidence that "good guy" funds perform as well or better than funds managed without regard to social policy issues.[40] Investment policies can be designed to reflect direct benefits from social investing.[41] Pension funds have an important opportunity to create value through socially motivated investments, and they should do so.

An equally important opportunity is for pension funds to promote welfare through exercise of their rights as owners. Shareholder resolutions calling for specific action can be more effective—and more cost-effective—than divestment. Pension funds can sponsor and support resolutions drafted for an individual company's situation. They can meet with management to discuss various options. Together, they can work for solutions that do well by doing good.

Social Investing, Part II:
Whose Money's Worth?

If politicians and others with a social policy agenda were the first to recognize the potential uses of pension fund money, corporate management was right behind them. If pension fund money can be used to bail out New York City, they reasoned, why can't we use it as well? What social policy goals could possibly be as important as the economic system of our own community? The issue here, again, is who decides what those goals are and how should they be implemented?

One of the most comprehensive examples of this second wave of social policy initiatives was the 1989 report prepared by the New York

State Task Force On Pension Fund Investment, established by Governor Mario Cuomo. This is the clearest example of an effort by politicians and representatives of business to consider how they can use state pension money. Although this kind of inquiry is useful and important, and other states have examined this issue without abandoning their primary commitment to state employees and retirees, we believe that the Cuomo commission recommendations shift the focus of the pension fund from retirement security for state employees to job security for state corporate management.

The report included recommendations on the role public pension funds should play in the economy and the way they should respond to the increasingly complex issues they face as fiduciaries and as shareholders. Its recommendations would permit a wider range of investments, based on a wider range of investment objectives, which are based on a broader interpretation of the notion of beneficiaries. It called for "optimizing" rather than "maximizing" returns on behalf of "stakeholders" rather than mere "shareholders."

The task force accepts without challenge and concludes without support that public pension funds play an important role in actions such as takeovers, which harm the economy of the state, that they should therefore be used as what amounts to a subsidy program for local businesses, and that doing so will in fact benefit pension plan participants and/or the state economy.

The task force reflects some of the compromises necessary for anything produced by a committee, especially one with membership as diverse as its own. But parts of the report are downright inconsistent. For example, it recommends that shareholders use "voice" rather than "exit"—in other words, that they use their ownership rights to express their views, rather than following the Wall Street rule of selling out, if they disagree with management. As enthusiastic supporters of active involvement by shareholders in corporate governance, we agree wholeheartedly with this recommendation—until we get to the fine print, where it says that the use of "voice" should not extend to the "shareholder rights" issues, thus removing the substance of the recommendation. Without shareholder rights to establish the framework, there may be a "voice," but whose voice, and what can it say?

The task force is also vague in answering the most important question, which is whether they are recommending that pension funds be used for investments that would otherwise not be considered prudent, in hopes of benefiting the state economy. They deny making such a recommendation, but if not, what are they talking about? The task force proposes the creation of a new state agency to identify, screen, and diversify the geographic and credit risk of "investments aimed toward economic development." The problem with this recommendation is that there is really no proof that the asset managers currently employed by public pension funds are not providing this function. Indeed, it can easily be argued that the issue is not whether these kinds of investments are being identified by the funds' current asset managers, but whether any truly investment-worthy opportunities are being missed. To the extent that such investments are not being identified by the wide range of commercial asset managers, using every kind of security analysis, market analysis, and innovative structuring of investments available, they are probably not prudent investments. Setting up such an agency could indeed interfere with the market's ability to structure such investment rather than enhance it. Furthermore, similar programs have performed poorly and have been vulnerable to political manipulation and abuse.

The task force also recommends that the state provide credit enhancement of pension fund investments, additional guarantees for pension funds trying to carry out new economic development–oriented investment policies. However, there is no evidence that worthy investments are not adequately guaranteed. To the extent that the investments contemplated here are more risky, why should the state—or the taxpayers—make up the difference? It is important to remember (as if the savings and loan bailout could let us forget) that guarantee programs are not free, and can sometimes be very expensive.

We have no problem with the notion of "optimizing" returns, if that means no more than permitting pension funds to take the long-term view in analyzing their options. But the sense of the report is that the factors to be considered are so broad and so diverse that virtually any action can be justified, no matter how adverse the impact on shareholders or pension beneficiaries. Although the task force claims that it is not talking about social investing, putting money into investments that do not meet traditional standards of risk and return is, in fact, social investing, and that is precisely what it is talking about.

The task force's bias is suggested by the title of the report: *Our Money's Worth*. Who is included in "our"? It is not "our" money; it is money that has been set aside to pay retirement benefits to state employees. It is only "our money" to the extent that it is managed poorly, requiring additional tax dollars to make up the difference. Broadening the range of constituent groups whose concerns must be considered may sound appealing, but accountability to everyone is accountability to no one, and without accountability the system falls apart. The critical point missed by the task force is that the accountability provided by a strict fiduciary standard for both pension fiduciaries and corporate managers is the best guarantee not just of pension fund security, but of a strong economy.

The Sleeping Giant Stirs

It is a measure of the long-time silence of shareholders that the first steps to involvement in corporate governance have been met with such alarm. "The Big Owners Roar!" proclaimed a headline in *Fortune* last year. In fact, progress has been significant, but hardly a "roar"—more like clearing its throat.

It's just that it is such a *big* throat. Institutional investor activism would not have been possible were it not for the legendary Gilbert brothers, who cleared the path. In 1932, Lewis Gilbert attended the annual meeting of New York City's Consolidated Gas Co. Gilbert, who held only 10 shares of the company's stock, was disturbed by the chairman's refusal to recognize shareholder questions from the floor.[42] Gilbert formed a group with his brother to purchase small amounts of a company's stock and attend its meeting to introduce proposals from the floor. When the SEC adopted Rule 14a-8 in 1942, requiring companies to put shareholder resolutions to a vote, the Gilberts were able to express their corporate governance concerns directly to shareholders via the proxy process. The Gilberts focused on expanding corporate democracy and making management financially accountable to owners, with proposals on such issues as locating meetings at sites that encouraged a large attendance, issuing postseason reports, and opening up the election process.[43]

With the social upheaval of the 1960s, shareholder activism began to focus on social responsibility. In 1966, Rochester, New York, radical Saul Alinsky aimed his two-year-old FIGHT (Freedom, Integration, God, Honor—Today) organization at Kodak. FIGHT, a coalition of over 100 black groups, targeted Kodak's minority hiring record. Kodak was by no means the worst offender, but it was Rochester's largest employer, representing 13 percent of the city's work force. FIGHT was hoping for a filter-down effect by selecting Kodak. When negotiations broke down over a plan for Kodak to hire and train 600 unskilled blacks, FIGHT took the issue to shareholders by asking them to withhold their proxies, assign them to FIGHT, or vote against management. Nowhere near enough proxies were voted in favor of FIGHT for any kind of mandate, but Kodak did agree to a less stringent minority hiring program. A similar proxy contest was waged at Honeywell over the manufacture of antipersonnel weapons in 1969, led by the heir to the Pillsbury flour company fortune, Charles Pillsbury.

Shareholder activism, however, was limited by Rule 14a-8 in what it could address through the proxy process. Specifically, 14a-8(c)(7) was particularly limiting, its vague language permitting the exclusion of any proposal "relating to the conduct of the ordinary business operations of the issuer." This rule evolved after the SEC allowed Greyhound to omit a 1946 proposal to exclude a resolution that it abolish segregated seating on buses, on the grounds that the rule enabling shareholders to file proposals was not intended to permit proposals of "a general political, social, or economic nature. Other forums exist for the presentation of such views."[44]

The commission formally amended its rules in 1952 to comply with the Greyhound opinion. The SEC explained this reasoning to Congress as necessary "to confine the solution of ordinary business problems to the board of directors and place such problems beyond the competence and direction of the shareholders. The basic reason for this policy is that it is manifestly impracticable in most cases for the stockholders to decide management problems at corporate meetings."[45]

But a different direction was taken in 1970 by a U.S. Appeals Court decision, *Medical Committee for Human Rights v. SEC,* overturning the SEC decision permitting Dow Chemical to omit a proposal requesting that the board "consider the advisability of adopting a resolution setting forth an amendment to the composite certificate of incorporation of the Dow Chemical Company that the company shall not make napalm."[46] In a way, Dow lost the argument by admitting in its own materials that its napalm operations lost money. The court pointed out the hypocrisy of claiming management's exclusive authority over ordinary business when that business lost money for owners: "Management in essence decided to pursue a course of activity which generated little profit for the shareholders and actively impaired the company's public relations and recruitment activities because management considered this action morally and politically desirable."[47]

In defense of its decision, the court cited the reasoning of *SEC v. Transamerica Corp.*: "A corporation is run for the benefit of its stockholders and not for that of its managers." The court concluded: "We think that there is a clear and compelling distinction between management's legitimate need for freedom to apply its expertise in matters of day-to-day business judgment, and management's patently illegitimate claim of power to treat modern corporations with their vast resources and personal satrapies implementing personal, political or moral predilections."[48]

After this precedent was adopted by the SEC, the floodgates were opened for social proposals. The SEC usually permitted them, provided they had some claim to the economics of the company and involved a legitimate public concern. The commission refined the ruling further in 1976, stating that 14a-8(c)(7) could exclude only proposals involving business matters "that are mundane in nature and do not involve any substantial policy or other considerations."[49]

Perhaps the most famous effort by social activists was Campaign GM. In 1970, four public interest lawyers set up the Project on Corporate Responsibility to reform public corporations. They decided to attack the corporation directly because, as one of the founders explained, "regardless of new laws or consciousness, [social objectives] would not be accomplished without a commitment of our corporate institutions, which have enough power to implement or deny national goals."[50] Once again, GM was selected not because it was the worst offender but because it was a symbol for the large American public corporation.

The project decided to run Ralph Nader for the GM board, but Nader declined the offer. Instead, the project submitted shareholder proposals for GM's 1970 proxy, calling for an amendment to the corporate charter stating that GM's operations would be consistent with "public health, safety and welfare," the establishment of a shareholder committee on corporate responsibility, and the expansion of the board to allow for three public interest representatives. Within three weeks six more proposals were added concerning auto safety, pollution control, mass transit, and minority hiring, but the SEC ultimately permitted all but two to be excluded from the proxy. The remaining two—concerning a shareholder committee and the expansion of the board—were enough to make the 1970 GM meeting a spectacle. Three thousand attended the May 22 meeting, which turned into a lengthy question-and-answer session regarding GM's commitment to social issues. Although neither proposal gained 3 percent of the vote, GM went on to create a public policy committee and a special committee of scientists to monitor the corporation's effect on the environment; it also appointed an air pollution expert and its first black director to the board. The project deemed Campaign GM enough of a success to launch Round two the following year, which focused lobbying on the 20 largest institutional investors, rather than the relatively small holdings of universities that were the target of the 1970 campaign. Round two, however, was not as successful, perhaps because GM had taken steps following Round one.

Although institutional investors began with social policy proposals, the takeovers of the 1980s and the defensive actions they prompted raised concerns about the impact on share value. They were too big to follow the traditional Wall Street rule—a sale of that size could itself depress share value. And these questions went beyond disagreement with a particular management; nearly 1,000 companies adopted poison pills without shareholder approval, and no one could sell out of all of them.

In 1987, institutional investors submitted their first governance-related shareholder proposals. These proposals, many calling for poison pills (called "rights plans" by management) to be put to a shareholder vote, received substantial support—from around 25 to 30 percent. The following year, two of these resolutions received majority votes, both at companies where a contest for director seats and attendant full-scale proxy solicitation provided the momentum.[51]

In 1989, institutional shareholders joined with a large individual shareholder (and with ISS) to mount a successful full-scale proxy fight over corporate governance issues. North American Partners, the California Public School Employees' Retirement System, the Pennsylvania Public School Employees' Retirement System, and ISS cleared proxy materials through the SEC. We circulated our own proxy card, asking shareholders to join us in opposing two items submitted for management approval by shareholders. The issue was not control of the company; there was no contest for seats on the board. The issue was two proposals by management—one to classify Honeywell's board so that only one-third of the directors would be up for re-election each year, and one to eliminate the right of the shareholders to act by written consent, so that they would not be able to take action at any time other than the annual meeting.

The question raised by these proposals struck at the core of the relationship between shareholders and management; could shareholders prevent management from changing the corporate charter to reduce accountability? The answer was yes. The success of the shareholders in defeating these proposals set the stage for more collective action. Instead of waiting for a company with disappointing performance to become a takeover target, with the acquirer reaping most of the gain, shareholders found they could join forces to enhance value and engage in a productive dialogue with management. Enhanced value was clearly demonstrated at Honeywell, where the announcement of the counter-solicitation sparked a sharp rise in the share price. Although takeover rumors played a role, the market was clearly reacting to the positive impact of active shareholder involvement; the market understandably recognizes the value of large institutions holding management accountable. The increase in share price exceeded the expense of the proxy solicitation by several orders of magnitude. Activism became one of the soundest investments of the season.

In 1990, shareholder resolutions again received significant support. Two poison pill resolutions sponsored by the Wisconsin state pension fund received majority votes, without any special solicitation effort.

But perhaps the most important development of the 1990 season was the way that governance issues affected contests for control. Harold Simmons led a proxy fight at Lockheed, running on a "platform" of support for the four pending shareholder proposals at the company. At the last minute, Lockheed management announced it, too, would support the proposals. They won,[52] but so did the proposals; majority votes were received for all of them, the highest 97 percent. Carl Icahn, instead of waging a battle for board seats at USX, submitted a shareholder proposal that the company separate its oil and steel businesses and spin off to shareholders at least 80 percent of the steel business as a special dividend. Rather than attempt to acquire the company, he used his position to try to influence management to implement a restructuring.

Most shareholder resolutions have fallen into either the social policy or the governance category, but three recent resolution issues are a kind of hybrid, with aspects of both categories. They are resolutions concerning tobacco, defense contracts, and the environment. The overlap of these social issues into the economic arena was reflected by the SEC Division of Corporation Finance's reversal of its prior policy that shareholder proposals concerning tobacco products could be rejected by management. Previously, tobacco company managers were protected by 14a-8(c)(7)—permitting the omission of a proposal concerned with the conduct of ordinary business actions—from any shareholder proposal that the company divest itself of tobacco operations. Not any more. The SEC staff decided that tobacco was an issue encompassing significant social and public policy issues.

The SEC explained its decision to overturn previous rulings: "Those prior letters failed to reflect adequately the growing significance of the social and public policy issues attendant to operations involving the manufacture and distribution of tobacco related products." Former SEC commissioner Bevis Longstreth, retained by Philip Morris, complained that the SEC had, in effect, "change[d] the meaning and operation of Rule 14a-8(c)(7) as applied to practically all products and businesses, since there are very few, if any, businesses that are immune from any important issues of social and other public policy."

But the SEC found that tobacco, increasingly stigmatized by the mass public, may no longer be a great investment. Although tobacco profits are currently sustained by massive exports to the third world and Asia, American society may not tolerate such behavior in the future. Shareholders, rather than see their company decline and fall with the erosion of the tobacco market, can decide as a group whether the company would do better with a spin-off by the year 2000.[53]

One Step Forward

One of the great success stories of shareholder activism is Texaco. James W. Kinnear, the president and CEO of Texaco, has begun to restore the element of trust in relations with his shareholders, which is ironic because the modern shareholder activism movement started with Texaco, or, more specifically, with California treasurer Jesse Unruh's objection to its greenmailing of the Bass brothers in 1983. Through all of the vicissitudes of the Pennzoil litigation, the appalling course of "Texas justice," and its resulting bankruptcy, Texaco may have unfairly symbolized to some the worst fears of capitalism. Kinnear had been part of a management that paid close to $400 million in greenmail. He had been at the company when the acquisition of Getty Oil led to the most expensive litigation in history, took the company into bankruptcy, and diverted significant shareholder resources to a contest with the company's largest shareholder. As Kinnear ascended to chief executive officer, he showed a commitment to the company's shareholders. He managed to keep the company viable for the future, even when it was forced into bankruptcy, and into the settlement with Pennzoil.

The Texaco bankruptcy was unusual in many ways, first because the company had substantial assets, and no one ever expected it to really go under. Thus, the shareholders had an importance in the Texaco proceeding for which there was little precedent. So much money was involved and so many parties had important but legally different roles that high confusion was inevitable. To begin with, some of the largest shareholders were public pension plans, which were excluded from the equity committee because bankruptcy law prohibits a government agency from participating. Against the opposition of the parties, with the exception of the U.S. Trustee, the California Public Employees' Retirement System and the Pennsylvania Public School Employees' Retirement System fought their way onto the equity committee as ex officio members by obtaining a court order. They were permitted to join the committee, along with six large individual shareholders and two smaller institutions. (The company's largest shareholder, Carl Icahn, who had newly acquired 14.9 percent of the outstanding stock, declined membership on the committee when it refused to make him chairman.)

The bankruptcy proceedings provided a rare forum for public debate over the charter and bylaw provisions concerning the governance of Texaco that would emerge from the bankruptcy proceedings. Originally, all of the ownership groups were anxious that Texaco give up its takeover defenses, especially its poison pill. Several participants also had a very special notion of appropriate additions to the board—themselves!

Under bankruptcy law, management has the prerogative of proposing a plan of reorganization. Shareholders can vote for or against it; they have no right to amend or to propose alternatives. That notwithstanding, Carl Icahn asked the court to permit a vote on his reorganization proposal, which was identical with the one proposed by Texaco management except for elimination of certain antitakeover proposals. The company wanted continuing "protection"; Icahn wanted freedom for the marketplace to decide. The institutional investors withdrew their support from Icahn's proposal, and the court ruled in Texaco's favor. The judge did not permit Icahn's proposal to be voted on by the shareholders.

Both Kinnear and Icahn appeared before a special meeting of the Council of Institutional Investors to state their cases. The sentiments of those in the room were geared slightly toward Icahn, when Kinnear appeared to make the first presentation. He made three simple points that won the entire room over. First, he said that he had every penny of his own money in Texaco. There is no better guarantee of scrupulous attention to shareholder value than a CEO whose net worth depends on it, and this had an enormous impact. Second, he said Texaco would never pay greenmail again. Third, he talked about the oil business and his plans for the future once the bankruptcy was behind them. Everyone in the room could feel his commitment, his enthusiasm, his expertise. Icahn came in. He did not give any specifics about his plans for the company, and he could not claim that he put everything he had into Texaco. The group was open-minded, but he just could not compete.

One condition of the reorganization plan approved by the court was that Kinnear and the Texaco board would not oppose certain charter amendments proposed by shareholders. In fact, after meeting with shareholders, Kinnear and the board went beyond that requirement and endorsed the proposals. This willingness to consider ownership concerns was again manifest in Kinnear's later publicly soliciting and using a list of nominees provided by CalPERS as a source for a new Texaco director.

Former congressman Brademas, the president of New York University, was an unexceptionable choice for director. His name could have been proposed from almost any source. And yet Kinnear went out of his way to credit PERS as being the source and to acknowledge the importance he placed on that recommendation. From that day to this, no representative of CalPERS has exchanged a single word with director Brademas. What happened is not that a large shareholder acquired power; what happened is that a sensitive management publicly acknowledged the importance of getting director nominations from outside sources. Compared to other company reactions, such as Northrop's "The nominating committee does not consider stockholder nominees for director,"[54] one can appreciate the true value of Kinnear's small step for healthy governance.

Shareholder Proposals in 1991

As we write, shareholder proposals for 1991 have been submitted. By the time this book comes out, they will be ready to be voted on. There are more of the same resolution issues that have become standard: poison pills, confidential voting, creation of shareholder advisory committees, annual election of directors, and opting out of state antitakeover laws. There are resolutions calling for reincorporation out of Pennsylvania, in response to the passage of the new antitakeover law and the evidence on its impact on share price. There are more proposals directed at board composition and structure, calling for a majority of outside directors, for nomination committees to be made up of outside directors, or for the chairman of the board to be someone other than the CEO. New York State Common Retirement Fund already abstains from voting for 10 to 13 percent of the boards of the corporations it invests in, for the sole reason that the company's boards do not have enough independent directors.

It is increasingly clear that institutional investors are focusing their attention on the composition of boards as well. CalPERS has worked with ISS in developing a director database, with information on the directors of the S&P 500. In the fall of 1990, CalPERS wrote to each of them, asking them to verify or correct the information and asking some other questions about their roles as directors. Looking to the successful example of PRO-NED, the clearinghouse/headhunter firm for directors established by Britain's institutional shareholders, we hope that the information we are assembling will make a difference with shareholders, who can make a difference with the companies they invest in.

7

Restoration of Trust

Corporate power without accountability creates two distinct problems. The first is financial and operational: Can the products and the securities of corporations like these be competitive in the world economy, or will corporations use their political power to create enclaves of protection, as predicted by Adam Smith? The answer is exemplified by the automobile industry's Voluntary Restraint Agreement of the 1980s and the other examples in Part II of this book. Without accountability, corporations will continue to "book" profits and simply decline to compete. Finally, they will just decline.

The second problem is political. How much political legitimacy can a system of corpocracy have? Business's size, focus, and resources — access to the money and talent for persuading, lobbying, and electing — raise the question of whether we have, or can continue to have, independent government.

Concerns about the failure of corporate governance as the foundation of corporate legitimacy go back more than a half-century. Proposed solutions range from Harvard professor Michael Jensen's suggestion that we have come to the end of the time of the public company, to the "focused shareholder" approach, as when Lester Pollack and Warren Buffett acquired preferential stock as compensation for monitoring on behalf of the whole class of owners (the Cummins Engine resolution is another example), to Martin Lipton's proposal for election of boards every five years instead of annually. All of these solutions assume that, because of collective choice, "rational ignorance," or the Byzantine labyrinth of the proxy voting system, it is out of the question for shareholders to assume their "legendary supervisory role."

We agree that change is necessary to permit this "legendary supervisory role." Healthy corporations need long-term commitment from involved owners. The solution is the undiluted fiduciary obligation of corporate managers and directors to shareholders who are themselves fiduciaries—the institutions. The existence of appropriate long-term shareholders and the restoration of the law and tradition of trust would create a kind of permanent financial infrastructure along the lines of the German banks and Japanese cross-ownership. It would provide support for long-term strategies and for directors committed to shareholder interests.

The good news is that no legislative action is required to make this happen. We can think of some legislation that would make things clearer, easier, or faster, but it really is not necessary. Change must come from the corporations themselves. This cannot happen without the leadership of the private sector, the heads of the great corporations who can recreate a healthy system of governance by establishing standards of ownership with respect to the portfolio holdings of their own pension plans. These corporations are, in a sense, as much a part of a system of cross-ownership as the Japanese. If they act, as fiduciary shareholders, to bring back the accountability of the companies they invest in, on behalf of their pension participant employees, corporate governance will be based on the "care, skill, prudence, and diligence" of those who, as corporate managers, have the best, most current understanding of trends, transactions, and business.

Trustees for the public and private pension systems are the long-term holders of 20 percent of the total equity of American corporations. Their beneficiaries have definable interests that are substantially congruent with those of society as a whole. They don't just want to retire with a comfortable income; they want to retire into a world where they can breathe the air and drink the water, where the economy is stable, the streets are safe, and criminals go to jail. In exercising their fiduciary responsibilities of ownership, pension fund trustees can restore accountability and global competitiveness to American business. They can provide a strong base of support and accountability. In this chapter, we show how it can be done, and we conclude with recommendations for making it happen.

Avoiding a Global "Race to the Bottom"

Our recommendations reflect the emerging global economy. Negotiations are proceeding with the Japanese to lower all manner of barriers to free trade. Among these are obstacles to access to capital markets and, ultimately, to control over corporations. At the same time we are trying to harmonize our governance notions with the Far East, the European Community (EC) is rapidly trying to develop common governance standards in anticipation of its 1992 consolidation. (Compare this to our own "race to the bottom" system of state control of corporate law.) Since EC rules will apply to all nations—our own as well as Japan—who wish to acquire companies located within the Community, they represent a kind of "world law of governance." This has required accommodation of the very different circumstances and legal structures now existing in the member states, such as the polar positions of the United Kingdom and Germany, so the compromises may well be precursor to how the United States, Japan, and the rest of the industrialized world ultimately decide to conduct their international governance. The principles underlying the emerging EC rules have been succinctly stated by Booz-Allen in a study submitted to the XVth Directorate in January 1990.

The Seven Principles of the EC

In our view, seven key principles should guide the development of a European Model for takeovers. They stem from the principles of a modern European democracy applied by analogy to the micro world of corporations and takeovers.

1. *"Ownership Democracy"*: This means that majority (51%) should rule. There should exist mechanisms both for control and changes of control to ensure, for example, that defense measures are sanctioned by a majority.

2. *"Periodic Reendorsement of Control Restrictions"*: The possibility of self-imposing limitations/restrictions to control structures (agreement rights, preemptive rights, . . .) should be available provided they are originally enacted, and periodically reendorsed, by a majority.

3. *"No Institutional Self-Control"*: Mechanisms whereby companies control themselves either directly (self-control) or indirectly (subsidiaries owning shares in parent, cross and circular ownership within same group) should be banned: they are unhealthy by definition.

4. *"Equal Opportunity for Shareholders"*: This principle ensures that all shareholders are treated fairly in that they all benefit from value

creation either as recipients of dividends/stock appreciation or as stock sellers in a takeover bid. . . .

5. *"Mutual Transparency":* All stakeholders should be accountable to each other; specifically, full disclosure of management accounts, free access to shareholder lists, disclosure of shareholders agreements, percentage holdings above certain thresholds and the like should be common practice in all Member States.

6. *"No Internal EC-Discrimination":* Executing a takeover in any of the Member States should be possible for any EC company under an "equal national treatment" principle.

7. *"Common Front to non-EC Countries":* As far as practicable, Member States should adopt a common policy vis-a-vis non-EC companies acquiring in the EC.

The United States and Britain are unusual in the industrialized world because public equity markets exist in which control over the listed companies can be acquired at an attractive price. In both countries, rules and governance norms have been developed to conform to the continuing existence of a market for the transfer of corporate control. As the European Community gains momentum, Britain must come to grips with the incompatibility of its governance structure with those of other Community members, where public markets involving access to corporate control do not exist. It now seems probable, for example, that its "takeover code," an immensely successful mechanism for coping with the potential for inequity in takeover situations, will be subsumed into a Community-wide requirement for formal legislation and a court-monitored system. Britain has to cope with the arithmetic of being in a unique situation, and part of the price it pays for membership in the Community will be loss of its distinctive governance institutions.

Similarly, it is unlikely that the United States, in its ongoing negotiations with Japan concerning nontariff barriers to trade, will be able to change the *keiretsu* system by which dominant voting power is retained in the "nonpublic" corporate constituents. Both Britain and the United States are presently confronting the reality that all other significant industrialized countries, lacking a pattern of publicly accessible portions of corporate equity, will need to have a different system of ensuring the compatibility of corporate power and the public interest. This presents three choices: we will continue to be different, they will change to become more like us, or we will change to become more like them. We cannot continue to be different. If we continue to live in a world where our currency and credit are relatively weak and control of our corporations can be acquired by anybody with enough money, we will quickly lose control over our industrial base. Our only protection would be recourse to political action; for example, the President could determine that a particular acquisition is contrary to the national interest. In turn, this would inevitably lead to erection of barriers elsewhere. Conceivably, as the post–World War II generation of corporate entrepreneurs dies and Japanese and German ownership patterns "mature," larger percentages of total share capital will be available in public markets. It does seem doubtful, however, that the significant percentage—in the range of 20 percent—held by the German banks and the Japanese *keiretsu* will disperse, at least so long as their governance practices continue to correlate with success in international competitiveness.

That leaves a choice between making them more like us or making ourselves more like them. There is no conclusive evidence as to which school of thought best serves the long-term interests of a democratic society. The German/Japanese model, where accountability is internal within a financial/industrial grouping, runs the risk of "inefficiency." Close ties between companies and financial and industrial affiliates raise questions of conflict of interest between equity holders and lenders on the one hand, and between equity holders and "group" members providing goods and services on the other. The involvement of banks as industrial operators can lead to an undesirable concentration of power.

The inefficiency of the system of accountability to public shareholders is documented throughout this book. What does seem to work, though, is accountability to a category of "permanent" shareholders, whether the public shareholders of the United Kingdom, the banks of Germany, or the cross-ownership of Japan. In the United States, the institutional investors, particularly the pension funds, can play that role.

The key to effective accountability today appears to be the existence of a class of "permanent" owners, holding approximately one-quarter of the outstanding equity, who have an incentive to monitor the operations of the corporation. This is essentially the system in Germany, Britain, and Japan. As both corporate operations and ownership seem likely to become increasingly transnational, the need for countries to be able to assert a purely national interest becomes more acute. In the United States, encouraging a pattern of domestic institutional ownership will be a way of ensuring the continuance of effective governance. The challenge, then, for the United States is to identify its "permanent" shareholder institutions and to ensure that they have the incentive and the ability to perform the monitoring function. This involves at the outset a clear expression of national policy so that the trustee institutions can assert authority and allocate resources within the parameters of their risk-averse nature. It further involves a need to clarify the desirability of institutions acting collectively in discharging their ownership responsibilities. At this point, the United States will have an institutional governance structure finely attuned to the competitive challenges of the world of the 1990s and beyond.

Corporate Governance in the 1990s and Beyond

The Institutional Monitor

After all, the monitoring financial institutions of which we speak are themselves corporations with disperse owners. Why should they not succumb to the same agency problems that affect public corporations? As a realistic matter, they often will succumb. But as long as their agency difficulties do not correlate with those difficulties afflicting the industrial companies in which they own stock, then beneficial monitoring could occur. The auditing analogy is again instructive. It suggests that an outside monitor without day-to-day operational involvement can provide a check often enough to be worthwhile.

Mark J. Roe

Source: "Legal Restraints on Ownership and Control of Public Companies," paper presented at "The Structure and Governance of Enterprise" conference, Harvard University, March 29–31, 1990, p. 30.

All of the ingredients now exist for the reestablishment of a traditional system of trust on which an ongoing and productive system of corporate governance can be built. The essential elements are a stable base of permanent shareholders represented by trustees who exercise care and loyalty. We will begin with the trustees and the emerging federal law of ownership that guides the way they function, then discuss the shareholders and the appropriate substantive agenda.

So far, no legislative or judicial thought has been given to how ERISA trustees should function as "owners" of portfolio companies. During the 11 years of Congressional consideration of this extraordinarily important statute, it was briefly recognized that ERISA funds would be very large—would indeed be the largest holders of American equity securities—but no specific attention was focused on the responsibilities of ownership.

Had they thought about it, they might have asked some of these questions: Should ERISA trustees follow the time-honored Wall Street rule and sell securities in companies whose management they do not approve, or should they function as the "legendary supervisor" and require meaningful corporate accountability that will address competitiveness and legitimacy? Put another way, can the country afford to let a huge percentage of corporate equity ignore its opportunity to become involved, which would be the result of a traditional view of ownership responsibility for ERISA trustees? Is ownership a useful concept for the governance of corporations? Is there a relationship between involved (real) owners and national competitiveness? Can we afford to condone any longer the single-minded mode of profit maximization in the stewardship of one-third of the nation's long-term capital?

The Visclosky Approach:
Right Question, Wrong Answer

In the last two sessions of Congress, Peter Visclosky (D-Indiana), a junior member of the House Subcommittee on Labor-Management Relations (who was, in fact, "bumped" off of the committee later in the session due to a seniority technicality), proposed legislation to change the trusteeship provisions of ERISA. Under the current system, the trustees are the top managers of the employer sponsoring the pension plan. Visclosky's proposal would require an equal number of employee and employer representatives as trustees. That the bill has made little legislative progress is not as important as the debate its introduction has engendered. From the point of view of ERISA corporation "plan sponsors," the proposition is intolerable. They are ultimately responsible for making up any shortfalls in the defined-benefit plan promises. If they are to lose control over plan administration, their liability appears unacceptably open-ended. (This is just another question of accountability, this time with corporate management on the right side.) Those opposing this bill appropriately pointed to the poor performance of pension plans that employ this kind of shared trusteeship, the joint employer-employee plans called "Taft-Hartley" plans. Why bring the better performers down to that level?

The reason we have pension plans, instead of relying on employees to make their own provisions for retirement, is that we believe there is some benefit to expertise. Just because Trip knows how to forecast the weather, make sneakers, compute accounts, design marketing plans, practice law, or play the violin does not mean that he knows how to manage money. We as a society do not want to bear the risk that he might make a mistake, because we know who would have to support him if he did. Although Congressman Visclosky was right in suggesting that the investment and management of pension fund assets should reflect the concerns of the employees who are the beneficial owners, he had the wrong approach. (The original proposal mandated an even split between the employer and employee trustees, guaranteeing gridlock.) The trustees should be financial experts. But the broader needs of the employees should be reflected in the trustees' actions.

Visclosky's proposal raises fundamental questions. In view of the emerging reality that funds held subject to ERISA are so immense that no planning or evaluation of the country's fiscal health or programs can be made without consideration of the pension system, is the continued total control over these assets by corporate plan sponsors tolerable? Is the criterion of achieving mathematically maximum investment results too narrow in view of the size of the assets and the other needs of society? Because the Pension Benefit Guaranty Corporation (PBGC) insures payments if the corporation fails, the public treasury carries the risk of loss. So the question of who should be trustees and how the assets should be managed is one with which the public is already concerned. The agglomeration of pension assets continues to be a tempting target. Eternal vigilance will be required to protect the primary mission of the statute—the funding of the pension promise—which has been so spectacularly achieved.

ERISA's "Fundamental Contradiction" Redux

ERISA has provided a useful legal structure with explicit provisions on delegation of responsibility. Typically, this has resulted in a "named

fiduciary"—an officer or board-level committee of the "plan sponsor"—
who then delegates the investment and management responsibilities to
outside firms. Other consultants are hired to "monitor" the first group.
As long as Trip's employer's involvement is limited to choosing outside
professionals, who actually make the buy-sell-hold-vote determinations,
and as long as that choice is prudently made (not the CEO's brother-in-
law, working out of his garage) and diligently monitored (someone has
to make sure they do not run off with the money), Trip's employer will
not be liable for any problems.

If, however, Trip's employer decides to handle the pension fund in-
house, his actions will be more carefully scrutinized. The Labor Department will need to determine whether the plan is being administered
"solely... and for the exclusive benefit of the plan participants." Although this is the same standard applied to the consultants that Trip's
employer hires, the fact that he is both running the business and managing the pension fund makes it a little tougher to meet. Whatever business Trip's employer is in, he will now also be managing stock—buying,
selling, voting, evaluating shareholder lawsuits—in his competitors, his
customers, his suppliers, companies he might consider taking over, and
companies that might consider taking him over. Was a pro-management
vote in aid of a higher share value of the company, in which case it
complied with fiduciary obligation to Trip and his fellow employees, or
was it a way to cement a relationship with a valued customer? If the
latter, it still could be justified as enhancing long-term value but could
no longer be characterized as the "exclusive" or "sole" reason for the
fiduciary act.

Assistant Secretary David Ball recently wrote me to express the Department of Labor's sensitivity in this area: "While I agree that the potential for a conflict may exist in certain investment decisions for the
corporate plan sponsor who is also a plan fiduciary... I believe that
you should note that the current system of plan sponsor control does
not appear to have led to major abuse, because of ERISA's rules against
self-dealing. [But] to be silent about this issue could encourage those
who believe that pension assets are fair game for suggesting that, under
current law, plan fiduciaries are not required to discharge their duties
solely in the interest of participants and beneficiaries."[1] ERISA thus
makes difficult direct involvement by corporations as owners of portfolio
securities in their ERISA plans. To be completely free from the appearance of self-dealing, the plan sponsor should recuse itself from acting
in situations where business relationships exist. This could mean that

a corporate officer would not be able to vote securities held in his corporation's customers, suppliers, and competitors. For the large companies, this will involve a great many situations in which they will have to find an ad hoc trustee to perform the requisite ownership functions.

ERISA was designed to encourage delegation to prudently chosen professional specialists, particularly "investment managers." If plan sponsors like Trip's employer want to manage the assets themselves, they must be prepared to take extraordinary care to protect themselves against real or apparent conflicts of interest. That is, after all, what it means to be a fiduciary. This care could include retaining an "ownership expert" and working with other shareholders on a common agenda. This both provides something of a reality check on exercise of ownership rights and helps to circumvent the collective choice problem. There is not much in the marketplace in the way of "ownership" expertise, and there is little experience with communication among institutions (due, in substantial measure, to the restrictions designed to level the playing field in contests for control); there is virtually no experience of working together. Yet both skills are well within the capacity of corporations to develop in a prudent and cost-effective manner.

To the extent that the ERISA plan sponsors prove capable of organizing themselves to deal with the potential conflicts of interest and of acting as owners in a manner that accords with the public interest, there will be decreased justification for amendments along the lines of Visclosky's proposals. What his initiative assumes is that the viewpoint of plan sponsors will be so short-term, narrow, and minimalist, so little concerned with a spacious view of the public good, that the only alternative is to add an essential supplementary viewpoint in the composition of the board of trustees. We have elsewhere discussed the plan sponsors' "taking back" ownership responsibility and the composition of boards of several public pension systems. Ironically, the liberal Democrat Visclosky may well have provided the answer to the question of Undersecretary Robert Glauber (referred to in Chapter 6): "How can we create other boards like CalPERS?" The ultimate guarantee is that the trustees, however they are selected and composed, be held to a fiduciary standard that is clear and consistent. So long as the trustee—whoever he may be—understands that his exclusive concern is to act in Trip's long-term best interest, ownership rights—whether exercised by investment managers or by Trip's employer—will give corporations the legitimacy, accountability, and support originally contemplated in the design of the corporate structure.

A New Federal Law of Ownership

Empty Skyscrapers

We have nothing left but our great empty corporation statutes—towering skyscrapers internally welded together and containing nothing but wind.

Bayless Manning

Although our recommendations do not require legislative action, they could certainly benefit from some, particularly at the federal level. Traditional arguments for leaving regulation of corporations to the states have, after 200 years, begun to erode, as we showed in our discussion of the race to the bottom in Chapter 4. It is increasingly evident that the current abuses are made possible by the failure of the states to enact effective laws. That is because the traditional justification of worthwhile experimentation being incubated by competition among the states has become overtaken by events like the antitakeover laws adopted specifically to protect local companies. As we explained in Chapter 4, competition and experimentation in state corporate law work only if the states must bear the costs of the benefits they provide to entice corporations. Delaware can make its laws as liberal as it wants because it bears such a tiny proportion of the consequences, and that proportion is vastly outweighed by the benefits of the tax revenue.

State after state has responded to the prospect of takeover of a local company—or the opportunity to get some of Delaware's corporate tax revenues—with self-serving antitakeover legislation. State laws governing the relationship of shareholders and management reflect the fact that state legislators, like corporate managers, have little accountability to shareholders, and the states have been shown to be powerless or worse in dealing with questions of abuse. We would like to see a federal law for corporations that sets minimum standards, with the states allowed to experiment and compete by imposing higher ones. There must be a point below which the race to the bottom cannot go, and only the federal government can establish it.

But we recognize that states jealously guard their franchise in corporate law. And there is an alternative that does not require new legislation. As traditional corporation law at the state level deteriorates into a kind of manual for management entrenchment, a new, possibly helpful trend can be detected in the emergence of a federal law of ownership, one that is set by regulation. Institutional investors subject to federal regulation now control a majority of the equity of American corporations. This has provided a foundation for meaningful recreation of corporate self-regulation through precise definition of the obligations of fiduciary owners to involve themselves in corporate affairs. The majority of fiduciary owners are obligated to manage their trust assets with the care of a "prudent expert" and with loyalty solely to their beneficiaries. As the obstacles to collective action by the institutional owners are reduced, it will come within their power to create a corporate governance system restoring the "constructive tension" of fiduciary responsibility. Through development of the specifics of a federal law of ownership, a national code for the effective self-regulation of corporations will emerge.

Traditionally, shareholder attributes have been defined by state corporate law.[2] However, several classes of shareholder—pension plans, investment companies, bank trusts—are fiduciaries under federal law. The nature and extent of their trustee responsibilities are matters of federal regulation, which supersedes the provisions of state law. Our consideration of this important trend begins with the private pension system, partly because it is the biggest category of institutional investor, and partly because the Pension and Welfare Benefits Administration (PWBA) of the Department of Labor (DOL) has taken the lead in outlining the new ownership law. ERISA creates a new law of governance because it preempts state corporation law in areas of conflict. The provisions of ERISA, therefore, and their interpretation by PWBA constitute an emerging federal law of ownership to the extent they require a code of behavior by fiduciaries. This standard has received general support from other federal agencies with jurisdiction over institutional investors, including the Internal Revenue Service, the Office of the Comptroller, and the Securities and Exchange Commission.

Although a federal law requiring shareholder-trustee involvement in corporate affairs is well developed in theory, there are only the beginnings of practical definition. PWBA has insisted that some entity must accept and discharge ownership responsibilities with respect to all outstanding shares of stock. PWBA considers ownership responsibilities "plan assets" under ERISA, and it will deem failure to discharge those responsibilities as a breach of trust. Fiduciaries, subject to federal law, are required to act as informed owners, if for no other reason than to forestall erosion of values,[3] and they must do so in ways that are unmistakably incremental to trust values.[4] Beyond this rests the challenge to develop a structure permitting efficient collective action and the commitment to form and maintain responsive institutions.

Pension Funds:
Permanent Shareholders

Corporate managers love to justify their neglect of shareholders by describing the institutional shareholder as "a 26-year-old in front of a CRT, ready to pounce on every quarter-point, with a 6-second attention span and a 10-second position in anything." Or, as Henry Schacht put it to us most compellingly, "They are not owners; they are investors." Although this, too, is something of a convenient myth (at least one study showed that takeover targets had lower-than-average institutional ownership),[5] as with most myths there is an element of truth in it. The short-term pressure is the result of two factors. First is the commercial pressure—money managers compete for business by pointing to last quarter's results. Second is a misunderstanding of a fiduciary obligation—the belief that it requires managers to jump at any premium. A major factor in the breakdown of the corporate form of organization is the conflict between institutional investors, who are seemingly obligated to act as short-term holders, and corporations, which need long-term commitment from owners. This is a classic case of unintended consequences. The effort to adapt a time-honored legal system—in this case, the law of trusts—to modern times has produced muddled results.

The law of trusts was conceived as a way for wealthy Englishmen to insure their descendants against the theft or neglect of inherited assets. It was called "the law of dukes." No one dreamed that it would one day constitute the operational force underlying half of all the equity capital of the United States. Trustees are directed to avoid risk; they are prohibited from sharing in the gains that result from successful risk taking; they are surcharged for losses caused by failure to act in the same manner as others similarly situated. Under traditional and present trust theory, a trustee, whether of a $4,000 portfolio managed on behalf of Aunt Mary's cats or of a $40 billion portfolio managed on behalf of the Chicago teachers,

252 The New Ownership Agenda

cannot refuse an offer of $20 in cash for a share of stock trading at $15. It is this factor, the essential short-term perspective of the trustee, that has damaged the corporate fabric. Ironically, lawyers like Marty Lipton try to tell corporate directors that they can "just say no" to such an offer, and at the same time Treasury and Labor department officials tell the ERISA fund managers they can do the same thing. But no one believes them, and until such a refusal is challenged and upheld—or, even better, until the acceptance of such an offer is challenged and overturned—no one will. Until then, they will continue to topple like dominoes.

We can try to resolve this dilemma by considering carefully the real needs of the largest institutional owners, the pension funds, and coming up with an expanded notion of fiduciary obligation by trustees that is designed for billion-dollar pension funds rather than feudal dukedoms.

Let's return to Boothbay Harbor and see how Trip fits in. Trip wants to be able to retire in 15 years in a country that has a stable and robust economy, a healthy environment, and a strong defense. He wants to be able to maintain a decent semblance of his preretirement standard of living. All the vagaries of inflation and foreign exchange mean little to him. Can the promise of a "real" pension for Trip be kept?

The many analyses of investment performance over the history of the United States share one conclusion: over the long run, common stocks outperform all other modes of investment. It is only by sharing in the growth of business enterprises that a passive investor has a chance to keep pace with inflation and to maintain purchasing power. Trip, therefore, wants his plan assets to be substantially invested in corporate equities. How should they be managed, and how can he be confident that he has picked the best person to do so?

Recent studies have made clear that active management of pension assets has not resulted in increased values for the participants and beneficiaries.[6] Wilshire Associates surveyed its data base of 222 live accounts over 7.5 years representing $40 billion in equities as of June 30, 1986. The performance of each stockholding in every portfolio has been calculated by Wilshire, representing 1,700 quarterly observations and a half million separate performance calculations. They came up with the following results: *"the net management effect is zero."*[7]

One must come to grips with the stark reality that, notwithstanding the optimistic expectations and billions of dollars in fees paid to money

Equity Managers' Box Score

How Managers Add (Subtract) Value

Management Activity	Incremental Performance
Market timing	(0.8%)
Sector weighting	0.7%
Stock selection	0.6%
Trading	(0.5%)
Net management effect	0.0%

Source: Wilshire Associates.

managers, consultants, and all manner of professional service providers,[8] the economic consequences for the objects of governmental bounty—the pension plan participants, our Trip—have been no better than if all the equity portion of the funds had been invested in market indexes.

If Trip's pension resources are invested in an equity index, he in effect becomes a permanent owner of corporate America. Although his interest is very small, it is real and can be understood by his trustee. What this means is that the ERISA fiduciary of indexed stocks has a very distinct blueprint of the beneficiaries' interests. Like Trip, they are American, they have a long-term interest in the prosperity of American business, and they are well served by commercial decisions that are sensitive to the quality of life at the time of retirement. All of the research, all of the theories, all of the fees that go into active management could be devoted to responsible exercise of governance rights to support and guide the corporations. This is at least as likely to protect and enhance share value as churning the shares by buying and selling.

Index funds are long-term shareholders. Indeed, they are permanent shareholders, unless, for some reason, one of the component companies drops out of the index. Many pension plans today are "indexed" with respect to their equity investments. Such prominent funds as the California Public Employees' Retirement System and State Teachers Retirement System and the public employees' fund of the State of New York are indexed. Congress has mandated by law that its own pension fund (FERSA) must be indexed. There are no definitive records of the extent of indexing, but based on those funds that can be identified, it is possible that 10 percent of total equity investment is held in index form.

There are two goals for pension fund investments. The first is to provide the best returns possible for the employees who participate in the plan. The second is to provide a stable, responsible base of equity investment. Both are best accomplished through index funds. We are not suggesting in any way that all ERISA funds should be indexed. Index funds benefit in part from the active managers. And fiduciaries should diversify. Even the ones we mentioned have separate portfolios, even more than one kind of index. But we would like to encourage greater investment in indexes. The best way to do this is for the secretary of labor, as the government official ultimately responsible for defining fiduciary standards under ERISA, to rule that investing the equity portion of a portfolio in an index constitutes a prudent "safe harbor." This would leave managers free to invest in any manner they deem appropriate but would leave them with the burden of proof that investment results that did not achieve the levels of the index were prudent, a burden that somone like GM's Gordon Binns could certainly satisfy.

It is worth noting that the only substantive investment provision in ERISA requires "diversifying the investments of the plan so as to mini-mize the risk of large losses, unless under the circumstances it is clearly prudent not to do so."[9] Indexing is the ultimate diversification, so the in-cremental restriction on trustee discretion involved in the adoption of an indexing "safe harbor" rule is not startling. Indexing the pension portion of the equity markets would reduce short-term trading and would provide a base of "permanent ownership" with a long-term view for American business. If the index used were the Wilshire 5,000, for example, pen-sion plan capital would be available to all publicly traded companies. At some level of indexing, the question would arise as to whether the bal-ance of market participants would be able to establish meaningful market prices on which to base the index.

As we noted in Chapter 4, pension funds have characteristics markedly different from those of other classes of institutional investors. For ex-ample, mutual funds, with their offer of daily sale or repurchase, have a self-evident need for liquidity. Private trusts, endowments, and insur-ance companies are all long-term investors but have varying needs for liquidity. Pension funds (specifically, defined-benefit plans) uniquely can extrapolate needs for cash into the future and thus confidently commit a portion of their assets "permanently" to the equity markets. We have shown that there is no evidence that participation through index funds, in contrast to active management, would *cost* beneficiaries.

"Permanent shareholders," constituting more than one-fifth of the total equity in American industry and a far higher percentage of the larger
companies, could have a positive impact in several respects. They would
constitute a filter for consideration of takeovers both by foreign and by
domestic interests; they would provide a stable constituency to encourage
managements to take a long-term view in their direction of companies;
they would provide the foundation for a system of corporate governance
based on ownership. As we discussed in the previous chapter, the enormous amounts of money building up in the pension system have stimulated interest from politicians and others who have imaginative ideas as
to its better use. It now seems that the optimal use of the equity portion
of pension assets is as the long-term owner of America's corporations.

This is where the leadership and participation of American corporations is indispensable. Their pension assets are the largest single element of institutional ownership. Public plans, notably CalPERS and
those overseen by New York's Ned Regan, have developed ownership
agendas and useful programs to promote governance concerns. However, in the absence of a parallel or even complementary effort from the
ERISA plans, needless and unproductive polarity has been created. On
the one side are the public plans; on the other is corporate management.
Public and private pension plans have more in common as "owners" than
they have differences. They should reflect this by working together on
an agenda that benefits them both.[10]

The Shareholder Agenda—and Its Limits

Shareholders, as a matter of law and policy, must keep to a very limited
set of issues. They do not have the expertise, the resources, or the right
to become involved in matters of day-to-day management. Their liability
is limited to the amount of their investment. Their only involvement
should be to make sure that the interests of directors and management
are aligned with those of the shareholders, and that when a conflict of
interest is presented, the shareholders make the decisions themselves.

Benjamin Graham and David C. Dodd, over a half-century ago, described the agenda for governance activity. They said that shareholders
should limit their attention to matters where:

> the interest of the officers and the stockholders may be in conflict. This
> field includes the following:

1. Compensation to officers—Comprising salaries, bonuses, options to buy stock.
2. Expansion of the business—Involving the right to larger salaries, and the acquisition of more power and prestige by the officers.
3. Payment of dividends—Should the money earned remain under the control of the management, or pass into the hands of the stockholders?
4. Continuance of the stockholders' investment in the company—Should the business continue as before, although unprofitable, or should part of the capital be withdrawn, or should it be wound up completely?[11]

We would add that governance must concern itself with preserving the full integrity—and value—of the characteristics of ownership appurtenant to shares of common stock. For example, the right to vote may be diluted by a classified board or by dual-class capitalization, and the right to transfer the stock to a willing buyer at a mutually agreeable price may be abrogated by the adoption of a poison pill. These kinds of issues, not contemplated at the time of Graham and Dodd's first edition, can also present conflicts of interest, as shareholders are interested in accountability and officers and directors are interested in protecting themselves.

This agenda says much about the powers, responsibilities, and intended relationship among shareholders, directors, and officers. It contemplates the restoration to owners of the power to make the critical decisions about a corporation, to resolve the conflicts of interest inherent in the corporate form of organization, and to be the source of nominations for director. The way for shareholders to affect corporations is through election and monitoring of appropriate individuals as directors. The fiduciary shareholder, in voting to elect directors, can hardly be said to be acting "prudently" by empowering a board that would dilute the ownership standards of the trustees themselves.

The Shareholder Agenda for Corporate Crime

The issue of corporate crime deserves separate consideration. Like the issues just discussed, it is one where shareholders and managers have a conflict of interest. One can argue that limited liability is conferred on shareholders on the express condition that the corporation not create liabilities for society to bear. To the extent that a corporation is enabled to avoid the consequences of activity for which an individual would be personally responsible, society is accepting the burden. Because the corporation itself has limited liability, it is impervious to court judgments, which may well encourage conduct not in the interest of society. As the corporation creates "externalities," the burden of its owners to abate those liabilities should increase. What will happen is that the cost structure of products will change. The citizenry may face higher product prices, but the net expense will not change. Consumers will explicitly pay for what they are now being charged in the form of higher government costs and diminished quality of life.

As we discussed in Chapter 4, no one has been able to design a system of appropriate deterrence to corporate violation of the law. Although many ingenious solutions have been suggested, including the "equity fine,"[12] none has been able to impose meaningful accountability.

Diffused Accountability

Companies have two kinds of records: those designed to allocate guilt (for internal purposes), and those for obscuring guilt (for presentation to the outside world). When companies want clearly defined accountability they can generally get it. Diffused accountability is not always inherent in organizational complexity; it is in considerable measure the result of a desire to protect individuals within the organization by presenting a confused picture to the outside world. One might say that courts should be able to pierce this conspiracy of confusion. Without sympathetic witnesses from within the corporation who are willing to help, this is difficult.

John Braithwaite

Source: Corporate Crime in the Pharmaceutical Industry, Routledge & Kegan Paul, Boston, 1984, p. 324.

There have been various efforts to place corporations "on probation," to require payments to societally useful causes, even to jail executives, but it is plain that nothing really works and that the problem is becoming more acute. Surely those with the largest stake in making societal and corporate interests compatible are the long-term owners.

Unless the long-term shareholders conclude that it will be "cost-effective" to continue to deal with the problems caused by corporate criminality on an ad hoc basis, some significant self-regulatory effort should be contemplated. There will always remain a need for legal sanctions: "[S]ome executives abstain from bribery because they are afraid of being punished. Most abstain from bribery because they view it as immoral. One reason that they view it as immoral is that executives who bribe are sometimes punished and held to public scorn. Do away with criminal punishment and you do away with much of the sense of morality which makes self-regulation possible. Self-regulation and punitive regulation are, therefore, complementary rather than alternatives."[13] And yet, "the firm is better positioned than the state to detect misconduct by its employees. It has an existing monitoring system already focused on them, and it need not conform its use of sanctions to due process standards. Indeed, if the penalties are severe enough, the corporation has both the incentive and, typically, the legal right to dismiss any employee it even suspects of illegal conduct."[14]

What is the role of the shareholder? Even in the days of Junior's investment in Boothbay Harbor, shareholders had no interest in and no ability to develop or impose internal corporate procedures. How a corporation establishes information flows, incentive systems, or review structures is far beyond the role of the shareholders. Their concern is to hold managements accountable for their conduct of the business in compliance with the law. Indeed, even Professor Milton Friedman's well-known aphorism that management's sole obligation is to maximize the value of the firm is conditioned on doing so "within the rules."

In a simplistic way, shareholders hire managers to run their business in a way that will encourage a governmental and societal climate supportive of capitalist enterprise.[15] An increasing level of corporate criminal activity is hostile to an attitude of public support in the future. Conceivably, management has been so caught up in the pursuit of short-term profit (institutional shareholders have their share of blame in this regard) that it has failed to grasp the utter unacceptability of a situation in which corporate criminal activity not only is rampant but apparently is beyond the power of any constituency to abate. Shareholders need to make unmistakably clear to those they hire that continued corporate crime will not be tolerated.

The best way to do that is in the election of directors. The most fundamental criterion in approving the continued service of particular individuals as directors is that they require the corporation to take every step to channel critical information within the corporation (in its extreme, this entails access of top management to "whistle blowers") and to structure incentives and penalties to ensure a crime-free environment. Setting forth the conditions of eligibility for service on the board of directors appears uniquely appropriate for shareholder concern and bylaw implementation. There is no question that the board of directors has the authority, indeed the responsibility, to promulgate basic corporate policies.

Specifying the Director's Role

More active stockholder participation might force greater corporate compliance with the law in some areas, although, as we have pointed out, their primary concern is often corporate stock growth and dividends. . . . Far reaching corporate reform, however, depends on altering the process and structure of corporate decisionmaking. Traditional legal strategies generally do not affect the internal institutional structure. . . . At present few clear functions are usually specified for corporate boards of directors; they frequently have served as rubber stamps for management. If a functional relationship and responsibility to actual corporate operations were established, directors would be responsible not only for the corporate financial position and stockholder dividends but also for the public interest, which would include the prevention of illegal and unethical activities undertaken in order to increase profits.

Marshall B. Clinard and Peter C. Yeager

Source: Corporate Crime, Free Press, New York, 1980, pp. 306–307.

Professor Christopher Stone's *Where the Law Ends* is perhaps the best-known work on this general subject. He concludes that the suspension of directors is the most effective way of dealing with the problems of corporate criminality.

Why is this better than what we have now? For one thing, the magnitude of the potential liability today has become so draconian that when we try to make the law tougher on directors the more likely effects are that corporate lawyers will develop ways to get around it, judges and juries will be disinclined to find liability, and many of the better qualified directors will refuse to get involved and serve. The advantages of the "suspension" provision, by contrast, are that it is not so easy to get around; it is not so severe that, like potential multi-million-dollar personal liability, it would strike courts as unthinkable to impose; but at the same time it would still have some effective bite in it—the suspendees would be removed from the most prestigious and cushy positions ordinarily available to men of their rank, and would, I suspect, be object of some shame among their peers.[16]

Removing the Impediments to Shareholder Action

Now that we have a stable base of permanent shareholders, led by corporations themselves, operating under a consistent federal regulatory structure, and limited to a restricted agenda, the final element is some structure for them to work together, to minimize the collective choice problem.

Institutional investors are apprehensive about collective action, and so are the corporations they invest in. We have already noted the extensive American tradition of mistrust of centralized financial power. Public plan trustees have set the pace so far. Inevitably, though, the leaders of corporate America will not permit that to continue. The Business Roundtable's initiative to get its members to reclaim the right-to-vote proxies from the investment managers responsible for their ERISA portfolios is just the first step. And the only way to develop effective governance through this process is to surmount the collective choice problem through collective action, through working together to share information and other resources, and to develop policies and initiatives.

The logistics of collective action are daunting as well as expensive. As we have already discussed, government policies favoring worthwhile goals such as liquidity (the registration of securities in "nominee" form) and privacy (laws protecting beneficial owners from having their identity disclosed) have led to a system where it is almost impossible for shareholders to identify each other, much less communicate. Another practical aspect, one that has become less of an impediment but is still significant, is the logistics of corporate elections. Corporate management counts the votes and sees how each proxy is voted and by whom. Although a small fraction of publicly held companies have adopted confidential voting procedures, most corporations are very aware of how each shareholder votes. There have been abuses in which corporate management has exploited commercial relationships to get money managers and banks to vote with them.[17] Beneficial owners, who do not know how votes are cast on their behalf, have no way to object. The one exception so far are the institutional investors of California, who, beginning in 1990, must report to their beneficiaries how they voted shares held in trust portfolios.

Once the legal and practical problems of collective action have been successfully overcome, there remains the reality that the proxy process itself is far from evenhanded. Shareholders underwrite both sides of any disagreement with management. A shareholder resolution may be included in the company's materials; however, management has the opportunity to respond to shareholder proposals, but the shareholders do not have the opportunity to respond to management proposals. The suitability of any particular subject for a shareholder proposal— it cannot be about "ordinary business"—is often the subject for expensive and technical quarrels before the SEC. Even when a proposal is permitted, it is only precatory; a company is free to disregard even a unanimous vote. Election of directors is even more troublesome. Edward J. Epstein points out that shareholder elections "are procedurally much more akin to the elections held by the Communist Party of North Korea than those held in Western democracies."[18] Except in the rarest of cases, there is only one slate of directors running for office, and management nominates the slate, controls the voting process, and counts the votes. Management has the opportunity to use the company materials to nominate directors; shareholders do not.

A firm commitment to act as a fiduciary, using ownership rights "for the exclusive benefit" of plan participants, fortified by a firm commitment from the Labor Department, SEC, and other agencies to enforce the policies and standards already in place, is the best way to counter the commercial pressures we described in Chapter 6.

The structure could follow the lines of the highly effective British National Association of Pension Funds or the Association of British Insurers. A small permanent staff is maintained to act as an information clearinghouse and analysis center for issues of interest to the members. Officers are "seconded" by the Bank of England and other sponsoring institutions, so the association never assumes a bureaucratic life of its own. Issues are closely analyzed, but all member institutions retain the full fiduciary responsibility to vote. As such, an association becomes supported by all of the institutions, and the problems of collective action are abated, if not eliminated.

The Ownership Focus

Imagine the difference it would make if pension funds, public and private, were enthusiastic and informed about ownership responsibility. Their ownership focus would have two special characteristics. First, it would be universal. The institutions not only own all of the companies that make up a particular industry, they own all of the industries that constitute the business component of the nation's economy. This permits decisions to be made on a larger scale than we are accustomed to. In considering the consequences of any act, the trustees must look at it from the perspective of the business segment as a whole. Thus, questions of pollution, unemployment, job training, and research and development expenditures can be considered from the perspective of the system as a whole. Second, these owners have a long-term viewpoint—that of their pensioner beneficiaries—and are literally permanent owners. What has changed is their view of creating value. Rather than picking and trading stocks, they organize themselves as owners to pursue long-term objectives that are characteristic of their beneficiaries'—and society's— real long-term interest.

We already have in the United States all of the elements that have been essential components for a competitive business climate elsewhere in the industrialized world. Management needs to be made accountable to someone who has the power, the motive, the perspective, and the ability to represent the public interest effectively. We have in the pension systems the necessary core of long-term shareholders. They should be committed once and for all to the long-term ownership of the country's companies. Once there is agreement on the ultimate use of pension assets, appropriate institutional development will be forthcoming. In the meantime, equity investment through indexes and reinforcement of the "exclusive benefit" rule for both public and private pension funds will provide direction and momentum. So long as trustees consider solely the long-term interests of plan participants, America can continue to have a competitive and legitimate corporate establishment.

Because trustees are by nature and profession risk-averse and are poorly suited to be out in the front of any pack, the federal govern-ment must make it clear that institutional responsibility as owner is their policy. With the assurance that what they are doing is "prudent," insti-tutions may well be able to make significant progress. The Securities and Exchange Commission has indicated that it plans to undertake a comprehensive review of its proxy rules, drafted for a time when the technology and the average shareholder were very different. This initia-tive could remove several regulatory obstacles to institutional collective action. Above all, what is needed is leadership from America's cor-porations. Corporate managers are the people who hire (and fire) the money managers. They can set the policy for investment and exercise of ownership rights. They must recognize that a system based on institutional ownership—with American business, through its benefit plans, the largest owner—is the best guarantee of competitiveness and productivity in the global economy.

From the Belzbergs to Ma Bell: Another Kind of Corporate Raider

Henry Schacht unsuccessfully tried to get his shareholders to act like owners, but found that they acted like investors. Junior would have stayed with him, but Trip cannot, or will not. In this environment, there are four possibilities.

1. There will be no more publicly held American industrial companies in cyclical industries with high requirements for capital and time (this is roughly Michael Jensen's point).
2. There will be semi-privatization along the lines that Cummins ultimately took, a *keiretsu*-like ownership pattern, with according voting restrictions.
3. The few—Ford, AT&T—will acquire the rest.
4. We will meaningfully deal with the "core issue" and take steps to make institutional investors genuinely long-term. There have been many suggestions in this direction: taxation for short holding periods and time weighted voting; our preference is "indexing."

The AT&T/NCR saga is both timely and topical. NCR says it is not for sale. "Ma Bell," the apotheosis of "touchy-feely" sensitivity for constituencies, is making an all-cash offer and staging a proxy battle for board seats. The line of questioning, the vocabulary of accountability, now comes from the heart of corporate America, rather than the maverick raiders. This is not the shouting of fringe characters with an ax to grind; this is the central question of corporate legitimacy being raised by the principal American corporation today. Will the combination of state legislatures, federal lassitude, and contrived governance provisions create an effective barrier to an all cash offer for all shares by the hypothetically ideal acquirer?

Power and Accountability

The dysfunction of the corporate paradigm in the United States is based on two factors. The first is failing to preserve "trust" as a relevant category in establishing the duty of directors and officers. The second is the tendency to "monetize" relationships, which inevitably focuses on the short term—in reality if not in theory. Both of these mistakes stem from failure to consider that corporations, are not simply another interest group whose demands and requirements can reliably be made compatible with societal interest through need to accommodate other interest groups. We have allowed corporations to become a separate source of power, a law unto themselves, and there must be within the corporation the element of "trust," or, looked at another way, accountability.

Our products and our investment instruments now compete in the global market. As that market becomes more global, the dominant mode of the expression of power in the world will be decreasingly political and increasingly economic, less military and more corporate. An escalating percentage of corporate activity will be conducted by companies having operations that cross national boundaries. The effective combination of culture, public opinion, and law that, in the past, has ensured the compatibility of corporate power with the public interest, will be insufficient for that purpose in the future. Restraints on corporate power based on the law of a particular domicile will tend to follow the pattern in the United States of a "race to the bottom" and will have little impact. We must therefore ensure a structure adequate to compel accountability of those in charge of corporations to some source outside of their organizations—and we have to accept that it cannot be left to individual countries' political systems. In law, economics, tradition, and common sense, the best place to start is with owners.

What Should Be Done Now

□ *By the President of the United States:*
Convene a *presidential corporate governance* task force, including representatives of every federal agency with jurisdiction over institutional investors, including the Treasury, Labor, and Justice Departments, the Securities and Exchange Commission, the Federal Reserve, the Comptroller of the Currency, and the FDIC, to study, make recommendations, and implement them on these issues:

  • The appropriate legislative or policy response to emerging EC standards on the role of owners in establishing corporate direction

- The desirability for a "minimum standards" federal corporate law

- The desirability of a "PERISA" or a federal law centered on ensuring public–trustee independence of governmental sponsorship in critical fiduciary areas and on imposing ERISA-type standards and responsibilities where state law and regulation are inadequate.

- The appropriate involvement of institutional shareholders in corporate governance

- The appropriateness of the pension system investing in equity primarily or solely through indexes

- The desirability of institutional investors acting collectively with respect to their equity holdings

- The appropriate legal structure within which they may best discharge this responsibility

- Convene a White House study group of lawyers and economists to prepare a legislative proposal that would revitalize private ownership of American business through the voting power of investors.

☐ *By the Majority Leader of the Senate and the Speaker of the House:*
Create an ad hoc joint committee to consider whether the laws that govern securities and institutional investors should be expanded specifically to cover control of business enterprises by their shareholders.

☐ *By the Securities and Exchange Commission:*
Completely reform the proxy rules to facilitate the constructive involvement of substantial owners in corporate direction, including the removal of impediments to collective action.

☐ *By institutional investors:*

- Establish explicit policies with respect to the discharge of ownership responsibilities of portfolio securities, and disclose voting records showing how proxies for the previous year were voted and why.

- Establish structures for collective action.

☐ *By private corporations:*
Commit the resources necessary so that the pension funds they sponsor can play a role appropriate to their status as the largest of institutional investors.

□ *By boards of directors:*

- Ask hard questions of management.

- Convene committees of independent, unaffiliated outside directors to make sure that management and director compensation is tied to performance, to meet with representatives of shareholders, and to act as a resource for finding new outside director candidates.

- When necessary, obtain advice from outside consultants, selected by independent directors, to review questions of performance, value, and compensation.

- Make sure that all matters involving a conflict of interest between management and shareholders are put to a shareholder vote.

□ *By owners and managers:*

- Work together to create an "ownership agenda" to ensure a strong base of support and accountability.

- Establish a registry for those interested in being directors to restore legitimacy to the process of selection.

□ **By you, the reader of this book:**

Pick up the phone and call your broker, banker, trustee, insurance company, and pension plan administrator. Ask them how they vote your stock and why. Ask them to send you regular reports on how they vote your stock, justifying their policies. After all, it's your money.

Notes

1
SHAREHOLDERS AND STAKEHOLDERS

1. Allanna Sullivan, "Exxon's Holders Assail Chairman Rawl over Firm's Handling of Alaska Oil Spill," *Wall Street Journal*, May 19, 1989, p. A3.
2. Announced at Exxon meeting for shareholders (New York, January 10, 1991).
3. Robin Toner, "Quiet Acts, Silent Halls, as a City Gives Thanks," *New York Times*, November 28, 1985, p. B6.
4. Maryann Keller, *Rude Awakening: The Rise, Fall, and Struggle for Recovery of General Motors*, William Morrow, New York, 1989, p. 20.
5. John P. Davis, *Corporations, vol. 1*, Capricorn Books, New York, 1961, p. 20, (originally published in 1905).
6. *Austin v. Michigan State Chamber of Commerce* (#88-1569), March 27, 1990.
7. *Ibid.*, Marshall opinion, pp. 6–7.
8. *Ibid.*, p. 5.
9. *Ibid.*
10. For the arguments of representatives from each field (Martin Lipton, Jesse Unruh, John Phelan), see Nathaniel Nash, "Shareholders' Rights: Three Views: Vying for Control of the Public Corporation," *New York Times*, February 15, 1987, p. D5.

2
WHY BAD STOCK HAPPENS TO GOOD INVESTORS

1. See *Austin v. Michigan State Chamber of Commerce* (for discussion, see Chapter 1).
2. Adam Smith, *An Inquiry into the Nature and Causes of the Wealth of Nations*, vol. 2, University of Chicago Press, Chicago, 1976, pp. 264–265.
3. Brandeis, dissenting in *Liggett v. Lee*, 288 U.S. 517, 458 (U.S. Sup. Ct. 1933).
4. John P. Davis, *Corporations, vol. 2*, Capricorn Books, New York, 1961, p. 246.
5. John C. Coffee, "No Soul to Damn, No Body to Kick: An Unscandalized Inquiry into the Problem of Corporate Punishment," *Michigan Law Review*, 79, January 1981, p. 388.

268   Notes

6. Harvey H. Segal, *Corporate Makeover: The Reshaping of the American Economy*, Viking, New York, 1989, pp. 5–6.
7. Smith, *The Wealth of Nations*, vol. 2. p. 265.
8. John Brooks, *Once in Golconda* (Harper & Row, New York, 1969), gives the account of the downfall of Richard Whitney, founder of Richard Whitney & Co., a prominent bond firm. Another prominent businessman who was forced to defend his business practices was Albert H. Wiggin, the head of Chase National Bank, who shorted the stock of his own firm, making $4 million on the 1929 stock market crash.
9. Segal, *Corporate Makeover*, p. 2.
10. Betty Linn Krikorian, *Fiduciary Standards in Pension and Trust Fund Management*, Butterworth Legal Publishers, Boston, 1989, p. 187. The discussion of the mechanics of the proxy system is adapted from pp. 187–193.
11. William Z. Ripley, *Main Street and Wall Street*, Scholars Book Co., Lawrence, Kans., 1972 (reissue of original edition of 1926), pp. 78–79. The quotation from Brandeis is not from his opinions on the Supreme Court, but rather from testimony before the Commission on Industrial Relations, January 23, 1913.
12. James Willard Hurst, *The Legitimacy of the Business Corporation in the Law of the United States: 1780–1970*, University of Virginia Press, Charlottesville, 1970, pp. 82–83. "[I]n *Dodge Brothers v. Ford Motor Company:* management's prime obligation was to pursue profit in the interests of shareholders and not to adopt pricing policies designed to promote the interests of wage earners or to effect wider sharing on the gains of improved technology." Interestingly, in light of the current "stakeholder" rhetoric, the court refused to enjoin the price reduction, observing that Ford's policies had benefited shareholders in the past and might do so again. The only thing the court ordered was a distribution of excess surplus.
13. *A.P. Smith Mfg. Co. v. Barlow*, 98 A.2d 581 (N.J. 1953).
14. Ripley, *Main Street and Wall Street*, p. 98.
15. Benjamin Graham and David C. Dodd, *Security Analysis*, 1st ed., McGraw-Hill, New York, 1934, p. 509.
16. *Ibid.*
17. Graham and Dodd, *Security Analysis*, 4th ed., 1962, p. 664.
18. Maryann Keller, *Rude Awakening: The Rise, Fall, and Struggle for Recovery of General Motors*, William Morrow, New York, 1989, p. 49.
19. The effects of increasing the number of shares, and thus holders, has become increasingly limited due to the rise of institutional investors.
20. Albert O. Hirschman (*Exit, Voice, and Loyalty: Responses to Decline in Firms, Organizations, and States*, Harvard University Press, Cambridge, Mass., 1970, p. 4) noted that deterioration in performance of an institution produces two options for its members and consumers: exit ("some customers stop buying the firm's products or some members leave the organization") and voice ("the firm's customers or the organization's members express their dissatisfaction directly to management or to some other authority to which management is subordinate or through general protest addressed to anyone who cares to listen").
21. Nathan Rosenbery and L.E. Birdsall, Jr., *How the West Grew Rich: The Economic Transformation of the Industrial World*, Basic Books, New York, 1986, p. 229. (Emphasis added.)

22. Pension plans in the aggregate own some 25 percent of all publicly held equity in U.S. companies (William Taylor, "Can Big Owners Make a Big Difference?" *Harvard Business Review*, September/October 1990, p. 5). Of this equity held in pension funds, two-thirds is in defined benefit plans.

23. Daniel Fischel and John H. Langbein, "ERISA's Fundamental Contradiction: The Exclusive Benefit Rule," *University of Chicago Law Review*, 55(4), September 1988, pp. 1105–1160.

24. John Brooks, *The Go-Go Years*, Weybright and Talley, New York, 1973, p. 155.

25. *Ibid.*, p. 181.

26. Edward Jay Epstein, *Who Owns the Corporation? Management vs. Shareholders*, Priority Press, New York, 1986, pp. 24–25.

27. Paul Zane Pilzer and Robert Deitz, *Other People's Money: The Inside Story of the S&L Mess*, Simon & Schuster, New York, 1989, p. 146.

28. In another sense, in terms of the role that the money played in the corporation, he turned stock into a bond. Thus, another of Milken's accomplishments was removing the limits imposed by accountability to shareholders. The investors in junk bonds were providing the kind of capital usually provided by stockholders, but they had none of a stockholder's ownership rights.

29. The Department of Labor in 1985 issued a release permitting incentive compensation in limited cases.

30. Randall Smith, John J. Kelle, and John R. Wilke, "AT&T Launches $6.12 Billion Cash Offer for NCR After Rejection of Its Stock Bid," *Wall Street Journal*, December 6, 1990, p. A3.

31. Doug Carroll, "UAL a Year Later: Still Up in Air," *USA Today*, October 9, 1990, p. 8B.

32. W. Michael Blumenthal, "How to Tell Good LBOs from Bad," *Washington Post*, January 1, 1989, p. B4.

33. One particularly heinous raider tactic was the "Saturday Night Special," whereby a raider would get agreements to purchase 51 percent of the stock and buy it all on a Saturday night. When the market opened on Monday, the deal was over. The Williams Act of 1968 put a stop to this tactic and "leveled the playing field."

34. Efficient market theorists argue that the initial offer for 51 percent would have to contain such a premium as to make the ultimate "blended" price a fair market value.

35. For discussion of the prisoner's dilemma, see Robert Axelrod, *The Evolution of Cooperation*, Basic Books, New York, 1984.

36. Ray C. Smith, *The Money Wars*, Dutton, New York, 1990, p. 145. See also "Majority of Large Corporations Have Adopted Poison Pills, IRRC Finds," *BNA Securities Regulation & Law Report*, 22(47), November 30, 1990, p. 1659.

37. Epstein, *Who Owns the Corporation?* p. 33.

38. See *Grand Metropolitan PLC v. Pillsbury*, 558 A. 2d 1049 (Del. 1049).

39. A third type of pill, the voting rights plan, hinges on the dilution of the acquirer's voting rights rather than financial dilution. Under this type of plan, should the acquirer trigger the pill, the target shareholders would receive supervoting rights for each share of stock they held, while the acquirer's would be nullified. Few companies have adopted this sort of pill, however, since Asarco's voting rights plan was struck down by the New Jersey courts in *Asarco, Inc. v. M.R.H. Holmes à Court*, 611 F. Supp. 468 (D.N.J. 1985).

40. See, for example: Analysis Group, Inc., *The Effects of Poison Pills on Shareholders: A Synthesis of Recent Evidence*, Belmont, Mass., November 4, 1988; Office of the Chief Economist, Securitities and Exchange Commission, *The Economics of Poison Pills*, March 5, 1986; Office of the Chief Economist, Securities and Exchange Commission, *The Effect of Poison Pills on the Wealth of Target Shareholders*, October 23, 1986; Michael Ryngaert, "The Effect of Poison Pill Securities on Shareholder Wealth," *Journal of Financial Economics*, 20, 1988, pp. 377–417; and Nancy Sheridan, *Impact of Stockholder Rights Plan on Stock Price*, Kidder, Peabody & Co., New York, June 15, 1986.

41. Analysis Group, Inc. *The Effects of Poison Pills on Shareholders: A Re-Analysis of Georgeson's Sample*, Belmont, Mass., December 1988; Ryngaert, "The Effect of Poison Pill Securities on Shareholder Wealth"; Richard Wines, *Poison Pill Impact Study*, Georgeson & Co., New York, March 31, 1988; and Richard Wines, *Poison Pill Impact Study II*, Georgeson & Co., New York, October 31, 1988.

42. T. Boone Pickens, *Boone*, Houghton Mifflin, Boston, 1987, pp. 156–157. Anyone who doubts the exorbitant fees of corporate lawyers need only read the next paragraph, when Flom simply suggests, "Why don't you make a Dome-Conoco offer?": "It was a million dollar suggestion, and that's about what he billed us."

43. Stephen J. Adler and Laurie P. Cohen, "Even Lawyers Gasp over the Stiff Fees of Wachtell Lipton," *Wall Street Journal*, November 2, 1988, p. A1.

44. 500 A.2d 1346 (Del. 1985).

45. Reply brief of appellants, John A. Moran and the Dyson-Kissner-Moran Corporation, May 7, 1985, p. 5.

46. "In addition appellants contend that the deterrence of tender offers will be accomplished by what they label 'a fundamental transfer of power from the stockholders to the directors.' They contend that this transfer of power, in itself is unauthorized. The Rights Plan will result in no more of a structural change than any other defensive mechanism adopted by a board of directors" [*Moran v. Household*, 500 A.2d 1346, 1354 (1985)].

47. *Shamrock v. Polaroid*, 559 A.2d 257, 267 (Del. Ch. 1989); also see 559 A.2d 278 (Del. Ch. 1989).

48. 559 A.2d 257, 274 (Del. Ch. 1989).

49. Although the Poloroid ESOP mandated that the trustee vote the unallocated shares, in the same proportion as the allocated shares, the Department of Labor has said that ESOP trustees are fiduciaries, and the "decision whether to tender employer stock held by a plan with regard to a tender offer for the plan sponsor is a fiduciary act plan asset management." Thus, the trustee has sole voting authority for the unallocated shares, regardless of how the allocated shares are voted. See letter from Alan D. Lebowitz, Deputy Assistant Secretary for Program Operations, February 23, 1989 (the Polaroid letter).

50. Benjamin J. Stein, "A Saga of Shareholder Neglect: Whose Interests Was This Management Protecting?" *Barron's*, May 4, 1988, p. 9.

51. Complaint filed in *NL Industries v. Lockheed*, case 90-1950 RMT (Bx) in the United States District Court for the Central District of California.

52. Coopers & Lybrand, *Barriers to Takeovers in the European Community*, vol. 1, the Department for Enterprise, Her Majesty's Stationary Office, London, 1989, p. 15.

53. *Ibid.,* pp. 11–12.
54. Hurst, *Legitimacy of the Business Corporation,* p. 104.
55. Michael Jensen, "The Eclipse of the Public Corporation," *Harvard Business Review,* 67(5), September–October 1989, p. 61.
56. *Ibid.,* p. 64.

3
THE DIRECTOR'S NEW CLOTHES

1. Bryan Burrough and John Helyar, *Barbarians at the Gate,* Harper & Row, New York, 1989, p. 93. The book also notes that "Johnson's two maids were on the company payroll."
2. *Ibid.,* p. 255.
3. See Committee on Corporate Laws of the Section of Corporation, Banking and Business Law, American Bar Association, *Model Business Corporation Act,* Prentice-Hall Law and Business, Englewood Cliffs, N.J., 1990, p. 781. "Thirty-two jurisdictions follow the language of the Model Act . . . the remaining 20 jurisdictions provide the corporation's affairs should be managed by a board of directors," p. 788.
4. Melvin Aron Eisenberg, *The Structure of the Corporation: A Legal Analysis,* Little, Brown, Boston, 1976, p. 140.
5. Benjamin N. Cardozo, *Meinhard v. Salmon,* 249 N.Y. 458, 464 (1928).
6. Robert Clark, *Corporate Law,* Little, Brown, Boston, 1986, pp. 33–34.
7. Arthur Fleischer, Jr., Geoffrey C. Hazard, Jr., and Miriam Z. Klipper, *Board Games,* Little, Brown, Boston, 1988, p. 3.
8. Jay W. Lorsch with Elizabeth MacIver, *Pawns or Potentates: The Reality of America's Corporate Boards,* Harvard Business School Press, Boston, 1989, p. 4.
9. Peter Drucker, "The Bored Board," in *Toward the Next Economics and Other Essays,* Harper & Row, New York, 1981, p. 110.
10. According to preliminary figures in the ISS Director Database, 843 out of 5,848 director positions in the ISS Director Database were "affiliated" outsiders, with some business connection to the company.
11. Lorsch, *Pawns or Potentates,* pp. 57–58.
12. Maryann Keller, *Rude Awakening: The Rise, Fall, and Struggle for Recovery of General Motors,* William Morrow, New York, 1989, p. 188.
13. Doron P. Levin, *Irreconcilable Differences: Ross Perot versus General Motors,* Little, Brown, Boston, 1989, p. 324.
14. Kim McQuaid, *Big Business and Presidential Power: From FDR to Reagan,* William Morrow, New York, 1982, p. 308.
15. Brief of petitioner The Business Roundtable, Case #99-1651, Court of Appeals, D.C. Circuit (August 22, 1989), p. ii.
16. McQuaid, *Big Business and Presidential Power,* p. 200.
17. *Ibid.,* p. 284.
18. Tim Smart, "Knights of the Roundtable: Tracking Big Business' Agenda in Washington," *Business Week,* October 21, 1988, p. 39.

19. The Business Roundtable, *The Role and Composition of the Board of Directors of the Large Publicly Owned Corporation* (available from The Business Roundtable, 200 Park Ave., New York, NY 10166), 1978, p. 3.
20. *Ibid.*, p. 8.
21. The Business Roundtable, *Corporate Governance and American Competitiveness* (Available from The Business Roundtable, 200 Park Ave., New York, NY 10166), 1990, p. 13 ("... while the CEO must be involved...").
22. *Ibid.*, p. 14 ("To ensure continuing effective board operations, the CEO can periodically ask the directors for their evaluation of the general agenda items for board meetings and any suggestions they may have for improvement").
23. *Ibid.*, p. 16.
24. An index fund is a type of "passive portfolio" that tracks an index. An example is the Standard & Poor's Index. Investment managers do not make buy/sell decisions based on analysis of individual companies but hold the stock as long as it is in the index.
25. The Business Roundtable, *Corporate Governance and American Competitiveness,* p. 16.
26. *Ibid.*, p. 9.
27. *Ibid.*, p. 14.
28. Letter from Bruce Atwater, chairman, Corporate Governance Task Force of the Business Roundtable, November 7, 1990.
29. "We suggest you advise your directors not to respond..." (*ibid*).
30. 45 U.S. 503 (1846).
31. 249 N.Y. 458 (1928).
32. *Ibid.*, pp. 466, 468.
33. Dennis J. Block, Nancy E. Barton, and Stephen A. Radin, *The Business Judgment Rule: Fiduciary Duties of Corporate Directors and Officers,* 2d ed., Prentice-Hall Law & Business, New York, 1988, p. 3.
34. *Joy v. North,* 692 F.2d 880, 886 (1982).
35. *Percy v. Millaudon,* 8 Mart. 68 (1829). Here directors were sued because of the behavior of the staff of the bank: "If nothing has come to their knowledge, to awaken suspicion of the fidelity of the president and cashier, ordinary attention to the affairs of the institution is sufficient. If they become acquainted with any fact calculated to put prudent men on their guard, a degree of care commensurate with the evil to be avoided is required, and a want of that care certainly makes them responsible." Quoted in *Briggs v. Spalding,* 141 U.S. 132, 148 (Sup. Ct. 1891).
36. 432 A.2d 814, 820 (N.J. 1981).
37. 795 F.2d 893 (10th Cir. 1986).
38. 237 N.E.2d 776 (1968).
39. C.A. No. 7583 (Del. Ch. May 9, 1984). Unpublished case.
40. *Danaher Corp. v. Chicago Pneumatic Tool Co.,* 633 F. Supp. 1066, 1072 (S.D.N.Y. 1986). See also *Danaher Corp. v. Chicago Pneumatic Tool Co.,* 635 F. Supp. 246 (S.D.N.Y. 1986).
41. 564 A.2d 651 (1988).
42. *Ibid.*, p. 658.
43. *Ibid.*, p. 652.

44. *Ibid.*, p. 659.
45. Joseph Nocera notes that a series of proshareholder decisions in Delaware ended after "fabled New York takeover lawyer" Martin Lipton wrote, in a "conspicuously leaked memo" to clients, "Perhaps it is time to migrate out of Delaware." Nocera concludes, "within two months the Court of Chancery began producing decisions that were more to Marty Lipton's liking. They've been doing so ever since." "Delaware Puts Out," *Esquire,* January 1990, p. 48.
46. 488 A. 2d 858 (Del. 1985).
47. *Ibid.*, p. 869.
48. *Unocal Corp. v. Mesa Petroleum Co.,* 493 A. 2d 946 (Del. 1985).
49. *Ibid.*, p. 956.
50. *Revlon, Inc. v. MacAndrews & Forbes Holdings, Inc.,* 506 A.2d 173,181 (Del. 1986).
51. *Ibid.*, p. 182.
52. *Ibid.*, p. 184.
53. *Norlin Corp. v. Rooney, Pace Inc.,* 744 F.2d 255 (2d Cir. 1984) (applying New York law).
54. 567 A.2d 1279 (Del. 1989).
55. *Ibid.*, p. 1282.
56. *Ibid.*, p. 1283.
57. *Ibid.*, p. 1286, 1287.
58. *Ibid.*, p. 1287.
59. *Ibid.*, p. 1288.
60. *Paramount v. Time,* 571 A.2d 1140, 1149, 1150 (Del. Sup. 1990).
61. "Skewered Shareholders: Roundtable on the Time-Warner Deal," *Directors & Boards,* 14(2), Winter 1990, p. 35.
62. *Paramount v. Time,* p. 1147.
63. *Ibid.*, p. 1148.
64. *Ibid.* (emphasis added).
65. *Paramount v. Time,* CCH Federal Securities Law Reporter, pp. 94, 514, 93, 269 (Del. Ch. 1989).
66. *Ibid.*, p. 93, 269.
67. *Ibid.*, p. 93, 284.
68. *Paramount v. Time,* p. 1140, 1155.
69. *Paramount v. Time,* CCH, pp. 94, 514, 93, 267.
70. *Ibid.*, p. 93, 277.
71. *Ibid.*, p. 93, 273.
72. Interview with Michael Klein, July 6, 1990.
73. *Sullivan v. Hammer,* CCH Federal Securities Law Reporter, pp. 95, 415, 97, 1064 (Del. Ch. 1990).
74. Michael M. Lewis, "Leveraged Rip-Off," *New Republic,* November 14, 1988, p. 27.
75. John F. Berry, "SEC Proposes Shareholder Protections," *Washington Post,* November 19, 1977, p. D9.
76. Charles W. Stevens, "Local Chairman's Buyout of Two Units Gives Him a Rewarding Second Position," *Wall Street Journal,* August 14, 1989, p. A5. The article notes that "if Mr. Schwartz spends the 10 hours a month he estimates will

be required of him as chairman of K&F, his K&F compensation would work out to at least $4,000 an hour."

77. Steve Mufson, "Breakdown of a Buyout: Plenty of Blame Passed around in UAL Takeover that Failed," *Washington Post,* Oct. 29, 1989, p. H1.

78. "A Wolf in Wolf's Clothing," *ISSue Alert,* 4(8), November 1989, p. 5.

79. Randall Smith, Michael R. Sesit and Robert L. Rose, "British Air May Balk at Any Haste in Reformulating a UAL Buy-Out," *Wall Street Journal,* October 18, 1989, p. A3.

80. Randall Smith, "Buy-Out Bomb: In a Failed Bid for UAL, Lawyers and Bankers Didn't Fail to Get Fees," *Wall Street Journal,* November 30, 1989, p. A1.

81. Courts have permitted companies to make such payments to outside bidders—only when they will increase the likelihood of superior bids, not prevent them.

82. Jeff Bailey, Asra D. Nomani, and Judith Valente, "Flawed Portent: Banks Rejecting UAL Saw Unique Defects in This Buy-Out Deal," *Wall Street Journal,* October 16, 1989, p. A1.

83. Benjamin J. Stein, "Watch Dog, Awake: A Fervent Plea to the New Chairman of the SEC," *Barron's,* November 13, 1989, p. 34.

84. All quotes are taken from a July 1990 interview with a source who was a member of the GAF board of directors during the buyout.

85. *GAF Corporation 1989 Proxy Statement,* p. 12.

86. *Ibid.,* pp. 14–15.

87. *Ibid.,* p. 15.

88. *Ibid.,* p. 21.

89. See Burrough and Helyar, *Barbarians at the Gate,* pp. 369–371.

90. James J. Hanks, Jr., "Non-Stockholder Constituency Statutes: An Idea Whose Time Should Never Have Come," *Insights,* 3(12), December 1989, p. 20.

91. Quoted in Leslie Eaton, "Corporate Couch Potatoes: The Awful Truth About Boards of Directors," *Barron's,* December 24, 1990, p. 22.

92. Ga. Code Ann. Sec. 14-2-202.5.

93. American Bar Association Committee on Corporate Laws, "Other Contituency Statutes: Potential for Confusion," *Business Lawyer,* 45(4), August 1990, p. 2261.

94. *Ibid.,* p. 2259.

95. F.A. Hayek, *Law, Legislation, Liberty. Volume 3: The Political Order of a Free People,* University of Chicago, 1979, p. 82.

96. The Business Roundtable, *Corporate Governance and American Competitiveness,* March 1990, pp. 3–4.

97. The previous version of the law, adopted in 1983, included a stakeholder provision similar to those adopted by many other states. However, the new version goes further than any other state has, so far, by expanding the list of interests may be considered and, more important, by establishing that no interest must be controlling (including the interests of shareholders), as long as the directors act in the best interests of the corporation. Other changes to the fiduciary standard include an explicit rejection of the Delaware "heightened scrutiny" test applied to directors' actions in change-of-control situtations.

98. "Outrage of the Month," *ISSue Alert,* 4(9), December 1989, p. 6.

99. *Fact Sheet on Act 36: The New Pennsylvania Anti-Takeover Law,* Klett Lieber Rooney & Schorling, October 17, 1990.

100. "A Stupid Law: If Pa.'s Anti-Takeover Bill Was So Great, Why Are So Many Companies Opting Out of It?" *Philadelphia Inquirer,* July 26, 1990, p. 18-A.
101. "When a State Protects a Company," *ISSue Alert,* 5(6), July/August 1990, p. 1.
102. Jonathan M. Karpoff and Paul H. Malatesta, *Evidence of State Antitakeover Laws,* University of Washington School of Business, July/August 1990, p. 1.
103. Stephen L. Nesbitt, *The Impact of 'Anti-Takeover' Legislation on Pennsylvania Common Stock Price,* Wilshire Associates, August 27, 1990.

4
THE SCARECROW OF THE LAW: THE FAILURE OF GOVERNMENT

1. Paul Houston, "Political Gifts, Fueled by PACs, Continue to Soar," *Los Angeles Times,* April 7, 1986, p. 9.
2. Stephen Taub, "The Auto Wars," *Financial World,* October 1, 1985, p. 12. Ford, for its part, went on to increase its market share, from 16.3 percent in 1981 to nearly 21 percent in 1989.
3. Jerry Flint, "'Best Car Wins,'" *Fortune,* January 27, 1990, p. 75.
4. Ronald Reagan, in David Jernigan, *Restrictions on Japanese Auto Imports,* Kennedy School of Government, Boston, p. 45.
5. This information is available in the annual company reports of GM, Ford, and Chrysler.
6. Paul H. Weaver, *The Suicidal Corporation,* Simon & Schuster, New York, 1988, pp. 88–89.
7. *Ibid,* p. 89.
8. See Robert W. Crandall, "The Effects of U.S. Trade Protection for Autos and Steel," Brookings Papers on Economic Activity, Washington, D.C., 1987, pp. 271–288.
9. Rachel Dardis and Jia-Yeoung Lin, "Automobile Quotas Revisited: The Costs of Continued Protection," *Journal of Consumer Affairs,* 19(2), Winter 1985, p. 19.
10. *Ibid.* Some auto industry sources say that the VRAs were by no means the only cause of profits. Higher capacity vibration and drastic cost-cutting measures on behalf of the auto industry, coupled with a growing automotive demand due to falling gasoline prices and growing household income, were major contributors.
11. We do not defend tariffs, an alternative approach, but at least with protectionism, the government increases its revenue, perhaps lessening the tax burden on citizens.
12. James Traub, "Into the Mouths of Babes," *New York Times Magazine,* July 24, 1988, p. 18.
13. Edwin Sutherland, *White Collar Crime. The Uncut Version,* Yale University Press, New Haven, 1983.
14. Marshall B. Clinard, Peter C. Yeager, Jeanne Brissette, David Petrashek, and Elizabeth Hartes, *Illegal Corporate Behavior,* National Institute of Law Enforcement and Criminal Justice, Washington, D.C., 1979.
15. Marshall B. Clinard and Peter C. Yeager, *Corporate Crime,* The Free Press, New York, 1980.
16. This section is freely adapted from Russell Mokhiber, *Corporate Crime and Violence: Big Business and the Abuse of the Public Trust,* Sierra Club, 1988, pp. 18, 19.

17. *Ibid.*, p. 19.

18. John C. Coffee, Jr., "No Soul to Damn, No Body to Kick: An Unscandalized Inquiry into the Problem of Corporate Punishment," *Michigan Law Review*, 79, January 1981, pp. 386, 387.

19. When Delaware passed an antitakeover law in 1987, one legislator explained the reasoning this way: "We have a $170 million corporate account in Delaware, and we take it very seriously. We nurture it." That year, Delaware received $170 million in franchise fees from 184,000 corporations. From Patrick S. McGurn, Sharon Pamepinto, and Adam B. Spector, *State Takeover Laws*, Investor Responsibility Research Center, Washington, D.C., September 1989, p. 4.

20. William L. Cary, "Federalism and Corporate Law: Reflections Upon Delaware," *Yale Law Journal*, 83(4), March 1974, pp. 663–705. Cary concludes by criticizing the legal establishment: "The absurdity of this race for the bottom, with Delaware in the lead—tolerated and indeed fostered by corporate counsel—should arrest the conscience of the American bar when its current reputation is in low estate."

21. 457 U.S. 624 (1982).

22. 481 U.S. 69 (1987).

23. Evan M. Kjellenberg, "The Model Control Share Act is the Best State Takeover Alternative," *Northern Illinois University Law Review*, 8, 1988, pp. 329, 331. Those states were Arizona, Greyhound Corp. (1987); Connecticut, Aetna Insurance (1984); Florida, Harcourt Brace Jovanovich (1987); Hawaii, International Holding Capital Corp. (1986); Kentucky, Ashland Oil (1986); Maryland, Martin-Marietta Corp. (1983); Massachusetts, Gillette Co. (1987); Minnesota, Dayton-Hudson Corp. (1987); Missouri, TWA (1985); New York, CBS (1985); North Carolina, Burlington Industries (1987); Ohio, Goodyear Tire (1986) and Federated Dept. Stores (1988); Oklahoma, Unocal (1985); Pennsylvania, Scott Paper Co. (1983); Washington, Boeing (1987); and Wisconsin, Heilman Brewing Co. (1987).

24. The amendment was originally introduced before the Belzbergs acquired the stock in Armstrong World, but the threat to Armstrong is what provided the momentum for passage of the bill.

25. An actual control share acquisition has never been implemented, so one can only speculate precisely how it would work. Theoretically, it creates a two-tiered voting system if a person or group acquires a significant amount of stock. If a shareholder crosses a certain threshold of ownership, usually around 20 percent, he loses voting rights. All shareholders then must vote on whether voting rights will be restored to him. The major shareholder, and often the management of the company, are excluded from the vote. Although a control share statute appears fair in that it allows noninterested shareholders to vote on whether a "voice" can be given to a large shareholder, it effectively exploits the barriers to shareholder rights already in effect.

26. "A Patchwork Approach to Takeovers," *New York Times*, February 12, 1990, p. A20.

27. Jason Zweig, "Damn the Shareholders, Full Speed Astern," *Forbes*, June 25, 1990, p. 64.

28. "Pennsylvania's Brave Experiment," *Wall Street Journal*, April 3, 1990, p. A20. For other criticisms of the Pennsylvania bill, see Diana B. Henriques, "A Paradoxical

Anti-Takeover Bill," *New York Times*, April 8, 1990, p. 15; Vineeta Anand, "Is Tough State Anti-Takeover Law a Dud?" *Investor's Daily*, July 26, 1990, p. 1; Leslie Wayne, "Many Companies in Pennsylvania Reject State's Takeover Protection," *New York Times*, July 20, 1990, p. A1; John Pound, "Shut Up, Shareholders—This is Pennsylvania," *Wall Street Journal*, December 13, 1989, p. A14; and Christopher Elias, "Turning Up the Heat on the Top," *Insights*, July 23, 1990, p. 8.

29. Jonathan M. Karpoff and Paul H. Malatesta, *Evidence on State Antitakeover Laws*, University of Washington School of Business, July/August 1990, p. 1.

30. From an interview with James W. Segal, Boston, August 9, 1990.

31. Lois Therrien and Peter Finch, "Mr. Rust Belt: Henry Schacht Did Everything Right, So Where Are the Profits?" *Business Week*, October 17, 1988, p. 72.

32. Charles R. Morris, *The Coming Global Boom*, Bantam, New York, 1990, p. 48.

33. The Cummins CFO told us the timing was coincidental, relating more to a change in the tax treatment of ESOPs than to the Hanson stock purchase.

34. As the federal official responsible for ESOPs, I gave the opinion that such a provision is contrary to federal law, a view in which all of my successors have concurred. See letter from Alan D. Lebowitz, Deputy Assistant Secretary for Program Operations, February 23, 1989 (the Polaroid letter).

35. *City Investing v. Simcox*, 633 F.2d 56, 61, 62 (1980).

36. Other sources say that she was removed because her brother was employed at a law firm retained by Cummins. However, both sides had previously waived objection to that possible conflict.

37. "Maddox Pressured Settlement," *Indianapolis Business Journal*, May 21–27, 1990.

38. One case where the market was able to set a price on voting rights was the case of Bergen Brunswig. Initially, Emil and Robert Martini offered to the public a class of common stock of Bergen Brunswig whose voting rights were limited so as to preserve the founders' capacity to elect a majority of the board of directors. In 1988, they decided (in anticipation of retirement) to restore full voting control to the public stockholders. Accordingly, over many months of negotiation during 1988, the shareholders approved a transaction that valued "control" at 11.5 percent over the quoted price of the stock. And at Resorts International, the voting stock traded for as much as $100 a share over the nonvoting stock.

5
PERFORMANCE ANXIETY

1. Robert Clark, *Corporate Law*, Little, Brown, Boston, 1986, p. 692.

2. The Business Roundtable's 1990 report on *Corporate Governance and American Competitiveness* is a good example, pointing to the "powerful accountability imposed by the markets" (p. 15).

3. "Who's Excellent Now?" *Business Week*, November 5, 1984, p. 77.

4. "Buchwald Suit: Profit Study Set," *New York Times*, October 23, 1990, p. D13.

5. Adam Smith, *Powers of Mind*, Random House, New York, 1975, pp. 3–4.

6. Dana Wechsler Linden, "Lies of the Bottom Line," *Forbes*, November 12, 1990, p. 106.

278   Notes

7. Business Roundtable, *Corporate Governance and American Competitiveness*, March 1990, p. 15.
8. Jeffrey R. Gates, *ESOP Expert Returns from Meetings with Soviet Economic Reformers*, paper from Powell, Goldstein, Frazer, & Murphy, Washington, D.C., September 14, 1990.
9. Securities Act of 1933, Rule 144A. See also Regulation D.
10. David Wessel, "Pentagon Spreads Coal Purchases over Five Years," *Wall Street Journal*, October 5, 1988, p. A-22.
11. Joseph A. Schumpeter, *Capitalism, Socialism and Democracy*, Harper & Row, New York, 1942, pp. 74–75.
12. Alfred Conard, "Beyond Managerialism: Investor Capitalism?" *University of Michigan Journal of Law Reform*, 22(1), Fall 1988, p. 165.
13. Alan Farnhan, "The Trust Gap," *Fortune*, December 4, 1989, p. 74.
14. Graef Crystal, "Cracking the Tax Whip on CEOs," *Business World (New York Times)*, September 23, 1990, p. 48.
15. Frederick W. Cook, "How Much Stock Should Management Own?" paper prepared for clients, dated February 28, 1990, pp. 2–3.
16. Michael C. Jensen and Kevin J. Murphy, "CEO Incentives—It's Not How Much You Pay, but How," *Harvard Business Review*, May–June 1990, p. 138.
17. Crystal, "Cracking the Tax Whip on CEOs," p. 48.
18. *Ibid.*
19. Graef Crystal, "Is There No Dignity?" *Crystal Report on Executive Compensation*, 2(3), May/June 1990, p. 12.
20. "Nuclear Executives in Japan Resign Over Recent Mishaps," *New York Times*, May 14, 1981.
21. Graef Crystal, "Pay for Non-Performance," *Crystal Report on Executive Compensation*, 2(3), May/June 1990, p. 10.
22. Conard, *Beyond Managerialism*, pp. 165–166.
23. Internal Revenue Code §422(b)(1).
24. Internal Revenue Code §423(b)(2).
25. SEC Rule 16(b)-3(a).
26. Kathy M. Kristof, "The Pay-for-Performance Myth," *Washington Post*, August 22, 1990, p. H3.
27. George B. Paulin, "Long-Term Incentives for Management: An Overview," *Compensation and Benefits Review*, July 1989, p. 36.
28. Graef Crystal, "The Great CEO Pay Sweepstakes," *Fortune*, June 18, 1990, p. 98.
29. Graef Crystal, "The Option Swappers," *Crystal Report on Executive Compensation*, 1(1), September/October 1989, p. 4.
30. Graef Crystal, "Bob Crandall and His Magic Safety Net," *Crystal Report on Executive Compensation*, 2(1), September/October 1989, p. 2.
31. Amanda Bennett."Reebok's Fireman Gets Hosed Down in New Pay Pact," *Wall Street Journal*, August 7, 1990, p. B1.
32. Bradley A. Stertz, "Chrysler Urges Its 100 Top Executives to Bet More of Their Pay on Firm's Fate," *Wall Street Journal*, April 2, 1990, p. A4.
33. Spencer Stuart, *Spencer Stuart Board Index 1990 Proxy Report: Board Trends and Practices at 100 Major Companies*, 1990, p. 32.

34. Korn/Ferry International, *Board of Directors' Sixteenth Annual Study, 1989,* New York, 1989, p. 9.
35. *Ibid.,* p. 11.

6
SLUMBERING GIANTS: THE INSTITUTIONAL INVESTORS

1. Fox Butterfield, "From Ben Franklin, A Gift That's Worth Two Fights," *New York Times,* April 21, 1990, p. A-1.
2. Carolyn Kay Brancato, "Breakdown of Total Assets by Type of Institutional Investor, 1989," Riverside Economic Research, February 21, 1991.
3. A comprehensive list of impediments to collective action by shareholders is included in Alfred Conard, "Beyond Managerialism: Investor Capitalism?" *University of Michigan Journal of Law Reform,* 22(1), Fall 1988. Impediments are vulnerability of voting rights, emptiness of shareholder proposal rights, liability of controlling persons, freezing stockholding, the forfeiture of short-term gains, and group filing requirements. See also Bernard S. Black, "Shareholder Passivity Re-examined," *Michigan Law Review,* 89(3), December 1990, pp. 520–608.
4. Melvin Aron Gisenberg, "The Structure of Corporation Law," *Columbia Law Review,* 89(7), November 1989, pp. 1461, 1474.
5. Daniel Fischel and John H. Langbein, "ERISA's Fundamental Contradiction: The Exclusive Benefit Rule," *University of Chicago Law Review,* 55(4), Fall 1988, pp. 1105, 1117.
6. *The Department of Labor's Enforcement of the Employee Retirement Income Security Act (ERISA),* Subcommittee on Oversight of Government Management of the Committee on Governmental Affairs, United States Senate, April 1986, S. Prt. 99–144, pp. 53–58. See also James E. Heard and Howard D. Sherman, *Conflicts of Interest in the Proxy Voting System,* Investor Responsibility Research Center, Washington, D.C., 1987.
7. David Bell, Assistant Secretary, Department of Labor, speech before the Financial Executives Institute, January 23, 1990.
8. Elmer W. Johnson, "An Insider's Call for Outside Direction," *Harvard Business Review,* March/April 1990, p. 54.
9. *Ibid.*
10. Karla Scherer, "Some Facts They Never Teach You in the Classroom," speech delivered at the Tenth Annual Awards Banquet, Wayne State University School of Business Administration, Detroit, Michigan, April 20, 1990.
11. The proxies at Fidelity are voted by a staff that is independent of the investment managers.
12. Mark J. Roe, "Legal Restraints on Ownership and Control of Public Companies," paper presented at the Conference on the Structure and Governance of Enterprise, Harvard Business School, March 29–31, 1990, p. 8.
13. James E. Heard and Howard D. Sherman, *Conflicts of Interest in the Proxy Voting System,* Investor Responsibility Research Center, Washington, D.C., 1987, p. 44.

14. "TIAA-CREF: A Concerned Investor," Teachers' Insurance and Annuity Association, 1990, p. 1.
15. William C. Greenough, *It's My Retirement Money—Take Good Care of It*, Richard D. Irwin, Homewood, Ill., p. 191.
16. Larry Rohter, "Corporations Pass Alumni in Donations to Colleges." *New York Times*, April 29, 1986, p. A-16.
17. Peter G. Gosselin, "BU Writes Off $16m of Seragen Stake," *Boston Globe*, December 29, 1989, p. 63.
18. Dana Wechsler, "Letting the Losses Run," *Forbes*, April 17, 1990, p. 116.
19. Nancy J. Perry, "Who Runs Your Company, Anyway?" *Fortune*, September 12, 1988, p. 141.
20. Richard H. Koppes, "CalPERS 1990 Corporate Governance Report," July 10, 1990.
21. Federal Employees' Retirement System Act of 1986, PL 99-335. ("FERSA").
22. Jonathan Alter, "The News that Didn't Fit," *Newsweek*, December 29, 1986, p. 57.
23. Judith Havemann, "U.S. Employees' Thrift Plan to Create New Capital Fund: New Benefit May Become Political Football," *Washington Post*, February 18, 1987, p. A1.
24. Robert A.G. Monks and Nell Minow, "The Federal Employees' Retirement System Act," *Barron's*, June 15, 1987, p. 44.
25. Report of the Committee on Governmental Affairs, United States Senate, To Accompany S.1527, Federal Retirement Reform Act of 1985, 99th Congress, 1st Session, Report 99–166, October 30, 1985, U.S. Government Printing Office, Washington, D.C., p. 87.
26. Brancato, *The Pivotal Role of Institutional Investors in Capital Markets*, p. 24.
27. Conference report to accompany H 2672, Report 99-606, p. 136 *et seq.*
28. See testimony by Robert A.G. Monks, before the Subcommittee on Labor-Management Relations of the House Education and Labor Committee, February 9, 1989, suggesting a "safe harbor" for ERISA funds invested in indexes.
29. Supplemental Information Regarding the Federal Emplyees' Retirement System Act of 1986, Report of the Committee on Governmental Affairs, United States Senate, 99th Congress, 2nd session, Report 99-184, October 1986, U.S. Government Printing Office, Washington, D.C., p. 29.
30. Hearings before the Committee on Governmental Affairs, United States Senate on S. 1527, S. Hrg. 99-754, p. 520 *et seq.*
31. See Jacqueline Campbell and Elizabeth S. Kiesche, "Koppers Battles to Repel a Suitor," *Chemical Week*, April 6, 1988, p. 13.
32. Beverly Ross Cambell and William Josephson, "Public Pension Trustees' Pursuit of Social Goals," *Journal of Urban and Contemporary Law*, 24(3), 1983, p. 47.
33. James A. White, "Divestment Proves Costly and Hard," *Wall Street Journal*, February 22, 1989, p. C-1.
34. See John H. Langbein, "Social Investing of Pension Funds and University Endowments: Unprincipled, Futile, and Illegal," in John J. Langbein, Roy A. Schotland, and Albert P. Blaustein, *Disinvestment: Is It Legal? Is It Moral? Is It Productive?* National Legal Center for the Public Interest, Washington, D.C., 1985, pp. 9–12.
35. Of course, the verdict is still out on divestment, an issue that divides institutional investors perhaps more than any other. When ISS recommended a vote against a New York State proposal for divestment of South Africa operations at

Echlin, Thomas Pandick, Director of the Office of Investor Affairs, wrote back: "In our opinion, continued presence in South Africa can have significant adverse financial impact on the company. Recent announcements by Mobil Oil and Goodyear cited the double taxation of profits earned in South Africa (Internal Revenue Code, § 911), resulting in an effective rate of 72 percent, as a major factor in their decision to disinvest. In addition, the increased incidence of state and local governments' refusal to contract for services and products with companies doing business in South Africa will certainly impact negatively on share values if the company losses a significant market portion as a result."

36. *Sgaglione v. Levitt*, 37 N.Y. 2d 507 (1975).

37. *Withers v. Teachers' Retirement System*, 447 F. Supp. 1248 (S.D.N.Y. 1978), aff'd. without op. *Withers v. Teachers' Retirement System* 595 F.2d 1210 (CA2 N.Y. 1979). See also the opinion of Ian D. Lanoff of Bredhoff & Kaiser, dated January 17, 1991, with reference to a local public pension plan investing in debt securities of the city of Philadelphia. The opinion concludes: "The Board lawfully may conclude that the purchase of the Notes would not cause the Municipal Retirement System to fail the qualification requirements of Section 401(a) of the Code" (p. 32).

38. *Regents of the University of Michigan v. Michigan*, 419 N.W. 2d 773 (1987).

39. Campbell and Josephson, "Public Pension Trustees' Pursuit of Social Goals," p. 84.

40. Matthew Bromberg, "Social Investing: The Good Guys Finish First," *Business and Society Review*, No. 67, Fall 1988, p. 32.

41. Edward A. Zelinsky, "The Dilemma of the Local Social Investment: An Essay on Socially Responsible Investing" *Cardozo Law Review*, 6, Fall 1984, p. 111.

42. This section is adapted freely from Lauren Talner, *The Origins of Shareholder Activism*, Investor Responsibility Research Center, Washington, D.C., July 1983, and Helen Booth, *The Shareholder Proposal Rule: SEC Interpretations & Lawsuits*, Investor Responsibility Research Center, January 1987.

43. Talner, p. 3.

44. *Peck v. Greyhound Corp.*, 97 F. Supp. 679 (S.D.N.Y. 1951). The court is citing SEC Release No. 3638, dated January 3, 1945.

45. *Medical Committee for Human Rights v. SEC*, 432 F.2d 659, 678. The court is citing Senate Hearings.

46. *Ibid.*

47. *Ibid.*

48. *Ibid.*, p. 681.

49. Booth, *The Shareholder Proposal Rule*, p. 10.

50. Talner, *The Orgins of Shareholder Activism*, p. 13.

51. One was an anti-greenmail resolution at Gillette, and the other was a poison pill resolution at Santa Fe Southern Pacific. Although both were precatory only, boards at both companies responded. Gillette adopted a bylaw provision prohibiting greenmail, and Sante Fe Southern Pacific, although not rescinding its poison pill, did amend it.

52. However, this "victory" is being challenged in federal court with reference to the validity of the ESOP votes (see pp. 61–64).

53. Michael Deal, "Should Philip Morris Snuff Out Marlboros?" *Business and Society Review*, No. 74, Summer 1990, pp. 36–39.

54. Northrop Notice of Annual Meeting of Stockholders and Proxy Statement, April 2, 1990, p. 5.

7
RESTORATION OF TRUST

1. Personal letter from David Ball to Robert A.G. Monks, September 4, 1990.
2. See *CTS Corp. v. Dynamics Corp. of America*, 107 S. Ct. 1637 (1987), respecting the voting power of shareholders in certain takeover situations.
3. For example, by not voting in a takeover, a shareholder in effect "gives" value to those who do.
4. A trustee would have a difficult burden defending action that was for the common interest of all owners if it resulted in charges that diminished the trust estate.
5. John Pound, Kenneth Lehn, and Gregg Jarrell, "Are Takeovers Hostile to Economic Performance?" *Regulation*, September/October 1986, pp. 29–30.
6. Richard A. Ippolito, *Pensions, Economics and Public Policy*, Dow Jones-Irwin, Homewood, Il., 1986; Richard A. Ippolito and John A. Turner, "Turnover, Fees and Pension Plan Performance," *Financial Analysts Journal*, November–December 1987 ("A CAPM-based analysis of the data reveals that, net of investment fees and turnover expenses, private pension plans underperform the S&P 500 by approximately 44 basis points per year"), p. 16; Stepen A. Berkowitz, Louis D. Finney, and Dennis E. Logue, *The Investment Performance of Corporate Pension Plans, Why They Do Not Beat the Market Regularly*, Quorum, Westport, Conn., 1988.
7. *The Equity Manager Box Score*, Wilshire Associates, Santa Monica, CA, 1987, p. 3.
8. Just how large this sum is may be approximated from Wilshire's work. "Brokerage commissions and even the impact of trades are small in comparison to the amount of fees paid to managers. Wilshire's clients tend to have large funds so the fee component for equity management is only about 0.4%" (*Ibid.*, p. 3). Total pension funds approximate $2 trillion, so fees might approach $8 billion per year.
9. ERISA Sec. 404(a)(1)(C).
10. Any doubt as to the legality of corporations acting collectively with respect to their ownership responsibilities for securities held in their employee benefit plans was dispelled by the ruling of (then) Assistant Attorney General Charles Rule to ISS in August 1987.
11. Benjamin Graham and David L. Dodd, *Securities Analysis*, 1st ed., McGraw-Hill, New York, 1934, pp. 510–511.
12. John C. Coffee, "No Soul to Damn, No Body to Kick: An Unscandalized Inquiry into the Problem of Corporate Punishment," *Michigan Law Review*, 79, January 1981, pp. 413–424.
13. John Braithwaite, *Corporate Crime in the Pharmaceutical Industy*, Routledge & Kegan Paul, Boston, 1984, p. 319.
14. Coffee, "No Soul to Damn, No Body to Kick," p. 408.
15. "Through the generally more active participation of their shareholders, cooperatives also offer the consumer greater control over management decisions than is provided to shareholders in large corporations" (Marshall B. Clinard and Peter C. Yeager, *Corporate Crime*, Free Press, New York, 1980, pp. 324–325).
16. Christopher D. Stone, *Where the Law Ends: The Social Control of Corporate Behavior*, Harper & Row, New York, 1975, p. 148.

17. *The Department of Labor's Enforcement of the Employee Retirement Income Security Act (ERISA),* Subcommittee on Oversight of Government Management, Committee on Governmental Affairs, U.S. Senate, April 1986, S. Prt. 99-144, pp. 53–58.
18. Edward Jay Epstein, *Who Owns the Corporation? Management vs. Shareholders,* Priority Press, New York, 1986, p. 13.

Index